T
G/Twins 16.12.95
14/1/92

Money, Inflation and Unemployment

Second edition

David Gowland

HARVESTER
WHEATSHEAF

New York London Toronto Sydney Tokyo Singapore

First published 1985
Second edition published 1991 by
Harvester Wheatsheaf,
66 Wood Lane End, Hemel Hempstead,
Hertfordshire, HP2 4RG
A division of
Simon & Schuster International Group

Typeset in 10/12pt Times
by Columns

Printed and bound in Great Britain by
Billing and Sons Ltd, Worcester

British Library Cataloguing in Publication Data

Gowland, David
  Money, inflation and unemployment. – 2nd ed.
  I. Title
  339.5

  ISBN 0–7450–0952–2
  ISBN 0–7450–0954–9 pbk

1 2 3 4 5 95 94 93 92 91

Contents

Preface

Galbraith, who turned the art of writing prefaces to second editions into an art form, said that their main function was to give authors the chance to be smug and self-satisfied in writing about the continued relevance of a successful book. I hope to avoid this temptation, but would like to explain the relevance of the arguments contained in this volume to current economic debates. The first edition did not have a preface in that the prefatorial material is incorporated into Chapter 1. Briefly, this states that the purpose of the book is to analyse the economic arguments in favour of a monetary target. The rival policy options are, on the one hand, discretion and, on the other hand, an alternative target such as an exchange rate target. To do this, it was necessary to explore at length the role of monetary factors in determining output and inflation. In the USA and Japan, this debate continues in its original form, that is of a choice between the three alternatives stated above.

In Western Europe, including the UK, the nature of the debate has been transformed by the success of the 'new ERM (exchange rate mechanism)'. Although established in 1979, the ERM was radically transformed in practice in 1984–5 and now works in a very different fashion. The UK joined in October 1990. Moreover, the European Community (EC) is debating moves towards a full monetary union. In the context of the UK, this represents a further round in the debate between internal (usually monetary) targets and exchange rate ones, which has raged since 1817, with Ricardo's classic contribution. The decision to join the ERM means a victory for the exchange rate fixers. Indeed, currently, the old-style Keynesian position (discretion and autonomy) is upheld by very few (notably Mrs Thatcher). Almost everyone else accepts the need for some target and the consequent discipline, although only a minority advocate monetary targets (notably Patrick Minford). The arguments are unchanged, whether contemporary practice includes a monetary target (as in the early 1980s) or rejects one (as now). Moreover, many of the arguments in favour of the importance of money-supply policy, are now cited as arguments against the 'narrow bands' version of the ERM. Similarly they are cited as arguments against full-scale European Monetary Union (EMU).

However, the move towards full monetary union merely changes the theatre of debate. The level of the European Community is necessary to determine many of the traditional issues of monetary economics: should there be a Europe-wide monetary target, should budget deficits be permitted, should there be an independent Central Bank? All of these and many other issues traditionally thought of as part of domestic monetary economics are currently under active debate, for example in the inter-governmental conference considering monetary union. Between now and 2000, the EC will have to decide not only on whether to form a complete monetary union, but on what the structure of such a union will be. Many of the decisions about the latter depend upon the importance of monetary factors as opposed to non-monetary ones in determining income: the theme of this book.

David Gowland
University of York
July 1991

1

Introduction

1.1 Necessity of monetary theory: money, income and causality

Everyone would agree that one of the most crucial tasks faced by economists is to explain the determination of income; that is, the level of prices and of output, and so of employment. Economists have disagreed for centuries about the relative importance of 'monetary' and 'real' forces in the determination of income. Some have argued that the money supply is largely responsible for determining prices and output, whereas others have argued that it is largely irrelevant: positions encapsulated by Samuelson in the propositions that 'money matters' and 'money does not matter'.

In the 1960s this controversy became widely publicised as 'the monetarist–Keynesian debate'. Both these groups were represented as holding the extreme positions '*only* money matters' and 'money does not matter *at all*'. In the late 1970s the use of the term 'monetarist' became less clear-cut, but the original debate is still of crucial importance to both economic theory and policy. In particular, it is the vital part of the controversy concerning the desirability of monetary targets, that is that control of the money supply should be the major objective of macroeconomic policy with the objective of achieving some quantitative target for the size of the money supply. A belief in monetary targets is not only the most basic tenet of the monetarist creed but that which distinguishes monetarism from other schools of thought. Through setting such targets, monetarists argue, governments can best seek to influence the level of prices, output and employment. As one of the pioneers of modern monetarism, Philip Cagan, put it:

> Monetarism is the view that the quanity of money has a major influence on economic activity and the price level and that the objectives of monetary policy are best achieved by targeting the rate of growth of the money supply. (In Eatwell *et al*, 1989, p.195)

It is the purpose of this book to explore this debate and so illuminate the processes whereby money might influence income, how money is created and how it may be controlled. In other words, to provide an introduction to monetary theory. In doing this, one obtains crucial insights into economic policy, since to quote Hicks' (1967) creed of the monetary economist:

> Monetary economics is indeed topical and relevant in a way that no other branch of the subject achieves.
>
> Monetary theory is less abstract than most economic theory; it cannot avoid a relation to reality, which in other economic theory is something missing. It belongs to monetary history, in a way that economic theory does not always belong to economic history. Indeed, it does so in two ways which need to be distinguished. It is noticeable, on the one hand, that a large part of the best work on money is topical. It has been prompted by particular episodes, by particular experiences of the writer's own time. All theorising is simplifying, cutting out the unimportant and leaving what is thought to be important in the hope that by simplifying we may increase understanding. Sometimes what is sought is a general understanding; but with monetary theory it is more often a particular understanding: an understanding directed towards a particular problem, normally a problem of the time at which the work in question is written. So monetary theories arise out of monetary disturbances . . . . Topicality is one way in which monetary theory is conditioned but there is another also . . . money itself has been evolving.

It is important to stress some key features of the monetarist–Keynesian debate. First, the debate is largely about empirical questions and so can only be understood within some theoretical framework. Various theoretical frameworks are presented in this book. They are complements to each other, each helping to illuminate a particular facet of the debate, rather than alternatives. Second, as the debate has done more than anything else to give economists their reputation for being quarrelsome creatures who 'put end to end, would not reach a conclusion', it is therefore important to stress just how much is common ground in this debate and how easy it is to take a moderate position; that money matters perhaps a great deal, but is not the only thing which matters. To simplify the issues, the debate is presented in textbooks (including this one) in simple black and white terms, but it should be remembered that the textbook monetarist and Keynesian are creatures of pedagogic utility rather than of real-world existence. All can agree that the debate is largely about empirical magnitudes within a theoretical framework. Indeed the difference in practice between monetarist and Keynesian analyses is usually very little but a great deal may hang upon that little. Policy makers have no choice but to make decisions; to raise or lower or leave unaltered interest rates, to influence exchange rates, for example by joining the exchange rate mechanism (ERM) of the European Monetary System (EMS), to intervene in money markets or not. The merits of a particular course of action are likely to depend upon the validity of one piece of monetary analysis compared to another and hence of a small but critical distinction.

A critic might ask why it is necessary to bother with monetary theory; cannot an elementary statistical analysis resolve the issue? It is easy to show that money and income are very closely correlated, so surely this is sufficient to prove monetarism without the need to theorise. This appeal to Occam's razor is attractive but, regrettably, unacceptable. First of all, it is necessary to point out that spurious correlation may exist; that is, two variables may be related statistically when the two have no real relationship at all. Examples are legion, two very famous ones being the birth rate in Sweden with the number of storks in Lapland, and the crime rate with membership of the Church of England. No one would conclude that any causality is involved. In 1977 a Cambridge biologist wrote to *The Times* to point out that the correlation between inflation and (lagged) money supply was 0.7; enough, he wrote, to convince any biologist. Two economists responded by pointing out that the correlation was even higher between inflation and the incidence of dysentery in

Scotland.[1] Hendry (1980) made a similar point, relating rainfall and prices. In fact, it is very easy to find spurious correlations involving inflation: any series which was high in 1974–5 and 1980 and low in 1977–8 and 1982 (or vice versa) would do admirably; the performance of Australian fast bowlers against England for example. This example illustrates another statistical point. Since I conceived it in 1983, it has continued to fit well – the low point of UK inflation coincided with England's clean sweep in 1986–7 and the acceleration in 1989 with Alderman's record-breaking series. In other words that a statistical relationship fits outside its estimation period is no guarantee that it is meaningful. However, Goodhart's law might well apply (p.6 below) that any observed statistical regularity will tend to collapse once reliance is placed upon it. If a well-meaning Australian government were to hamstring its bowlers it is unlikely that inflation would fall in the UK.

The imaginary critic might well, legitimately, intervene at this point and say that he or she is well aware of the existence of spurious correlation and doubts if anyone believes that the money–income link is spurious. This is true, but money and income (like any other two variables) may be economically linked in any of four ways:

1. Money causes income. This is the monetarist proposition.
2. Income causes money. This is the Keynesian proposition. Even monetarists agree that it can occur if policy makers pursue an accommodating monetary policy. If whenever income rises, the authorities respond by increasing money then income does cause money – as certainly happened in the UK in the 1950s.
3. Each causes, and is caused by, the other. This two-way causality, called feedback by statisticians, requires a more complex model but is, *a priori*, the most plausible.
4. Both variables are caused by another. This proposition is frequently put forward by Keynesians. In one of the most famous and bitter of all monetarist–Keynesian debates (Friedman, 1970a; Kaldor, 1970) this was the essence of Kaldor's position; that income and money were both determined by the budget deficit (the budget deficit–money supply link is explained in Section 1.3 and Chapter 11; the

government spending–taxation impact on income is a fundamental Keynesian proposition).

Thus, an economically meaningful relationship between money and income could exist in a variety of different forms, each of which bears a different interpretation: Keynesian, monetarist or neither. The critic has one remaining argument before accepting the view that the debate can only be understood within the relevant theoretical framework. This is to argue that surely if changes in money occur before changes in income, this would be sufficient to show that money caused income (or vice versa). Unfortunately, this, the famous doctrine *post hoc ergo propter hoc*, is invalid. Temporal precedence does not establish causality. To explain that it is necessary to rely on the seeming paradox that an event today may have been caused by something which has not yet occurred. A good example is that the purchase of wedding rings precedes weddings, but one would regard the purchase of a wedding ring as being caused by a marriage, not as the cause of it. The equivalent of monetarism in this context is the view that people purchase wedding rings for reasons which are obscure and irrelevant. Carrying the ring around leads to an irresistible desire to get married. Hence if one wishes to influence the number of marriages, one targets the wedding ring supply. Goodhart made a similar point in his influential article (1970) concerning tickets for boxing matches. In many, probably most, cases temporal precedence does coincide with causality, but not always. In the case of money and income some Keynesians argue that a similar relationship, called the finance demand for money (see pp.65ff), exists. A simple example of this concerns an individual who, learning of a forthcoming inheritance, decides to buy a new car. He orders it and withdraws £5,000 from a building society to pay for it. He lodges this in a bank account. The car arrives and he pays for it by cheque. An observer would note that the increase in this individual's money balance preceded his purchase. Nevertheless, it would not be true to say he bought the car because his money balances rose. Rather, his decision to purchase the car led him to make the necessary arrangements, one of which was to increase his money balances. Hence this is a perfect example of the Keynesian proposition that a change in money precedes one in expenditure or output but that the change in money is, nevertheless, caused by the change in other factors, in this case wealth but normally income.

The precise relationship between money and income can only be determined within the context of an economic model. Only in this way can it, for example, be determined whether money is merely an indicator, as Keynesians avow, or can be (or should be) a proximate target, as monetarists claim. An indicator merely registers the change in another variable, whereas to change a proximate target is both sufficient and necessary to change the goal variable, in this case income. Formally the chain of causality runs through the proximate target but not the indicator. The distinction between proximate targets and indicators can be elucidated with the aid of an analogy. Thermostats and thermometers frequently look alike but are crucially different within a heating system. A thermometer is a good indicator of temperature, but the heat of a room cannot be altered by direct manipulation of the thermometer (for example, by plunging it into ice or heating the bulb with a lighter). Such, Keynesians believe, is the relationship between money and income. A thermostat, on the other hand, is a proximate target since manipulation of its dial is both necessary and sufficient to change the room temperature. Monetarists believe money is akin to a thermostat in its relationship to income. A number of important points are true both in the analogy and the real world. The response of the room temperature to manipulation of the thermostat may not be fixed and may vary from day to day. Similarly, the impact of monetary policy will only be felt after a 'long and variable lag', to quote the most famous of all monetarists, Friedman (1970b).[2] Moreover, the thermometer is more closely related to the room temperature than the thermostat. If one turns the thermostat up every time one feels cold and down when feeling hot then the thermostat reading could actually be negatively related to room temperature. Similarly, Keynesian theory actually implies a closer relationship of money to income than does monetarism. An attempt to use an indicator as if it were a proximate target not merely fails to change the goal variable but renders it useless as an indicator; putting a thermometer in ice not only leaves the room temperature unchanged but also means that the thermometer ceases to register it accurately. The economic equivalent is often referred to as 'Goodhart's law': to try to control a definition of money will distort its relationship to income (Goodhart, 1984, p.96). Finally, it is perfectly reasonable to control the room temperature by adjusting the thermostat without even the haziest idea of how the central heating system works, or even knowing whether it is gas or oil fired. A guest in a hotel room is frequently in this position. A similar monetarist proposition was that it does not matter how money affects income; it is simply sufficient to know that it does. This view which originated in the eighteenth century with Hume (see Rotwein, 1972) was often called 'black box monetarism' because the economy was considered a black box, the inner workings of which were unknown and unimportant. By the 1970s nearly all monetarists had accepted the alternative view that it is necessary to say how and why changes in monetary aggregates influence income. To answer this is to explain the means by which developments in financial markets are transmitted to real ones, so it is usually the *transmission mechanism* of monetary policy. An important monetarist–Keynesian debate has concerned the nature of the transmission mechanism. Keynesians have usually denied the possibility of a direct transmission mechanism, as exemplified by the quantity theory. Instead they postulate an *indirect* transmission mechanism, whereby monetary forces matter but only through their effect on intermediate variables such as interest rates or exchange rates, see Table 1.1. The structure of such a model is that

(a)   there is a change in the money stock, which
(b)   leads to a change in the intermediate variable, which, as a consequence
(c)   leads to a change in income.

The crucial importance of this to the monetarist–Keynesian debate is that the logical response to such a structure is to 'target' the intermediate variable, and not the money supply. The authorities decide on an optimal level of the intermediate variable (as part of their overall stabilisation policy), and the money supply is allowed to adjust to whatever level is necessary to achieve this. The monetarist direct transmission mechanism, on the other hand, implies that the money supply should be the target variable. The classic example of such a model incorporating an indirect transmission mechanism is the elementary IS–LM

Table 1.1 Possible intermediate targets

	Monetarism	
Money supply	Quantity	Milton Friedman
	Non-monetarist targets	
Exchange rate	Price	Young Keynesians–Buiter European Monetary System
Credit	Quantity	Ben Friedman
Interest rate	Price	Old Keynesians–Harrod
Share prices/rates of return on shares	Either	Tobin
Nothing		Lawson, Waud
PSBR	Quantity	Lawson
High employment budget deficit	Keynesian artefact	Ward and Neild (1978)
Fiscal leverage	Keynesian artefact	Musgrave (1968)
Domestic credit expansion	Quantity	IMF
Nominal income	Quantity	Meade
Money base	Quantity	Minford (instrument)

model (see Chapter 4) but a more modern one involving the exchange rate is discussed in Chapter 2. Interestingly, the view here called 'Keynesian' does describe Keynes' view of the workings of monetary policy – not always true of 'Keynesian' models.[3]

The debate about the role of money is frequently said to be a debate about its exogeneity. An exogenous variable is an independent variable determined outside the system, in contrast to an endogenous variable which is determined within the system and so is dependent upon the values of the other variables in the system. The relevance of this distinction to the debate about the direction of causality between money and income is obvious. Nevertheless, the crux of the debate is not whether money is exogenous but, rather, with respect to which variables is money endogenous? Money is not an entity caused by nothing but causing other variables, like Aristotle's unmoved movers. Every economist believes that the size of the money supply can be explained by some variable or variables (see Chapter 11). The important issue is whether these variables include income or variables determined by income. The monetarist needs to show that money is largely determined independently of income. If it is, given that there is an economically meaningful relationship between money and income, money must determine income. All of the other three possible relationships are ruled out. The monetarist also needs to show that the government can control the money supply. Without this, the monetarists' policy prescription is empty. Indeed the exogeneity debate is considered as one about the controllability and income dependence of money. The rest of this book provides an analysis of monetary theory, through which these important questions can be answered: does money determine income and, if so, how and to what extent?

1.2 The monetary sector

The main characteristic which distinguishes a modern from a primitive economy is that a modern economy is a monetary one. Transactions either involve the use of money or are expressed in monetary units, as when credit is extended. Individuals rarely exchange their labour directly for goods. Instead, they work for wages specified in a monetary unit and use their earnings to purchase goods, the price of which is also expressed in terms of the monetary unit. Similarly, goods are usually not exchanged directly for other goods but are sold in exchange for money. This all-pervasive use of money is the major institutional datum of developed Western economies. These economies are not barter economies, nor have they large subsistence agricultural sectors.

So crucial is this brute fact – as Clower (1969) put it in a seminal article, 'Money buys goods and goods buy money, but goods do not buy goods' – that at first sight it is surprising that it is ignored in most economics. Conventional microeconomics, even general equilibrium theory, implicitly assumes a barter economy or as Keynes put it, a real exchange economy.[4] So does the elementary (Keynesian) national income model, based on planned injections being equal to planned withdrawals. Strictly, these models and those using them do not so much assume that economies are barter ones but that they can be analysed as if they were barter ones; that is, that the existence and use of money has no effect on the goods and labour-market equilibrium. This assumption is sometimes called the 'classical veil' or 'classical dichotomy'. An alternative interpretation of 'orthodox' analysis, whether microeconomic or Keynesian, is that it ignores altogether the problem of how exchange takes place. Perhaps Clower (1971) best encapsulates both views: the problem is ignored by assuming that barter will take place.

It is the task of monetary economics to explore the implications of relaxing this assumption. In this respect economics follows the classic scientific methodology; the general equilibrium and Keynesian models are built resting upon an assumption. Economists then test the effects of relaxing it. This has been the starting point for all monetary economics since Aristotle.[5] Different economists reach very different conclusions about the implications to be derived from the existence of a monetary economy. Nevertheless, the analysis of these implications is the starting point of monetarism, on the one hand, and 'post Keynesianism' on the other (see Dow and Earl, 1982; Eichner, 1979; Sawyer, 1982). These two doctrines present radically different policy prescriptions, but the divergence seems more comprehensive once the common starting point is recognised.

Moreover, some implications are clear. Monetary economics cannot ignore the nature of monetary history in the way that other branches of economics can. Crucially, monetary economics has to be a policy-orientated subject or topical, as the doyen of monetary economists, Hicks (1967), put it, see above.

All economists tackle monetary economics by constructing a model of the monetary or financial sector. This is usually a conventional economic model in that it is based upon an equilibrium condition, usually that the supply of money should equal the demand for money.[6] The standard approach is then to seek to link this model to the real or goods sector. Most models use the rate of interest as the link; they operate in such a way that any shock in either sector changes the rate of interest, and this change throws the other sector into disequilibrium and so transmits the shock. It is possible to calculate the new equilibrium which will emerge once this interactive process has ended. The rate of interest is a suitable transmission mechanism because it is both a financial phenomenon and a real one; it is the inverse of the price of financial assets and equal in equilibrium to both the rate of return on capital and to the time preference (discount) rate. There are alternatives as in the flow-of-funds approach, where quantities are the link rather than price. Nevertheless, most economists use the rate of interest as the link often interpreted as asset prices (pp.99–101). This is the reason why so much attention has been paid by economists to the rate of interest, since it is representative of all the other links between the two sectors in addition to its intrinsic importance. This is the basis of most theories of the determination of the rate of interest. Any such theory necessarily analyses how the two sectors interact to determine the rate of interest in a model which also incorporates government influences. Elementary texts often call the real influences 'loanable funds' and the financial ones 'liquidity preference'.

It is not easy to determine exactly what money does in an economy and still less to explain why this peculiar institution has arisen. Some functions are clear. Money can act as a medium of exchange and as a means of payment; such functions are closely related but distinct (Goodhart, 1975). Money acts as a *numeraire*, that is, the unit in which all other prices are expressed. However, money performs other functions. Most decentralisation is only possible because of the existence of money; non-monetary economies, like those of the Aztecs and Incas, are highly authoritarian. A trivial example of this is a gift voucher. Because it is expressed in a monetary unit, the recipient can choose what to buy rather than the donor making the decision. Similarly, decision making can be delegated within a family or from higher to lower units within a government or firm. The decentralisation of education following the 1987 Education Reform Act illustrates this principle: the Locally Managed School is left free to spend or budget independently of the LEA. Money is also the main method of conveying information; a willingness to buy or supply goods or labour is expressed through money and so conveys information about preferences and opportunity costs. This, the pure theory of money, is a fascinating subject (see Hahn, 1982, Chapter 2). Nevertheless, it will hereafter be ignored in this book for three reasons. It is complex, inconclusive and, most important, irrelevant to policy. Possibly the inconclusive and complex nature of the literature has arisen through seeking a generality which, as Hicks argued (p.2 above), is unnecessary and sometimes counter-productive.

The definition of money is more immediately relevant to monetary policy. The classic definition of money is that it is 'any asset generally acceptable in payment for a debt'. This is still the best definition, although it does not fully capture the subjective nature of any definition of money. This definition does, however, imply that the most appropriate definition of money may vary from place to place and time to time. Money is any asset which its holder regards as money; so, like beauty, 'moneyness' lies in the eye of the beholder. For monetarists, 'moneyness' is often defined in terms of its effect on behaviour; money is anything which burns a hole in your pocket. Another useful definition is that money is a perfectly liquid asset. Liquidity is a very useful concept in its own right, being a measure of how easily an asset can be turned into goods, or how easily it can be converted into purchasing power. There are three aspects to this: speed, cost and certainty. The speed element is straightforward: the longer it takes to convert an asset into purchasing power, the less liquid it is. Sometimes conversion to purchasing power involves a cost, either a fixed penalty or a brokerage fee (or other transaction costs both psychological and real). To convert a house, for example, involves a number of costs, some predictable (for example, solicitors' fees), others less so (for example, advertising). Cost and time are often interrelated. Many building societies, for example, offer investments where a penalty is charged for instant withdrawal but not if notice is given. The final aspect of liquidity is the degree of certainty about the amount an asset will realise. Many securities, especially those traded on markets, would be very liquid on the first two criteria but very illiquid because of this third consideration. This aspect of liquidity is not independent of the first two. It is often only possible to realise assets quickly by accepting a low price (and so accepting a cost); for obvious reasons, one is far less certain about the price to be received if one must accept the amount offered by the first bidder than if one waits.

There are two final considerations to be taken into account in a discussion of liquidity. The first is that the liquidity of an asset may vary over time. A house is much more liquid in the middle of a housing boom (for example, 1972–3 or 1978 or 1986–9) than at a time when the market is depressed as in 1990. The other consideration is that an asset's liquidity may also be measured in terms of the ease with which one can borrow against it. If an otherwise illiquid asset would be accepted instantaneously as collateral for a bank loan, it is highly liquid. This led to a famous aphorism that 'a man is as liquid as he feels' (Radcliffe, 1959), since the perceived ease of borrowing is largely a subjective matter (see Lewis in Creedy, 1990, pp.290–330).

Liquidity, then, is a complex concept, but one that is essential to any idea of portfolio management. It is worth noting that Keynesians tend to believe in a 'liquidity spectrum': that assets can be ranked by liquidity with only very small differences between them (that is, money is perfectly liquid but some other asset, near money, will only be slightly less liquid, and so on). Monetarists believe that there is a crucial gap in such an ordering between their concept of money (cash and those assets which are almost perfect substitutes for it) and all other assets.

As Clower (1971) said, 'It is one thing to construct a theoretical definition of money and quite another to decide what collection of objects in the real world correspond to this.' Friedman (Friedman and Schwartz, 1963) argued that the problem should be resolved empirically, by seeing which variables have the closest relationship to money – 'money is what does the work of money'. In the last resort there is no alternative to such a pragmatic approach. In practice it is generally agreed that money should be defined as 'non-bank private sector holdings of currency plus (at least some) bank deposits'.[7] Some definitions, such as M_3 in the USA and M_4 in the UK, include all bank deposits within the definition of money. These are usually referred to as *broad* definitions. The *narrow* definition traditionally excluded interest-bearing bank deposits and sought to include only demand or sight deposits (that is, for private individuals, a cheque account). These are labelled M_1 (or variants, such as M_{1B} in the USA); the UK definition formerly included some interest-bearing deposits over £100,000 and certificates of deposit, a type of large deposit. In the USA this is called M_2. Many variants are possible: for example, by including or excluding public sector deposits, non-resident deposits or foreign currency deposits by residents. A final problem is the definition of a bank. For example, some have argued that building societies in the UK are banks in all but name and should be so defined. Hence, private sector liquidity (PSL_2), later M_5, was calculated, which was M_3 except that 'bank' was redefined to include building societies as well as self-styled banks. Similarly, the UK M_2 also includes building society deposits. The permutations of defining money are such that the Federal Reserve Bank of New York has over forty definitions. Some Keynesians argue that it is absurd to try to control an economy by manipulation of a variable that cannot be precisely defined. This is disingenuous since their concepts are equally fuzzy (for example, autonomous expenditure, investment, fiscal leverage). Moreover, similar implications can usually be derived from the different series relating to M_1, M_2, M_4, etc. The definitional problem is one argument for multiple targets (Gowland, 1982, p.153). Otherwise it suffices to be aware of its existence. However, the appendix to this chapter provides more detail for the masochist.

1.3   Creation of money

Money can be created in four and only four ways. These are shown in the flow-of-funds equation below (formally derived later, pp.135ff):

Δ Money supply = Public Sector Borrowing Requirement
  + Δ Bank lending to non-bank private sector
  − Δ Non-bank private sector lending to the public sector
  + Overseas impact on money supply

(Δ *means 'change in'*)

The money supply can change through and only through these variables. A change in one of these variables is a necessary counterpart to a change in the money supply. In this section it will be shown how each of these leads, *ceteris paribus*, to a change in the money supply.

(i) *The public sector borrowing requirement (PSBR)*

This is the difference between the government's outlays and its receipts. Its outlays are its expenditure on goods and services, its expenditure on transfer payments, including interest payments, its purchase of assets, and its loans. In Keynesian analysis each of these would have different effects. However, as far as the influence on money creation is concerned, each has the same effect. Public sector receipts consist of taxation, various miscellaneous receipts, from charges etc., and the proceeds from sales of assets. The PSBR, as its name implies, is the amount the government must borrow. *Ceteris paribus*, there will be an increase in the money supply of exactly the same amount as the PSBR. Government expenditure of £100 will, *ceteris paribus*, lead to a rise of £100 in the money supply. The process is simple. In some recent years, the PSBR has been in surplus in the UK. It has been renamed Public Sector Debt-Repayment (PSDR). None of the analysis changes since $(PSDR) = -(PSBR)$. A PSDR of £100 will lead to a fall in money supply of £100, *ceteris paribus*.

For an example, it is assumed that the government is paying a grant of £100 to a student, Miss X. It can do this in two ways. First, it can send her £100 in notes. In this case the money supply has risen because Miss X holds the £100 of currency. The government has financed the expenditure by putting currency into circulation. (This is sometimes called 'printing money'. The epithet is misleading as the crucial feature is not printing money but putting money into circulation.) Alternatively, the government could send Miss X a cheque. (In practice it does this through an intermediary, her local authority, but this does not affect the process.) Miss X will pay this cheque into her bank account. At this moment, money is created because she has acquired a claim on the bank and the bank's liability to her, the £100 deposit, is part of the money supply. In exchange the bank has acquired a claim on the government (the cheque for £100). Thus, the bank's balance sheet constraint has been satisfied. Its liabilities and assets have both risen by £100 – its new liability is Miss X's deposit; its new asset is the cheque for £100. The government now owes the bank £100 (more than it did before).

In other words, the government has indirectly borrowed £100 from the bank. *It is only by this indirect process, usually called residual finance, that a government can borrow from a bank.* There is no direct transaction between a bank and a government, whereby the government can increase its indebtedness to the bank, at least given the UK's institutional arrangements. The bank is unlikely to continue to hold the cheque but will exchange it for another public sector liability, usually either a central bank deposit or a Treasury Bill. However, this merely transforms the form of the bank's claim on the public sector. It changes neither the size of bank loans to the public sector nor the size of the money supply. Money creation occurs as a direct and inevitable consequence of government expenditure (unless this is financed by taxation or by borrowing from the non-bank private sector; in this case money creation still occurs but is exactly offset by the money destruction caused by taxation or by non-bank private sector lending to the public sector).

Taxation (or a PSDR) leads to money destruction by the converse of the process described above. If, for example, Ms Z has to pay £100 in income tax, there will be a fall of £100 in the money supply. Ms Z can pay the government the £100 in the form of currency. In this case the money supply must fall, as private sector holdings of currency are £100 lower. Alternatively, Ms Z can write the government a cheque for £100. In this case her deposit is reduced by £100 and the bank has a liability of £100 to the public sector, which automatically reduces the government's debt to the bank usually in the form of the commercial bank's deposit with the central bank. Thus the money supply has fallen by £100 because Ms Z's deposit has been reduced by this amount. Moreover, the bank's balance sheet constraint has been satisfied. Its liabilities have fallen by £100 (Ms Z's reduced deposit) but so have its assets, because the bank's claim on the public sector has been reduced by this amount.

(ii)   *Bank lending to the private sector*

This creates money. As the old adage puts it, 'every loan creates a deposit'. Moreover, this relationship is a strict one: a loan of

£100 creates a deposit of £100. This stems from the fact that a bank in making a loan exchanges a claim on itself for a claim on the borrower. The claim on itself is obviously a bank liability and so, by definition, part of the money supply. This process is seen clearly in the case of a personal loan in the UK, or any loan in the USA. In this case the bank loan takes the form of an increased deposit for the borrower. If, for example, Mrs Y borrows £100 from the bank, she will be given a bank deposit with £100 in it (or her existing deposit increased by £100). This process is clearly illustrated in the ubiquitous TSB advert when a cash register shows the bank balance increase. In this case the link between the increase in bank assets and liabilities is obvious and the increase in the money supply consequent upon Mrs Y's borrowing self-evident. Moreover, the deposit is created even if Mrs Y never spends any of it – as might be the case with a compensating balance.[8] Often, in the UK, the borrowing is in the form of an overdraft. This is slightly more complicated, because the bank agrees to increase the deposit of a third party at the request of the borrower; that is, the bank agrees to honour the borrower's cheque. Nevertheless, the essence of the process is the same.

(iii) *Non-bank private sector lending to the public sector*

The effect of this on the money supply is exactly the same as that of taxation. Thus, for example, if Mrs W lends £100 to the public sector by purchasing £100 of national savings certificates, the money supply will fall by £100. The purchaser of a government security, such as savings certificates, must pay for it either by writing a cheque to the government or by handing bank notes to the government. The consequences are just the same as if these had been done to pay taxes. Moreover, the motive and object of an individual writing a cheque or handing over bank notes is irrelevant insofar as its effect on the money supply is concerned. In similar fashion, if the government repurchased £100 of its securities (for example, a holder of savings certificates redeemed them), the money supply would rise by £100. This is often called an open-market operation.

(iv)   *The overseas impact on the money supply*

While this is the most complex of the four, its essential features are simple. If the government acquires foreign currency by buying it with sterling and its reserves rise, the money supply will rise. Government expenditure on the acquisition of foreign currency influences the money supply just like other government spending although it is treated differently in government accounts. If it sells foreign currency, the money supply falls. For example, if a UK citizen, Ms V, decides to go on a skiing holiday in France, she will buy some foreign currency. Indirectly this may be supplied by the government from its reserves, through her bank. If she purchases 1,000 French francs for £100, the money supply will fall by £100 just as if she had purchased national savings certificates for £100 or paid £100 of income tax. Similarly, if an exporter, Mr W, sells foreign currency to the government for £1,000, the money supply rises just as if he had been paid £1,000 as a salary (and the PSBR been higher) or as a repayment of a government security he owned (and private lending been lower). This necessarily occurs when the government intervenes in the foreign exchange market to influence the exchange rate. Thus, an exchange rate fixing mechanism such as the ERM of the EMS, means that a government cannot simultaneously control the money supply. The obligation to intervene in the foreign exchange market to maintain a fixed or semi-fixed parity means that the overseas influence on the money supply is determined by the actions of the foreign exchange market. This is a crucial monetarist argument against fixing exchange rates since the monetarists feel that maintaining control of the money supply is more important than influencing the exchange rate. Finally, a bank loan creates a deposit irrespective of who the borrower is. As a matter of definition, foreign holdings of bank deposits are excluded from the UK money supply, so it is necessary to deduct from the deposits created by the methods described above any which finish up in foreign ownership. Similarly, if someone pays for a foreign holiday by writing a cheque on a UK bank and the recipient pays this into a UK bank, all that has happened, in effect, is that the ownership of the deposit has been transferred. However, this transfer from resident to non-resident ownership also reduces the money supply. Hence the money supply is reduced by:

1. government sale of foreign currency
2. an increase in foreign deposits with UK banks

and increased by:

3. government purchase of foreign currency
4. an increase in bank loans to non-residents.

The sum of (1) to (4) is the overseas impact on the money supply. In general a balance of payments surplus makes the overseas impact positive.

This account of the process of money creation is not a complete model of the supply of money unless it is augmented by a description of why the transaction takes place, of why the participants wish to engage in it and why they can do so. This usually depends upon government policy and the level and structure of interest rates (see Chapter 12; also Gowland, 1982, 1984a). Moreover, the four variables need not be independent of each other. Indeed, many real-world transactions may combine more than one transaction described above. For example, if Ms Z had borrowed from the bank to finance her tax bill or Ms V to finance her holiday, the money-creation effect of this bank loan would have offset the negative effect described above. Similarly, if Mrs Y had used her bank loan to buy savings certificates, the money supply would have been unaffected. This does not diminish the above analysis of money creation, but instead makes it possible to make statements like the following:

1. Government spending will cause the money supply to rise unless financed by taxation or sales of debt (or foreign currency) to the non-bank private sector.
2. Non-bank private sector borrowing from a bank will increase the money supply unless the loan is used to buy foreign currency or government securities.

Nevertheless, it is usually simpler to maintain the *ceteris paribus* assumption and analyse the transaction separately. A final point is that some models of the money supply assume that the banking sector's desire to lend to the non-bank private sector depends upon the size of its loans to the public sector. These would make bank lending a function of the PSBR less non-bank private sector purchases of public sector debt. If this relationship is positive, the resultant model is called a multiplier model (see p.243). It can, however, also be negative, as in Jaffee's model (see Section 11.3; also Jaffee, 1975 and below).

Finally it is worth noting that the first three items in the flow of funds relationship can be relabelled 'Domestic Credit Expansion' or DCE. Hence

$$\Delta \text{ Money} = \text{DCE} + \text{Overseas impact on the money supply}$$

The IMF and European Commission wish governments to target DCE, that is what their economies' monetary growth would be if the overseas influence were zero. This ensures that countries with a balance of payments deficit would have growth in money which was less than DCE. This relative deflation would tend to reduce their demand for imports. Surplus countries would have monetary growth in excess of DCE and thus a more rapid growth of income and prices. In consequence they would import more. DCE targets tend therefore to eliminate balance of payments surpluses or deficits. Hence, DCE targets are the good behaviour rules of organisations like the EMS; as has been the practice of international financial organisations since Polak (1957) but formalised in McKinnon (1979, Chapter 1). Hence, a consequence of UK membership of the ERM is that it will have to have a DCE target consistent with maintaining its parity. This may be explicit, for example, arising from macroeconomic policy co-ordination through a European Central Bank. Alternatively, it could be implicit, arising from the need to maintain the parity. Either way, membership of an exchange rate fixing mechanism implies some loss of control of domestic macroeconomic policy, here represented by DCE. This was one of Mrs Thatcher's and Minford's arguments against the UK membership.

1.4   Money and credit

Monetarist authors in the 1950s and 1960s frequently argued that Keynesians confused money and credit. Formally, the distinction is clear. Money is an asset owned by someone; credit is a debt owed by someone, although sometimes public sector borrowing is counted as part of credit and sometimes not. Bank liabilities are money, whereas bank assets are credit. Statistically, the two are linked in that, of course, the creation of credit is likely to involve the creation of money and vice versa. For example, a bank loan to a private individual simultaneously increases both the quantity of money and credit. Nevertheless, the two are separable. There are many institutions which extend credit but whose liabilities are not money, including many retail shops. Institutions whose liabilities are money but whose assets are not (private sector) credit are rarer but not unknown; the National Savings Bank in the UK is an example.

Keynesians, without exception, accept that credit can influence spending. In recent years there has been a créditiste revival spearheaded by a prominent Keynesian, Ben Friedman (1983). He and Blinder (1989) emphasised the importance of credit in Keynesian analysis. Expenditure may be influenced by the cost of borrowing, since a high cost is likely to deter expenditure. The other terms attached to a loan may be important, especially the collateral (security) required and the period of repayment. Keynesians, however, have usually stressed the availability of credit, hence the availability doctrine.[9] The rationale of this is that both individuals and companies are unable to carry out their spending plans because of a lack of credit to finance them. Thus the availability of credit is a binding constraint upon expenditure. This, of course, assumes that borrowers cannot borrow as much as they would like, given prevailing interest rates; that is, there is non-price rationing in credit markets, either as a consequence of official policy or because of market imperfections. This is critical to the modern Keynesian defence of the Keynesian consumption function, Chapter 8, and to Keynesian modelling of financial markets, Chapter 11.

Monetarists would not deny the possibility of this but claim that Keynesians assume that this is the only possible transmission mechanism for monetary policy and so treat monetary policy as synonymous with credit policy. Keynesians, for example, frequently suggested in the 1950s that monetary policy could restrict expenditure but that expansionary monetary policy would not necessarily lead to an increase in expenditure; Radcliffe's dictum that you could lead a horse to water but could not make it drink, whereas you *could* stop it drinking (1959). This asymmetry is almost self-evident if credit availability is the transmission mechanism – no one can be forced to borrow more but it is possible to prevent borrowing.

To monetarists who lay stress on the effect on behaviour of holding an asset (money), this Keynesian critique seemed bizarre. In a crude sense monetarism is the belief that money burns a hole in your pocket. When money and credit are simultaneously increased, the Keynesian looks at the borrower, whereas the monetarist looks at the effect on the holder of the deposit. If someone borrows £1,000 to buy antique furniture, the Keynesian would say that it would have no effect on output (unless it stimulated the production of fakes!), whereas the monetarist would expect the seller of the antiques to be influenced by the £1,000 (or strictly to behave differently because the loan and deposit were created). A final point on which monetarists laid great stress was that the rate of interest was the price of credit not of money, but this is better left until later (see p.126) since both parties agree that in this context the rate of interest is the opportunity cost of holding money.

Of course, both parties might be right in their analyses. If an economic agent receives a circular informing him or her that he or she is eligible for a new credit card with a £5,000 loan limit, the Keynesian expects his or her behaviour to be significantly influenced while the monetarist does not. On the other hand, the holder of a term building society deposit might receive a circular saying that in future unlimited withdrawals could be made by cash machine without penalty. This would seem significant to the monetarist, as non-money asset had become money, but not to the Keynesian. In practice many agents would be influenced by both circulars.

1.5 Summary and conclusions

The relationship between money and income can only be analysed within the context of a theoretical model since it is impossible to deduce anything about the direction of causality between money and income from statistical evidence alone. The objective of the monetary theorist is to analyse the consequences of the pervasive use of monetary systems of exchange by modelling the interrelationships between the monetary and real sectors. The link between these, the means by which a change in the money supply causes a change in income, is called the transmission mechanism. This may be direct or indirect. Important examples of indirect transmission mechanisms are the rate of interest and the exchange rate.

Money is defined as those assets which are generally acceptable in payment of a debt. These assets are normally currency (notes and coins) plus bank deposits. Money creation can be analysed through the flow-of-funds equation, described earlier:

Δ Money supply = *PSBR*
+ Δ Bank loans to non-bank private sector
− Δ Non-bank private sector loans to public sector
+ Overseas impact

Although an increase in money and in credit frequently occur together, it is important to distinguish them.

Appendix: Defining money

It is difficult to measure almost any concept; for example, see Graham (1980) for a discussion of the problems of measuring unemployment. Sen once observed that while it was impossible to quantify inequality, he nevertheless hoped that his grandchildren would live in a world in which there was less of it. The attitude of monetarists to monetary growth is often very similar. It is easy to identify periods − for example, 1986–8 when monetary growth is too fast. Similarly, one can make relative statements − for example, the money supply grew less in the UK in 1990 than in 1988. Philosophers have debated the problems of how to define and measure concepts since Plato. Philosophy students usually discuss these in the context of the problem of defining 'dog'. The first set of problems are conceptual; is a wolf a dog? The equivalent problem in defining money is identifying the characteristics of institutions that are banks. In what sense is a money-market fund a bank? The second set of problems are more practical. The author of a definition may be clear what he wants to include but find it difficult to put this into a clear-cut operational definition. For example, it is difficult to think of a definition of a dog that excludes wolves, but includes dingos. Similar problems arise with concepts such as sight deposits. It is clear that the idea is money that is instantly obtainable. However, one faces the problem of deposits where only a portion is instantly obtainable. Alternatively, the deposit may be obtainable in one way (for example a cash machine) but not another. Finally, there are practical problems in that data may not be available in the form that the statistician requires. It may be that the concept involves a dog but data is only available for pets. Similarly, it may be that a definition of money should include deposits held by individuals but not by companies. However, data may not be collected on this basis. It may even be that a bank does not know which of its deposits are held by, for example, non-residents and which by residents.

The following describes the solutions to these problems. The first comprehensive and regularly published monetary statistics for the UK were the M_1, M_2 and M_3 series described in the *Bank of England Quarterly Bulletin*, Volume 10, No. 3 (September 1970) pp.320–6.

M_1 was defined as being notes and coin in circulation, plus sterling current accounts with UK banks.

M_2 was equal to M_1 plus sterling deposit accounts, with 'deposit banks', that is, interest-bearing accounts (other than CDs) with large well-known banks.

M_3 was equal to M_2 plus other deposit accounts, public sector deposits and residents' deposits in foreign currency with deposit banks. The distinction between deposit banks and non-deposit banks was largely one of statistical convenience.

There were various breaks in the series in the 1970s due to the inclusion of new banks. However, consistent series are available on request from the Bank of England.

Following negotiations with the IMF, in December 1976, a new definition of money was introduced, sterling M_3 (£M_3). This was described in the *Bulletin*, Volume 17, No. 1 (March 1977) pp.39–42. This excluded foreign currency deposits from M_3. Thus, it included notes and coin in circulation, plus all sterling deposits held by UK residents with UK banks. Unlike the definitions used by many other central banks it included public sector deposits.

Current accounts were traditionally non-interest bearing demand (NIB) or sight deposits. Later M_1 was defined as including all sight deposits. As an ever larger proportion of these became interest bearing, a new aggregate NIB M_1 was introduced which excluded interest-bearing sight deposits. Subsequently, sterling £M_3 was renamed M_3 and M_3 was renamed M_{3C}. The M_2 series was dropped because the distinction between deposit and non-deposit banks became meaningless. New series, $M2$, $M4$ and $M5$ were introduced to reflect the fact that building societies were becoming more like banks. All of these definitions in different ways treat building societies as if they were banks. Eventually, with the conversion of the Abbey National from a building society to a bank, the distinction became meaningless and M_3 and similar statistics ceased to be published (*Bulletin*, Volume 29, No. 3 (August 1989) pp.352–3). The new aggregates were described in the *Bulletin*, Volume 22, No. 4 (December 1982) pp.530–37. The subjoined list includes for reference, all aggregates used for policy purposes in the 1980s, whether or not they are still published.

1. *Notes and Coin in Circulation*. This excludes notes and coins held by banks.
2. NIB M_1. This is equal to 1, plus non-interest bearing sterling sight deposits.
3. M_1. This is equal to 2, plus private sector interest-bearing sight bank deposits.
4. M_2. This is equal to 2, plus private sector interest-bearing retail sterling bank deposits. Retail refers to deposits which are not wholesale ones, that is, made in large quantities on organised money markets.
5. M_3. This is equal to M_1, plus all private sector time deposits and CDs. It also includes public sector bank deposits.
6. M_{3C}. This is equal to M_3, plus private sector foreign currency bank deposits.
7. M_4. This was originally called private sector liquidity$_1$ (PSL_1).

It excluded bank deposits that had an original maturity of over two years. However, it included private sector holdings of building society shares and deposits.

Private sector M_4 excludes public sector deposits. M_{4C} included foreign currency deposits and was intended to be analogous to M_{3C}.

8. M_5 was originally named PSL_2. This included various money market instruments and private sector holdings of national savings.

9. M_0. This includes all notes and coin in circulation, that is, it includes those held by banks. In addition, it includes banker's balances with the Bank of England.

Notes

1. For the original correspondence see *The Times*, 4 and 6 April 1977.
2. Friedman's writings (for example, 1970b, p.23) are actually much more specific than the usual textbook citations of this phrase suggest. It seems to be the fate of the few memorable phrases in economics that they are frequently cited (often out of context) and usually misinterpreted; Keynes' dictum that 'in the long run we are all dead' has suffered similarly.
3. Keynes may have believed not only that the only influence of monetary policy on the economy was through its effect on the rate of interest but also that the money supply was the only determinant of the rate of interest. See Chick (1983), especially pp.219–28; Keynes (1971), Vols. XIII and XIV. In general I use the term Keynesian to refer to the views generally called Keynesian without consideration of whether they were actually held by Keynes. Keynesian views seem to me to be the proposition that, at least in some circumstances, increased government spending can reduce unemployment combined with an opposition to monetary targets. Here it seems important to concentrate on what influences the levels of unemployment and inflation rather than on exegetical questions, fascinating as these may be. Of the voluminous literature on Keynes: life and times: Moggridge (1976, 1980) is the most readable, although Skidelsky (1983), of which only volume 1 has appeared, will be the definitive life. Keynes (1975) is the best of the many memoir volumes. Bleaney (1985) provides the best study of Keynesian ideas in theory and practice. Interpretation and reinterpretation of his economic writings: Leijonhufvud (1968), Chick (1983), Coddington (1983), Gilbert (1982). Studies of Keynes' role in public policy and his contemporary relevance are equally

voluminous, of which Hamouda and Smithin (1988) and Vicarelli (1983) are perhaps the best (see also p.190, note 1).

4. Keynes put it as follows:

[There is no] monetary theory of production. An economy, which uses money but uses it merely as a neutral link between transactions in real things and real assets and does not allow it to enter into motives or decisions, might be called for want of a better name – a real-exchange economy. Most treatises on the principles of economics are concerned mainly, if not entirely, with a real-exchange economy; and – which is more peculiar – the same thing is also largely true of most treatises on the theory of money . . . . The theory which I desiderate would deal, in contradistinction to this, with an economy in which money plays a part of its own and affects motives and decisions and is, in short, one of the operative factors in the situation, so that the course of events cannot be predicted, either in the long period or in the short, without a knowledge of the behaviour of money between the first state and the last. And it is this which we ought to mean when we speak of a monetary economy.

This can be found reprinted in Chick (1983) pp.2–3; Keynes (1971), Vol. XIII, pp.408–11. For Clower see p.185.

5. Aristotle's writings on money can be found in Book IV of the *Nicomachean Ethics* (Ross, 1954). Modern commentaries can be found in Roll (1961) and Finley (1974). It is obviously easy to read anachronistically so that any passage seems to contain ideas that the author never intended, but Aristotle's ideas are distinctly modern in his derivation of both an asset and a transactions demand for money, and in his proposition that the equilibrium in a monetary economy may not be the same as that in a barter economy (because speculation is possible in a monetary economy).

6. Post Keynesian and Austrian models often eschew equilibrium concepts.

7. Or as one Bank of England official put it 'some liabilities of someone'.

8. In many countries, notably the US, a condition of a bank loan is that a proportion of it be left on deposit with the bank. This is called a compensating balance. The reason is to evade usury laws or to facilitate price discrimination (by having different proportions for different customers). Usury laws are evaded because the effective rate of interest is increased – if a customer wishes to spend $70 with a 30 per cent compensating balance he or she has to borrow $100 – and pay interest on it!

9. The availability doctrine is discussed in Mattesini (1990) pp.15ff. He includes a discussion of the origins of the doctrine. A less ephemeral version is forthcoming, Mattesini (1992).

2

Quantity Theory and Portfolio Balance

2.1 Old quantity theory

The quantity theory of money is a hypothesis that money determines *nominal* income. Nominal income is the price level times output, so a nominal income of £1 million might be 100,000 units of output at £10 each or 10,000 at £100 each or any of a myriad of other combinations. The quantity theory is only a theory of aggregate demand and so cannot in itself explain the breakdown of a level of nominal income into a price level and a level of output, and so employment. For this, an aggregate supply curve is necessary (see Gowland, 1983a, Chapter 4, or 1990, Chapter 5). Hence, various schools of quantity theory arise because of the incompleteness of the basic quantity theory – Keynes' 'fatal ambiguity' and 'great fault' (Weintraub *et al*, 1973) or Friedman's 'missing equation' (in Gordon, 1974). Besides its significance in the history of economic thought, the quantity theory has had a large influence on modern monetary theory. A critic like Desai (1981) regards monetarism as 'but the [old] quantity theory writ large'. Avowed monetarists like Laidler (1982) stress its significance in the development of monetarist thought; indeed Friedman's first major step in the monetarist counter-revolution was to reformulate the quantity theory (1956a; reprinted in Friedman, 1969). Certainly the quantity theory is the most important basic model in which money determines income. Moreover it contains the simplest and clearest example of a direct transmission mechanism from money to income.

The quantity theory postulates a proportionate relationship between money and income so that an x per cent increase in the supply of money will necessarily cause an x per cent increase in nominal income. Monetarists, to use the modern term invented in 1968 by Brunner, have argued for this proposition since at least Oresme's writings in the fourteenth century (see Johnson, 1956). Indeed, for many centuries monetary theory was synonymous with the quantity theory. There were, and are, many varieties of quantity theorists. The best known school, usually referred to as classical monetarists, assumed output to be fixed in the short term. Thus they regarded the quantity theory as a theory of the price level, since if output is fixed, any change in nominal income must be a change in the price level. Others, termed monetary heretics by Keynes (1936), such as Mun, believed that changes in the quantity of money were more often the cause of changes in output. Indeed, an essential element in mercantilism, widely held in the eighteenth century, was the doctrine that governments should seek to promote exports and restrict imports. Despite the derision with which Adam Smith (1776) treated it, this was a perfectly logical piece of macro-economic analysis. A balance of payments surplus increases the money supply and so income. If, like the mercantilists, one believes that a balance of payments surplus is the only way to increase the money supply, it becomes a desirable policy objective, akin to Keynesian arguments for export-led growth. In fact French monetarists like David and Melitz still present models in which money determines output because prices are determined exogenously by cost factors. Anglo-Saxon textbooks often read as if classical monetarism were the only legitimate variety but the other strain has a longer pedigree and equal intellectual validity. More sophisticated variants are possible of which the best known is Friedman's: output adjusts in the short term but price in the long term (see p.166ff).

Despite its antiquity, the old quantity theory was only formally derived in its present form early in the twentieth century, by Irving Fisher (1911). Fisher derived the famous, or infamous, equation of exchange. This is an identity (that is, something which is necessarily true). This is because it is merely two ways of stating the total value of transactions which is equal to the number of transactions (T) multiplied by the average amount involved in each transaction (P). This follows from the definition of the word average, P is the value of transactions divided by T, so PT must equal the value of transactions. The other formulation of the total value of transactions is slightly more complex. If a medium of exchange (M) is used in every transaction, then the average number of times it is used can be calculated by dividing the total value of transactions by the stock of the medium of exchange. This is called the velocity of circulation of the medium of exchange (V). For example, if milk must be paid for with tokens, as used to be the case with the Co-operative dairies, and there are 1,000 tokens issued in an area and sales of milk are 4,000 pints per week, by definition the velocity of circulation is four. Necessarily, the stock of the medium of exchange items times its velocity must equal the value of transactions because of its method of calculation. Thus, Fisher derived the famous identity:

$$MV = PT$$

This identity is virtually useless for economic analysis in this form. Amongst other problems, the following stand out:

1. The total of transactions refers to all transactions, not just transactions in final goods. In addition, financial transactions (for example, a building society deposit), transactions in second-hand goods, transactions in real assets, transactions in intermediate goods and, on some interpretations, gifts are included.
2. The average amount per transaction can change when the quantity of goods per transaction changes as well as when price changes. If pubs started to sell beer in quarter pints (instead of halves and pints) the amount spent per transaction on beer would fall but few drinkers would regard this as a fall in the price of beer.

To be economically useful, PT must be replaced by the level of nominal income, usually written as PQ where P has changed its meaning from the average value per transaction to the price level. To make this double substitution of P and Q for P and T, it is first of all necessary to replace all the transactions by only those transactions which involve real output. This assumes that the ratio of final to total transactions is unchanged, so that, for example, there is no change in the degree of vertical integration. As the *number* of transactions in real output must be replaced by the *quantity* of output, it is necessary to assume that the amount per transaction is unchanged. This assumption is sometimes stated as being an assumption that the structure of payments remains unchanged. It is violated, for example, when firms start to package goods differently; for example, if cigarettes were to be sold in thirties instead of twenties, or when consumers make fewer trips to shops, as has happened with the growth of supermarkets in place of corner shops. Thus, it is necessary to make a series of assumptions about how the economy is organised before T can be replaced by Q. The same assumption plus one other are necessary before P can change its meaning. The additional assumption is that the ratio of the price of final goods to other prices – share prices, house prices, antique prices, etc. – is constant. The quantity theorist needs to make two further assumptions before deriving the crucial proposition, that money is proportional to nominal income. The first is that a medium of exchange exists and can be termed money; that is, a fairly constant set of assets are used for purposes of exchange and nothing else. The other is that velocity is constant. The monetarist can thus derive the basic tenet, that money is proportional to income:

$$M \propto PQ$$

or

$$M = kPQ$$

The monetarist, in fact, can rely on a weaker assumption about velocity: that it is independent of income, prices, output, money and any other economically relevant variables. The quantity theorist, in effect, is committed to the belief that the velocity can be predicted for a given year on 1 January without the prediction being at all conditional upon the outcome of these variables. Hence, velocity can depend upon structural, but not short-term, factors. Thus, a quantity theorist would accept and incorporate a proposition that velocity changed because of the invention of credit cards, but not that it was affected by the level of unemployment. This assumption, sometimes called exogeneity, about velocity is challenged by Keynesians of all varieties. The extreme Keynesian argues that the velocity of money is totally dependent upon the quantity of money and so is as economically meaningful as the sardine velocity of circulation: one can divide the level of income in the UK by the number of sardines (S) in the world and call the result sardine velocity (V). If this is multiplied by the number of sardines, income is once more obtained ($Y = VS$) but no one would regard it as saying anything about the determination of income. Extreme Keynesians similarly regard the velocity of circulation as a meaningless concept, merely an arithmetic artefact invented to link two unrelated variables. If income and money were totally independent, $MV \equiv PQ$ would still be true by definition, because $V \equiv PQ \div M$. Moderate Keynesians argue that V is a meaningful concept but is dependent upon income, prices, output and, critically, the rate of interest (and, indeed, perhaps on the expected level of any of these variables). In other words, it is totally endogenous to the model and cannot therefore be treated as an independent variable.

There are two conclusions worth noting in the old quantity theory. The first is that the monetarist–Keynesian debate can be reduced to an empirical controversy about the nature of velocity. The other is that the quantity theory rests upon assumptions that are more likely to be true in the short term than the long term.

2.2 New quantity theory

The old quantity theory is cumbersome and the assumptions needed to derive it are strong. Hence the monetarist counter-revolution began with Friedman's restatement of the quantity theory (1956a; reprinted in 1969). This reformulation is presented here in simplified form. It is interesting that Friedman's approach is in part derived from the Cambridge cash-balance equation, which was also Keynes' starting point. Indeed, as he himself pointed out, Friedman's whole approach is in some ways derived from Keynes (Gordon, 1974 – especially Patinkin's contribution). Patinkin made a similar point at greater length in Patinkin (1969) where he contrasted Friedman's views with the traditional and in his view authentic quantity theory. Friedman's analysis has two key features. The first is that the quantity theory is formulated as a theory of the demand for money. The other is that it is a theory of stocks, money and assets, in contrast to the Keynesian textbook model, which is only concerned with flows (savings, consumers' expenditure, output, investment and all the rest are flows). This emphasis on the importance of stocks is one of the most valuable features of the monetarist counter-revolution and is considered further in Section 2.4. Keynesian stock models can and have been devised – notably by Tobin (1969), Chapter 5. In a stock model expenditure and so income are determined as a by-product of stock adjustment. As Goodhart (1989a) puts it

> . . . the discrepancy between the stock of money created by credit expansion and the stock that would be demanded in equilibrium sets up subsequent portfolio readjustments involving purchases/sales of a wide range of goods, services and assets, until full equilibrium is restored.

It is a critical feature of Friedman's analysis that emphasis is put upon asset markets. This is the most valuable and widely-shared feature of his approach. In the UK the most important asset markets are in houses and in consumer durables (cars, etc.). Analysis of these asset markets is crucial to the understanding of contemporary monetary policy.

A simple direct transmission mechanism of the sort Friedman envisaged works as follows. Suppose individuals always want to hold money balances equal to about x weeks' income (or alternatively to x weeks' expenditure; given the national income convention, the two are identical). More formally, it is assumed that individuals wish to keep approximately constant the ratio of the value of:

1. Their holdings of money (M)
2. Their expenditure of their income – at an aggregate level income and expenditure are equal – which equals the price (P) times output (Q) (that is, nominal income)
3. The value of their holdings of assets other than money; this is their price (P_A) times their quantity (Q_A)

$$M \propto PQ \propto P_A Q_A$$

or

$$M = k_1 PU = k_2 P_A U_A$$

Friedman's is thus a macroeconomic theory which rests very solidly upon a foundation of a theory about individual behaviour if a simplistic one. An individual might well choose to hold money balances equal to say, six weeks' income and to hold other assets equal to five years' income (these other assets might comprise a house, a car, a building society deposit and a hi-fi system). This is certainly not an unreasonable simplification of behaviour, and, moreover, it is easy to make the model more realistic, as Friedman did. What is crucial is that individuals regard it as vital whether or not they hold their preferred quantity of money and whether, if they are forced away from this equilibrium, they will make a major effort to reattain it. The quantity theory is the result of such efforts.

The following story illustrates the effect of a fall in the money supply, but the example can be reversed.

(a) Individuals always want to hold money balances equal to about x weeks' income (or alternatively to x weeks' expenditure; given the national income convention, the two are identical. In the USA x might be 6 if the definition of money were M_1). In economic jargon there is a stable demand for money.

(b) The government reduces the money supply.

(c) It is assumed that the money market was previously in equilibrium, so that economic agents held the quantity of money they desired. In consequence of the reduction in the money supply individuals no longer hold as much money as they did before. So at least some individuals no longer hold as much money as they wish to. In other words the money market is in disequilibrium because demand is greater than supply.

(d) Individuals, therefore, seek to rebuild their money balances. They can do this either by spending less on the goods they normally buy, or by buying fewer assets, or by selling assets they already own.

(e) As a consequence of (d) there is excess supply in both goods and assets markets. This may have arisen because of reduced demand or because of increased supply, that is people may have bought less or sold some of their existing holdings.

(f) Hence the excess demand for money caused by monetary policy has been transmitted to goods and asset markets as excess supply.

(g) Excess supply means that either prices will fall or output will fall or both depending on the elasticity of supply. As a macroeconomic level this means that a fall in the money supply will lead to a fall in either prices, output or both.

This process must continue until equilibrium is reattained. This will occur only when the demand and supply of money are once more equal. This can only be when both PQ and P_AQ_A have fallen by as much as the money supply. Hence, the proportionality of money and income has been established. Moreover, this result was obtained in a model in which money causes income, so that the quantity theory has been derived. It is possible to elaborate this model in many ways, but it would be pointless as the basic mechanism would remain unchanged. Two steps to greater realism are the introduction of more than one asset besides money, and the introduction of the rate of interest as an extra factor influencing the desired level of the demand for money. These are important but best considered as separate models; namely, Tobin's model (see Chapter 6) and the IS–LM model (see Chapter 4), respectively. The quantity theory is best analysed in this simple version. The assumptions and transmission mechanisms are clear-cut. Resting upon a demand for money relationship, changes in the quantity of money cause disequilibrium in the goods and asset markets. Nominal income (and asset prices and quantities) adjust according to the elementary laws of microeconomics.

Different monetarists have different opinions about which of price or output changes in response to a change in the money supply. Classical monetarists believe that it is always price which changes, whereas French monetarists tend to emphasise that it is output which changes. Friedman believes that output changes in the short term and price in the longer term. It is also possible that the extra demand will lead to a change in neither price nor output. This occurs when the demand is satisfied from foreign sources at previously prevailing prices (or where excess supply is absorbed by the world market). This is true by definition for a small economy. In this case variations in monetary policy lead only to a balance of payments surplus or deficit: *the monetary theory of the balance of payments* or international monetarism, Section 2.3 below. However, the exchange rate may also adjust, in which case the international monetarist model becomes indistinguishable from the Keynesian model, see Section 2.4. Hence the resulting hybrid is the basis of much advanced macroeconomic theory and modelling, for example the Bank of England model in the UK.

The key features of modern monetarist analysis are:

(a) A change in the money supply causes disequilibrium in the money market which is directly transmitted to the goods market.
(b) Adjustment occurs via the asset market.

The latter is common to all modern models of monetary policy, whether Keynesian or monetarist. For most consumers, two assets predominate: houses and consumer durables – washing machines, cars, etc. The main asset for companies is stocks of raw materials and finished goods; most of the latter are consumer durables. Hence monetary policy is likely to have a disproportionate effect on the housing market, the market for consumer durables and (to some extent) that for raw materials. Hence expansionary monetary policy will lead to a rise in the demand for houses and consumer durables. In consequence house prices will rise – expansionary monetary policy led to explosions in house prices in 1972–3, 1978–9 and 1985–8. Builders respond to higher house prices by building more houses (Table 2.1).

Undoubtedly, the monetary expansion in the UK after 1984 caused the explosion in house prices. This generated a rise in housebuilding but it also caused serious social problems as well as impeding labour mobility. More generally unbalanced demand management (fiscal tightness and monetary laxity) led to the concentration of growth in a few sectors of the economy and a few regions, notably the South East. Monetary policy was not the only factor leading to the North–South divide but it was probably amongst the most important.

Table 2.1 Money supply and housebuilding

	Money supply increase (per cent)	Housing starts one year later (000)
1979	13	88
1980	19	112
1981	13	138
1982	9	170
1983	11	160
1984	10	168
1985	14	168
1986	18	194
1987	23	211
1988	21	233

Extra demand for consumer durables will largely be met from foreign sources, especially in the UK with imports from Germany and Japan. Hence expansionary monetary policy will lead to a large balance of payments deficit as in 1973–4 and 1988, when the current account deficit was £15 billion; in 1989 it was £20 billion.

From a theoretical viewpoint Friedman emphasises:

1. The quantity theory is in the first instance a theory of the *demand* for money. It is not a theory of output or money income or of the price level. Any statement about these variables requires combining the quantity theory with some specifications about the conditions of supply of money and perhaps about other variables as well.
2. To the ultimate wealth-owning agents money is one kind of asset, one way of holding wealth, and the ultimate wealth-owning agent is to be regarded as dividing his or her wealth among (the numerous forms possible) so as to maximise utility subject to whatever restrictions affect the possibility of converting one form of wealth into another (Friedman, 1956b, p.176).

2.3 International monetarism

One criticism frequently lodged against the quantity theory is that it is a closed economy model which ignores the existence of the overseas sector. In response to this some economists have developed the monetary approach to the balance of payments, or international monetarism. Despite its name, this model is antithetical to monetarism in that it denies the direct money–income (prices) link essential to orthodox monetarism. The school is, nevertheless, quite close to monetarism in its approach and methodology but radically distinct in its conclusions. The simplest form of international monetarism can be derived as a variant on the quantity theory model used in the section above. One further assumption is made: the economy is a small one, that is, it is a price taker which is unable to influence the world price of any good. The story proceeds as before· until the increase in the money supply has created an excess demand for goods and assets. This excess demand is met by foreign suppliers (at the previously prevailing prices). Hence, there is no change in either domestic prices or output, so income in unchanged. Similarly, the price of assets is unchanged and no new domestic ones are produced. The effect of the increase (reduction) in the money supply has merely been to create a balance of payments deficit (surplus) by the purchase of foreign goods and assets. This balance of payments deficit creates a negative overseas impact on the money supply. The money supply is thus reduced and this continues until it reverts to its original level. In this model, equilibrium in the money market is restored not by a change in income as in the quantity theory but, instead, by a balance of payments surplus or deficit. In consequence, any payments surplus or deficit is nothing but a temporary symptom of disequilibrium in the money market. These features remain in all international monetarist models.

In more advanced models, changes in the money supply do affect income but only indirectly, through changing the exchange rate. Hence, international monetarist models are Keynesian in two senses: changes in the money supply may not affect income; if they do, the changes are made through an indirect transmission mechanism.

The basic mechanism of this approach is that the exchange rate is the price of pounds in terms of dollars etc. and so is likely to depend upon the relative quantities of pounds (the UK money supply) and dollars in existence. Reducing the quantity of pounds should increase the exchange rate and vice versa. When the

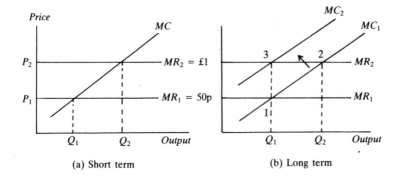

Figure 2.1 The effect of the exchange rate on the economy

money supply changes the price which adjusts to equilibriate the market is now the exchange rate instead of the interest rate.

The effect of a variation in the exchange rate is illustrated in Figure 2.1. The underlying idea behind this analysis is that most UK firms are price takers in markets (both in the UK and abroad) in which the price at which they sell is determined by the world price and the exchange rate. (The world market may be competitive or the UK producers may be relatively small firms in a market in which a foreign price leader or cartel determines the price.) Figure 2.1(a) illustrates this for a representative UK producer – and thus for the entire UK economy. The diagram shows the marginal cost and revenue curves for a producer of a representative good, 'leets'. 'Leets' have a world price of $1. Originally the exchange rate is $2=£1, so the world price expressed in pounds is 50p, the world price divided by the exchange rate. The UK producer faces a perfectly elastic demand and marginal revenue curve at this price. Hence his output of leets is Q_1 at a price of P_1 (50p).

The exchange rate then falls to $1=£1. The world price expressed in sterling is now £1. Hence the fall in the exchange rate causes the *MR* curve to shift upwards to *MR*=£1. Output of leets rises to Q_1 and price to P_1 (£1). This can be generalized:

a fall (rise) in the exchange rate will lead domestic producers to increase (decrease) their output and prices. Hence a fall in the exchange rate increases output (and so reduces unemployment) but at the cost of higher prices (more inflation); a rise in the exchange rate will reduce inflation but at the price of more unemployment.

However, this result only applies in the short term. The lower exchange rate causes a rise in prices. This means domestic producers will face a rise in costs because:

(a) costs of raw materials and inputs have risen; if raw materials and other inputs are imported, then their price necessarily rises when the exchange rate depreciates. Much more importantly, if they are produced within the economy, then their price rises for exactly the same reasons as applies to the output of the final good analysed in Figure 2.1 (a).

(b) real wages are lower and marginal value product higher. Hence whatever model of the labour market is used, wages will rise.

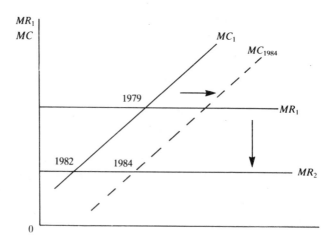

Figure 2.2 The UK economy in the 1990s

The rise in marginal cost is shown in Figure 2.1 (b). The *MC* curve shifts upwards from MC_1 and ultimately reaches MC_2, where output has fallen back to Q_1 – that is, the economy moves from 1 to 2 to 3. This diagram can be reversed to show the effect of an appreciation. This is one way to illustrate the UK economy in the 1980s, Figure 2.2. The appreciation in sterling caused a fall in output and price, hence the economy reached the point marked '1982' in that year. Thereafter the supply curve shifted rightwards as marginal cost was below the level it would otherwise have been and output rose steadily until the effects of Mr Lawson's policy changes in 1985 worked through. The spirit of this model has influenced UK governments since 1974. Whenever they have wanted to reduce inflation they have sought a high exchange rate (1974–5, 1977–8, 1979–80, 1988–9). On other occasions they have sought a lower rate to reduce unemployment (1976, 1985).

It is possible to integrate the two aspects of international monetarism into a single diagram. In Figure 2.3, *MC* is the

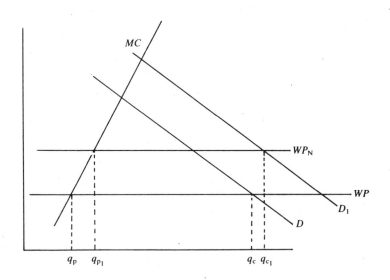

Figure 2.3 The complete model

domestic MC curve and D the domestic demand curve. WP is the world price expressed in pounds. Hence q_p is produced and q_c consumed. Thus there is a balance of payments deficit of $q_p - q_c$. The money supply is increased. In consequence D shifts outwards to D_1 and the exchange rate falls so WP shifts upwards to WP_N. Hence in the short run output rises to q_{p1} and consumption to q_{c1}. The short-run effect on the balance of payments is ambiguous. Once long-run analysis is incorporated – a shift of MC – the ambiguities become still greater. Indeed the whole message of international monetarism is that nothing is certain and paradoxes are likely.

2.4 Portfolio models

Both the new quantity theory and the international monetarist model described above are examples of portfolio (or asset) models. The portfolio approach to monetary policy dominates advanced treatment of the subject (as, for example, with the Tobin model described in Chapter 6 or with Brunner and Meltzer's analysis). The essence of this approach is that it analyses the stock equilibrium (balance) of wealth holders, both corporate and personal. These own a collection of assets, called a portfolio, which includes money. A change in the money supply necessarily means that at least some wealth holders are forced out of equilibrium. They seek to reattain equilibrium by purchasing or selling other assets. This affects the price of other assets and so makes it more attractive to produce them, thus boosting output. For example, an increase in the demand for cars or houses would lead to increased employment as well as higher prices.

The disequilibrium need not be the result of an increase in the quantity of money. For example, an article in the *Bank of England Quarterly Bulletin* suggested that the upsurge in consumer spending in 1982–3 might in part be the consequence of an attempt to readjust portfolios because housing was an excessive proportion of personal sector wealth.[1] Arguments about this continued throughout the 1980s, see Spencer (1990) and Spencer and Muellbauer (1990). Hence, people were borrowing against the security of their homes to increase their holdings of other assets – in particular cars and other consumer durables. Of course, this may have been the indirect effect of an increase in the money supply, since this had caused the rise in house prices, which had unbalanced portfolios in the first place.

Contemporary theories of monetary policy thus give pride of place to the analysis of the impact of monetary policy as the reattainment of stock equilibrium by asset holders. This is analogous to modern theories of investment, which are also usually models of adjustment of the real capital stock rather than models of flow. This similarity is not accidental and means that the effect of monetary policy on corporate spending is easily modelled.

An interesting treatment of investment is the valuation ratio model invented by Tobin (1972) and applied to the UK by Fleming (1976a) and Jenkinson (1981). This is dealt with more fully in Chapter 6, but its essential feature is that monetary policy affects share prices and thus the market price of companies. This is, in effect, the market price of second-hand factories since the purchase of a company involves the purchase of its assets. Other firms thinking of expansion can choose between a new factory (investment) and the purchase of a second-hand one (via purchase of an existing company). A rise in share prices makes the former relatively cheaper. This process can be seen clearly in the case of oil companies. The 1987 stock market crash made acquisitions of oil companies (such as Britoil) a cheaper method of acquiring reserves than exploration. The most thoroughgoing portfolio model is Minford's equilibrium model (for example, 1981) which treats all economic transactions as phases of stock disequilibrium. Godley and Cripps (1983) derive elementary Keynesian results in a stock adjustment framework.

Modern portfolio models are largely the result of the addition of sophisticated techniques of financial analysis to Friedman's basic framework. The quantity theory results are only special cases in these models but the nature of the transmission mechanism and the qualitative results are similar. The market impact of monetary policy on asset prices is as vital a feature of these models as it has been a stylised fact in the UK since 1970. This is, of course, one of Friedman's arguments for relatively stable growth in the money supply, since the rapid rises in house prices in 1972–3, 1978 and 1985–8 had relatively little effect on housebuilding but produced adverse effects on both equity and efficiency. An implication of the portfolio approach is that the effect of monetary policy may be largely (at least initially) on the demand for durable goods rather than on a broader spectrum of goods. However, stocks held by shops and manufacturers are likely to spread the impact. A tightening of monetary policy will lead shops to try to reduce their stocks by, for example, special 'sales', as seen in the UK in 1981–2 and on a much smaller scale in 1989–90. This is the 'stock accelerator'[2]. Similarly, the boom in 1982–4 was largely caused by an upsurge of consumer expenditure on durable goods.This is a very simple effect of asset portfolio disequilibrium but very important in both the UK and USA, where the 'stock (inventory) cycle' accounts for half the variations in output. One implication of this is that a switch to the Japanese-style 'just in time' method would have significant macroeconomic affect. Under this system inventories are less sensitive to changes in output so the accelerator mechanism does not apply (Morgan, 1991).

2.5　Summary and conclusions

The quantity theory of money is the hypothesis that changes in the money supply are the sole determinants of changes in nominal income and, moreover, do so proportionately such that a 1 per cent increase in the money supply leads to a 1 per cent rise in nominal income. The quantity theory can be analysed either by using the equation of exchange ($MV = PT$), sometimes called the old quantity theory, or by using Friedman's reformulation. The latter is valuable in highlighting a direct transmission mechanism whereby excess demand (supply) for money leads to an excess supply (demand) of goods and assets. In its emphasis on the reattainment of stock equilibrium, Friedman's analysis heralded portfolio models which have dominated monetary theory in recent years. Friedman's results do not always follow in these models; for example, international monetarist models suggest that monetary policy largely affects the balance of payments. An important result derived from portfolio models is that changes in macroeconomic conditions will be largely experienced in asset (housing and consumer durable) markets. This theory fits in with the UK experience.

Notes

1. See *Bank Bulletin*, Vol. 22, No. 3 (Sept. 1982), p.390 and Vol. 23, No. 3 (Sept. 1983), p.333.
2. If optional stocks (or inventories) are a fraction of sales then when sales fall, output falls by much more as with the fixed investment accelerator.

3

Demand for Money

3.1   Keynesian motives analysis

Friedman's restatement of the quantity theory was as a theory of
the demand for money. In this, as in virtually all macroeconomic
models, the equilibrium condition is that the demand for money
should equal the supply of money. These are good illustrations of
the crucial importance of the demand for money in modern
monetary theory. The debate about the nature and form of this
demand was the earliest, longest-running and arguably most
important of all the monetarist–Keynesian debates.

There are two distinct approaches to the demand for money.
One is the neoclassical approach; the other is the motives
approach of Keynes, based upon the famous trinity of precautionary, transactions and speculative demands for money. The
model based upon these concepts is usually called the Keynesian
model. This may be misleading in that while Keynes used the
concepts, neither were they the totality of his demand for money
theory (see Section 3.5) nor is it clear that he would have
approved of the modern 'Keynesian' theory. The crucial feature
of this is that each of the three demands is separately analysed
and calculated. The total demand for money is calculated by
summing the three separate demands. This is done at both the
individual and aggregate level. Thus, an individual might hold
transaction balances of £400, speculative balances of £1,000 and

precautionary balances of £600, and so his or her demand for money would be £2,000. The aggregate demand for money is obtained by summing the money demands of all economic agents – individuals, companies and the remaining economic entities (co-operatives, charities, etc.). Both these features are challenged by the adherents of the alternative neoclassical approach, but first the three motives must be examined. The *transactions* demand is straightforward; agents need to hold money for everyday purchases. These would include such items as food for an individual and wages for a company. These balances, Keynesians suggest, are largely dependent upon the volume of transactions and so upon income (and sales for companies). Modern Keynesian theorists would also include interest rates as a determinant of transactions demand (see Section 3.3). The *precautionary* demand arises because it is necessary to hold balances to deal with emergencies which might arise (for example, car or house repairs) and more welcome, but equally unpredictable, sources of expenditure, such as invitations to weddings or weekends with friends who live several hundred miles away. Precautionary balances were little analysed but usually loosely assumed to depend upon income and interest rates. Modern work on precautionary balances such as Sprenkle and Miller (1980) is best considered as an extension of the transactions approach, as in Section 3.3. Finally, *speculative* balances would be held when the price of some other asset was expected to fall; for example, an individual would sell shares or bonds when he or she expected their price to fall and so would hold money instead.

This motives approach is subject to a number of weaknesses. First, in a world of uncertainty, the precautionary and transactions demands are indistinguishable. The theory assumes that transactions are either certain or totally unpredictable. In fact, no transaction is either; instead there is a range of possible transactions which may occur with varying degrees of certainty. Many categories of expenditure obviously lie between the two suggested by the Keynesian approach (such as clothes); but even for the 'certain' ones like food, neither the timing nor the amount spent is determined. Hence the combined treatment in Section 3.3.

Second, the speculative demand for money does not stand up

to analysis. This is a valid criticism and is sufficiently important to be the subject of a separate section (see Section 3.4).

Third, one of the objections to the speculative demand is that it is based upon a fallacy of composition; that is, while valid for individuals, it is not valid as a macroeconomic theory because the aggregation necessary to convert the one into the other is invalid. A similar objection can be lodged against most of the other aggregations necessary to convert a microeconomic theory into an aggregate theory because stringent if not implausible assumptions are always necessary for aggregations.

Finally, a still more serious objection is laid against the other aggregations involved: the summing from motives to the total demand for money. Laidler, a leading neoclassicist (1985), argued that this was like summing the ice cube and cold milk demand for fridges. A fridge, or money, can perform many functions, and the motives approach would imply that several fridges would be purchased whereas one would suffice. Similarly, money holdings could fulfil more than one purpose. Returning to the above example (transactions demand £400, speculative £1,000, precautionary £600) why should one add the three? Why not take the largest (£1,000) and assume that the same balance performs all three roles? Why not add the transactions demand to the larger of the other two – since the speculative balance is also available for precautionary purposes and it is difficult to see why an additional precautionary balance is necessary.

The gravamen of the neoclassical objection to the motives approach is also contained in Laidler's quip. This is that the motives approach is contrary to conventional economic methodology. One should not construct a theory in this way, but money should instead be analysed just like any other durable good.

3.2   Neoclassical approach

The neoclassical approach was largely the work of Friedman (1969), although its origins lie in a famous suggestion of Hicks of 'how to simplify monetary theory' (1935). Laidler (1985) has been the most prominent of 'British' economists to advocate and develop the theory.[1] Friedman argued that the motives approach ignored the key insights of Keynes' analysis. In particular,

Keynes had suggested that the demand for money was not special but should be analysed in exactly the same way as the demand for any other good. For any normal good, economists believe that it will have a positive income elasticity and a negative price elasticity; indeed, this is the definition of normal. There is no reason to believe that money should not be considered a normal good. Hence, the theory of the demand for money should be merely a specific application of conventional microeconomic theory.

Again, following Keynes, Friedman pointed out that the price of money is the opportunity cost of holding it (that is, the return foregone by holding it rather than another asset). In this respect money is like any durable good such as a television or car. In comparing the cost of watching films on a purchased television or at a cinema, the opportunity cost of the funds tied up in the TV must be allowed for (or in deciding whether to rent or buy a TV). The best known example of such a calculation is the AA's estimates of the cost of travel by car.

Rational individuals will hold money up to the point where its marginal benefit (return) will be equal to the marginal cost of holding it. However, there is no need to specify the nature of the return or the services derived from it for exactly the same reason as one postulates a downward sloping demand curve for any other durable good, such as a television, without specific analysis of the 'news demand', the 'opera demand' and the 'Dallas demand'. The opportunity cost of holding money is the rate of return on those assets which money holders regard as direct alternatives to holding money. What these assets are is a matter for empirical investigation since, *a priori*, individuals might regard anything as a substitute for money. Indeed, the argument about the nature of these assets is at the core of the monetarist–Keynesian debate (see p.93). Monetarists argue that all other assets are potential substitutes for money and so would regard the rate of return on all other assets as an influence on the demand for money. Friedman, for example, stressed that the relevant rates of return include those on equities (ordinary shares) and real assets. He proxied the latter by the expected rate of inflation since the rate of return on real assets measured in monetary terms should move in line with inflation: if all prices rise by 20 per cent, the value of a ton of copper will rise by 20 per cent in money terms. Hence, there is a return on holding copper, rather than money, of 20 per cent less storage costs. If inflation were only 5 per cent, the return would be 5 per cent less storage costs, so it would be lower by 15 per cent, the difference in the rate of inflation. Keynesians accept that theoretically the rate of return on all other assets should be included in a demand for money function. Indeed, there is no alternative, since the argument for doing so is exactly the same as that for the fundamental price theory proposition that the demand for any good depends upon the price of all other goods.

However, Keynesians assume, on *ad hoc* grounds, that most of these other assets are not significant substitutes for holding money, rather as someone interested in the demand for marmalade might ignore its cross-price elasticity with holidays to France so as to concentrate on the elasticities with respect to jam and honey. Keynesians believe that in practice money is only a direct alternative to holding short-term financial assets such as building society deposits. In other cases, Keynesians believe the transaction costs and inconvenience are such that the conversion of cash balances to copper ingots as an investment is so rare as to be ignored *de minimis*. Hence, the rival schools agree that the demand for money depends upon the rate of return on those assets which are viewed as direct alternatives to holding money. They disagree about what these alternatives are and so what is the opportunity cost of holding money. However, they are agreed that the rate of return is that on other assets relative to that on money. Hence, if the rate of return on money were to vary, this variation could influence the demand for money. This is analogous to the demand for televisions; for example, the introduction of an extra channel would shift the demand curve and must be introduced into the analysis even though there is no need to analyse the demand for Coronation Street and sum it with the demand for the Olympics. Usually the relevant aspect of the return for holding money is interest paid on bank deposits. Nevertheless, there are also services paid in kind, such as remitted charges for banking services or even free gifts such as piggy banks or book tokens. These rarely affect the marginal rate of return, however, and in principle can in any case be added to the interest paid to calculate the return on a bank deposit in cash and kind – usually termed the 'own rate'. In fact Friedman

(1956a) considered this. The elasticity with respect to this is positive since a higher rate of interest on bank deposits should, other things being equal, lead to a higher demand for money. This has become of greater relevance as ever-greater proportions of demand (checkable) or sight deposits became interest bearing. In the UK, in 1984, the total of interest-bearing sight deposits exceeded non-interest-bearing ones for the first time and the proportion of the former continued to grow. Personal (retail) customers could obtain interest-bearing current accounts only in special circumstances, such as if they held a minimum balance of £1,000. Even so by October 1988 such accounts (£14 billion) already exceeded orthodox, non-interest-bearing ones (£12 billion), when the Midland Bank followed by the other 'High Street' banks introduced interest-bearing current accounts which did not involve minimum balances or other restrictive features. It was estimated that the change would reduce Nat West's profits by 14 per cent.

The income elasticity is much less controversial but has been debated at some length because of Friedman's distinctive view on the matter. He argued that the microeconomic proposition is that demand for a normal good increases when the budget line is shifted outwards in a parallel fashion. This is not necessarily the same as an increase in real income. Instead, Friedman suggested that the appropriate budget constraint should be defined in terms of wealth or permanent income. Money is an asset. Hence one should look at holdings of it as part of an overall portfolio of assets. This is logical in view of the asset price transmission mechanism or monetary policies, Chapter 2. However, in principle a similar point applies to the demand for any good. The different specifications have relatively little impact on economic policy (for the exception, see Chapter 7). There have also been arguments about whether or not money is a luxury with an income elasticity above one as Friedman thought. The counter-argument is based on the Tobin–Baumol model below, that there are economies of scale in holding money.

The final influence on the demand for money is the price level. If there is not money illusion, the demand for money should rise proportionately with the price level because the demand for real balances should be invariant with respect to the price level. This is another basic microeconomic proposition.

Hence, the neoclassical theory of the demand for money is that it should depend upon:

1. The general price level, with a positive elasticity: on theoretical grounds this should be equal to unity, at least in the long run.
2. The level of real wealth, with a positive elasticity.[2] Friedman included 'human wealth': the discounted present value of future earnings.
3. The level of real income (or output), with a positive elasticity.
4. The rate of interest on short-term financial assets, with a negative elasticity.
5. The rate of return on other assets, including real assets with a negative elasticity.
6. The own rate of return, with a positive elasticity.

The list is comprehensive and any theory of the demand for money can be treated as a special case of the theory. The neoclassical theory is thus the most general of the rival theories. Indeed, it would probably be unchallenged if it were not for the policy significance which attaches to specific numerical values of the various elasticities. These can be estimated empirically, but supporters of the motives approach believe that theoretical analysis can throw additional light upon these values. The appeal of this has not been diluted by the poor performance of empirical equations in recent years – described in the *New Palgrave* as 'in a bit of disarray', Goldfeld in Eatwell *et al* (1989).

3.3   Transactions demand and inventory theory

Tobin (1956) and Baumol (1952) constructed similar theories of the demand for money. Theirs is known as the inventory theoretic approach because they used models originally designed to calculate optimal stock (inventory) levels for a firm. In fact the Tobin–Baumol approach was anticipated by Allais (in 1948); see Tobin and Baumol (1989) for their discussion and translations of Allais. A car-producing firm has to decide how many windscreen wipers to have in stock. If it has too few, the entire assembly line may be brought to a halt (if, for example, a strike halts deliveries). On the other hand, if it holds too many wipers it foregoes interest on the money tied up in this stock and incurs storage costs. The firm has to trade-off these costs and benefits. Tobin and Baumol discovered that there was an extensive literature devoted to this problem which could easily be adapted to the demand for money. Ironically, at the same time Japanese engineers sought to make this redundant by the 'just in time' approach – not without its parallel in the demand for money literature, see the section on the discussion of sweep accounts below.

The Tobin–Baumol model was derived using the very simple example of an individual who receives income periodically (discretely) but spends it continuously; for example, someone who receives an income of £720 per month and spends £24 per day (in fact, as set up, the model assumes £1 per hour, 1.4p per minute, etc.). This is merely a convenient mathematical formulation of the problem that faces most individuals, because they receive income infrequently but make many (smaller) purchases. It is quite easy to generalise the model to make it more realistic; for example, by adding lumpy payments like gas and electricity bills. An individual (John James) who receives his income at the start of the period could choose to hold it all as money; a separate analysis is needed to determine how much is held in cash and how much in a bank account. In this case he would receive no interest. Alternatively, he might hold the amount in interest-bearing form, such as a time deposit or a building society account. In this case he receives interest. However, he incurs costs in that he must visit the building society to make a withdrawal each time he wishes to make a purchase (that is, to convert an interest-bearing asset into money). Each trip will involve a number of costs. Some of these are psychological – the time and effort involved in visiting the building society. Others are pecuniary, such as the petrol or bus fares involved. Still other costs would be an interest penalty on making a withdrawal (as with a bank time deposit) or a fixed or variable fee for making a withdrawal. The individual can calculate the income and deduct from it the transactions costs incurred to see which course of action is preferable. For example, if the individual visited the building society daily, he could earn interest equal to that obtained for half a month of his salary (£720): since his deposit would be £720 for one day, £696 on the second day, etc., concluding with £0 on the thirtieth day, he would have held an average deposit of £360. In general, average money holdings must be equal to half those at the starting point since they decline continuously to zero. If interest rates were 6 per cent per annum (0.5 per cent per month), he would receive £1.80 in interest. To earn this, he would have to make thirty trips to the building society, so he would prefer to hold his salary as cash unless the transaction costs were less than 6p per trip. However, there are many intermediate possibilities. He could, for example, pay £360 into the society and withdraw it after a fortnight. In this case his average money holding would be £180 – since on each occasion he starts with £360 and this declines continuously to 0. This earns 90p interest and involves only two trips per month so is preferable to holding nothing but money, unless the transaction cost exceeds 45p.

Tobin and Baumol sought to calculate the optimal number of trips made and so the average money holding. To restate, income divided by the number of trips equals his or her money holdings after each conversion of interest-bearing assets. Average money holdings equal this value divided by two. If the individual makes no trips (that is, holds all money), his or her average holding is £360 (£720 on Day 1, £690 on Day 2, down to £0 on Day 30). If he or she makes two trips, as in the final example, he or she only holds an average of £180 (since he or she holds £360 at the beginning of each month) and so on. The optimal number of trips is the one which maximises income received in the form of interest, net of transaction costs; in fact, Tobin and Baumol minimised transaction costs less interest received. This is the same thing, of course, but made the problem analogous to the firm deciding on the stock of wipers it would hold. The optimal quantity clearly depends upon:

1. The price level (P).
2. Real volume of transactions per period (T).
3. Interest rate received on the interest-bearing asset (r). This was misleadingly termed bonds by Tobin. The usual alternative will in fact be a capital certain short-term asset such as a savings deposit.
4. Transaction cost, or as termed by Tobin, the brokerage fee (b).

Tobin and Baumol (see Appendix 1, p.67) showed that money holdings (M^*) would equal:

$$M^* = P \sqrt{\frac{Tb}{2r}}$$

Hence, this theory is often called the square-root rule. It implies that the price elasticity is unity and all the other elasticities are equal to 0.5 to negative in the case of interest rates, positive for the brokerage fee and the volume of transactions (see Appendix 2, p.69). The fact that the elasticity with respect to the volume of transactions is less than unity means that there are economies of scale in money holding; that is, the optimal size of money balances rises by less than real income.

Tobin and Baumol had thus achieved their aim of producing a model which gave precise, numerical values for elasticities and one which, moreover, had other interesting implications, especially the hypothesis that economies of scale exist in money holding. Their models proved easy to expand and generalise. Policano and Grossman (1977) produced the most interesting and elegant addition. They treated the number of trips made to purchase goods as another variable. The Policano–Grossman representative consumer still receives, say, £720 per month and *consumes* £30 per day of goods. However, this consumer also decides whether to visit the shops once a day and purchase £30 of goods each time or once every two days and purchase £60, or the various other possibilities. Each trip involves a transaction cost in terms of time, inconvenience and transport costs. Hence there is an incentive to minimise the number of trips. However, each trip incurs an extra cost because the outlay is made earlier, so an opportunity to earn interest is lost. This may be partly balanced by any saving brought about by purchasing goods earlier if prices are rising. Thus, the individual has to make a further trade-off to determine the optimal number of trips to the supermarket. As this model means the individual has these assets available (that is, goods as well as money and interest-bearing assets), this has implications for the optimal quantity of money held. The consequence is that two further items enter the Tobin–Baumol formula: the rate of inflation, with an elasticity of $-\frac{1}{2}$, and the costs of purchasing goods, $\frac{1}{2}$. Critically, Policano and Grossman have produced a Friedman-type demand for money function in a

Keynesian framework in that inflation is a cost of holding money. The cost of shopping term proves vital in more advanced analysis, see Blanchard and Fischer (1989, p.171). They choose to optimise the time between shopping trips, not as Policano and Grossman did, the goods obtained per trip, but the two are merely inverses in the simple model. One can also easily incorporate an own rate of interest with an elasticity of ½. If the own rate of interest exceeds that on alternatives, all assets are held as money and the average value of money holdings is *PT*/2.

It is possible to make the Tobin–Baumol model more realistic in other ways. Tobin's reworking ensured that only an integral number of conversions could be made; the Baumol version allowed for the absurd possibility of a fractional number of visits to the building society. The Tobin–Baumol model is simple, elegant and produces very specific values for elasticities.

Hence it seems possible to generate an apparently rigorous and plausible model of the demand for money which offers some insights into elasticities on theoretical grounds.

Effectively, Tobin and Baumol assume that the cost of not having money is infinite. In fact there are at least two alternatives: not performing the transaction or borrowing. These possibilities are perhaps most relevant when the timing of receipts and payments is uncertain. However, they are also relevant even in the certainty case; expenditure patterns are not inviolate. It is possible that an individual will be unable to make a transaction because he or she has no money (for example, a student whose grant cheque is delayed in the post and who has to forgo a planned trip). This is called a 'stock-out' cost because it is analogous to the problem faced by a car firm which runs out of windscreen wipers (see, for example, Thorn, 1974).

Of the many other features that have been grafted on to the Tobin–Baumol models, the most important is the possibility of borrowing, since it is conceivable that an individual would choose to have an overdraft rather than cash an interest-bearing asset, or not perform a transaction at all. The attractiveness of doing this depends upon the rate of interest on bank loans relative to that on interest-bearing *assets*, and upon the cost of encashment. Rama Sastry (1970) developed an elegant model in which the possibility of borrowing was integrated within the Tobin–Baumol framework. Optimal money holdings (M^*) were shown to be the following, where r_c is the rate of interest paid on loans:

$$M^* = P\left(\frac{bT}{2r}\right)^{1/2}\left(\frac{r_c}{r+r_c}\right)^{1/2}$$

This is, of course, the Tobin–Baumol formula multiplied by

$$\left(\frac{r_c}{r+r_c}\right)^{1/2}$$

It is possible to calculate either partial interest elasticities (that is, holding r_c constant) or total ones (that is, allowing for changes in both r and r_c simultaneously). When the partial elasticity is calculated, it equals:

$$-\frac{1}{2}\left(1+\frac{r}{r+r_c}\right)$$

Tobin–Baumol's square-root formula implicitly assumes an infinite cost of borrowing (since it is impossible), in which case

$$\left(\frac{r}{r+r_c}\right)$$

equals zero, so the elasticity is indeed $-\frac{1}{2}$. In general, however, the possibility of borrowing increases the interest elasticity.

Nevertheless, this model has been subject to much criticism, notably by Orr (1970), Sprenkle (1969, 1972) and Goodhart (1975). Among other points that have been made are:

(a) The possible gains for an individual seem so trivial relative to the costs that the rational individual would not bother. This point is illustrated by the fairly realistic figures cited in the original example; it is in practice unlikely that anyone 'would think it worth visiting a building society to gain 45p'. In general it can be shown that no switches will take place between the interest-bearing asset and money unless the brokerage fee is less than one-eighth of the interest rate times the individual's income (both measured per period). Presented formally this is:

$$b < \frac{PTr}{8}$$

Using this formula with plausible specific values suggests that few individuals will wish to switch at all; for example, even with a very high net income of £1,000 per month, and (after tax) interest rates of 7 per cent per annum, the brokerage fee has to be less than 80p for any transactions to be worthwhile. Indeed, if the brokerage fee includes a time element of at least fifteen minutes, and if time is valued at the average wage rate, as is conventional in cost–benefit studies, there will be no switches between money and interest-bearing assets at an after-tax interest rate of 7 per cent, assuming monthly payments of salary (if the interest rate were 10 per cent, the time element has to be twenty minutes to eliminate any transfers). For a theoretical analysis of the value of time see Fisher (1989, pp.43–7), largely based on Karni's work (for example, 1974). Thus it has been suggested that the model is more relevant to companies than persons.

(b) However, US corporate holdings of money are 100 times larger than implied by crude Tobin–Baumol models (Sprenkle, 1972). If Tobin–Baumol can only explain 1 per cent of money holdings, the model is of little practical value; to quote Sprenkle, it is 'useless'. By contrast, in the UK money holding tends to be below the Tobin–Baumol formula level (Phillips, 1979; Dow and Saville, 1988).

(c) The specific values of the elasticities generated by Tobin and Baumol are very much special cases. As Orr (1970, p.47) put it, 'a proper choice of departure from the Baumol model can generate elasticity predictions which differ significantly from his'. An early and crucial result was Brunner and Meltzer (1967), who showed that if the brokerage fee were proportional to the value of the transaction (instead of a constant), the correct real income elasticity was unity and so the economies of scale in money holding disappeared and the quantity theory reappeared. Insofar as time is the major element of the brokerage fee, the Tobin–Baumol formulation is probably the more plausible of the two. A more general model can be developed in which

$$b = b_0 + b_1 V$$

where b_0 is a fixed element and b_1 is proportional to the value of the transaction (V). In this case the elasticity is between ½ and 1, collapsing to ½ when $b_1 = 0$ and to 1 when $b_0 = 0$.

Nevertheless, the specificity of the model is one of its major virtues and this disappeared once it had been shown that $-½$ was only a special case. Moreover, the square root was not even the minimum value that the elasticity could take. Sprenkle (1970) and Miller and Orr (1966) showed that an elasticity of ⅓ (that is, below the square-root rule) could be derived on very plausible assumptions. Tobin–Baumol assume that payment is received in non-money form so that one transaction is necessary to obtain any money – for example, one receives a pay cheque. Instead, one's salary may be paid into a bank account – the Sprenkle case. Akerlof and Milbourne (1978) deal with two further problems. One is that individuals save part of their income: in other words interest-bearing assets are acquired as long-term holdings as well as for short-term 'Tobin–Baumol' reasons. The other is aggregating from an individual to the entire community. Problems arise because it pays some individuals but not others to make Tobin–Baumol conversions. They demonstrate that almost any elasticity can be derived, depending on the propensity to save and the proportion of income earned by those who do not make any conversions.

Hence, Tobin–Baumol models do not seem to add anything to the neoclassical theory as a (macroeconomic) theory of the demand for money, since no further variables are suggested, nor can any specific values be derived for elasticities. Nevertheless, variables which are important in the neoclassical theory have been made explicit; in particular, loan rates and structural change (for example, Johnston, 1984). However, the theory has been of crucial importance as a prescriptive microeconomic theory, since many firms now practise cash management policies based on these models. Computer packages which carry out the calculations are available to the smallest firm at minimal cost and some banks will do the work for their customers. The Royal Bank of Scotland and certain building societies offer modified versions to the individuals. Hence, Tobin–Baumol models may be becoming more relevant as descriptions, despite innovations like credit cards, which might seem to render them obsolete. However, Tobin–Baumol models also seem in danger of being outmoded by important features of the advances in cash management engendered by both technical progress and competition amongst financial institutions. In many ways these are analogous to the 'just in time' approach to stocks. The sweep account automatically converts any cash balance to interest-bearing form at the end of the working day. In effect it is Tobin–Baumol with '*b*' equal to zero and so money holdings are zero! However, there may be very heavy costs of setting up such a mechanism to switch between interest-bearing and non-interest-bearing assets, but the marginal brokerage fee is usually trivial. For example, Goodhart shows that this is so in the case of companies, with access to overnight wholesale money markets. Even individuals and small businesses can make use of 'sweep accounts' (provided by Bristol and West Building Society and various banks). These automatically transfer all excess balances from current account to interest-bearing form. The Alliance–Bank of Scotland account works in reverse. All inflows are placed in interest-bearing form, but transfers are made to current account balance whenever it falls to the minimum level to avoid bank charges. These types of procedure mean that:

1. When interest rates rise it pays some people to switch to a sweep account or other scheme whereas previously they found it too costly.
2. Thus the elasticity is with respect to *changes* in interest rates, not actual levels.
3. When interest rates fall, it pays no one to cease using a scheme, since the initial expenditure is not recoverable. Thus, the elasticity is zero for falls in interest rates.
4. All participants in such schemes have a zero-interest elasticity.

It would be both churlish and misleading not to emphasise the enormous role of Tobin–Baumol models in the development of both (academic) portfolio theory and (practical/microeconomic) cash management practice. Nevertheless, the motives-approach analysis of transactions demand seems pointless for the objectives of macroeconomic monetary theory.

It is therefore worth examining the role of Tobin–Baumol in the 1990s when most current accounts pay interest at close to market rates:

(a) They may explain cash holdings, especially by individuals. With an interest-bearing current account and the brokerage fee the cost of visiting a cash machine, the basic model seems perfectly apposite. It could be used for macro-economic purposes, for deciding the capacity of banknote printing works or to enable banks to decide on optimal provision of cash machines – that is, what is the effect of reducing b by providing more cash machines?

(b) Much of the work which incorporates Tobin–Baumol is vital in advanced theory. For example, the so-called general equilibrium version (Blanchard and Fischer, 1989, pp.168–80) incorporates Tobin–Baumol into an overlapping generations model (p.161) to investigate many crucial issues of economic theory. Clower uses the approach in his brilliant analysis of a trader (1986, pp.166–84) who produces and purchases various goods. Clower makes particular use of 'bunching costs', that is an assumption that one would prefer not to do all one's dealing on the same day – at an individual level one does not wish to buy new clothes, a new hi-fi and visit the supermarket all on the same day. This enables him to derive various discontinuities which challenge the neoclassical approach and therefore fit in with a new Keynesian approach, see Section 8.4 below.

(c) It provides a suitable framework within which to incorporate uncertainty about the timing of receipts and payments. Cash management is really a problem of how to deal with a stream of receipts and bills when it is unclear exactly when they will materialise. Such a problem is really a hybrid transactions–precautionary demand and is still relevant, even in a world of sweep accounts. The seminal version of such models was devised by Miller and Orr (1966) and Orr (1970). It incorporates floors and ceilings – replenish money balances when they fall to £x and transfer money to a higher-yielding form when balances exceed £z (for floors and ceilings see Cuthbertson, 1985, pp.28–31, 35–7). If one can model the nature of the receipts and payments specific elasticities can be devised, for example $(-)\frac{1}{3}$ if they are binomial. Sprenkle and Miller (1980) include overdraft facilities. In this case agents normally simultaneously hold large quantities of liquid assets and have overdrafts – a real-world feature observed by Dow and Saville (1988) – even when the latter's cost is below the former's yield.

3.4   Speculative demand for money

The Keynesian speculative demand for money was originally devised to justify the hypothesis that the demand for money was infinitely elastic, the liquidity trap (see pp.73 and 89). The proposition was basically simple: individuals would not hold assets whose price was expected to fall, but would hold money instead. Hence, if the price of an asset, in particular bonds, were expected to fall, wealth holders would sell them and hold the proceeds as money. Thus the demand for money was dependent upon expected changes in bond prices. Bonds (see Appendix 3, p.71) are marketable assets whose price moves inversely with interest rates, because they give the holder a fixed income. The attractiveness, and so the value, of such a fixed sum obviously varies according to the rate of interest. Indeed, in the case of an infinite bond, its price is the inverse of the rate of interest; see Appendix 3 for a fuller explanation of the bond price/interest rate relationship. Hence, individuals will hold money when they expect interest rates to fall. The Keynesian theory then argued that individuals believed that there was a 'normal' rate of interest, and that if interest rates were above this, interest rates would be expected to fall, and vice versa. Hence, whenever interest rates were below the normal rate, there would be a speculative demand for money. This would, in fact, be so large that a minute fall in the interest rate below the normal rate would lead to an enormous demand for money by the erstwhile bond holders. Thus the interest elasticity would be (almost) infinite.

This simple and plausible theory has been attacked on several grounds:

(a) Expectations in the bond market are extrapolative, not regressive, as implied by the Keynesian theory; that is, when interest rates fall they are expected to fall still more, not rise as adherents of the speculative demand suggest.

(b) The theory suggests that individuals hold either bonds or money but not both. In fact, all of those wealthy enough ever to own bonds, own both all of the time. Tobin modified the theory to accommodate this objection, in a famous article entitled 'Liquidity preference as behaviour towards risk' (1958). He assumed that individuals held expectations about future interest rates which were uncertain, and not necessarily the same for all individuals, as in the simple version. Hence, if the normal rate were 14 per cent and the actual rate 13 per cent, the Tobinite speculator might believe there was a 10 per cent chance that rates would fall further, a 50 per cent chance that they would rise to 14 per cent and a 40 per cent chance that they would rise even higher. Normal risk aversion would make the individual choose to hold some bonds and some money. Holding only money deprives the asset holder of any income, holding only bonds is excessively risky. If, instead, interest rates were 12 per cent, the asset holder would hold fewer bonds but would still hold some. This resurrection of the theory avoids the problem but no longer produces an infinite elasticity between interest rates and the demand for money. Moreover, the concept of a normal rate is unnecessary in this model; individuals merely hold expectations about future interest rates. Hence, Tobin's reformulation drops the two crucial elements of the theory. Moreover, it is still not immune to the two final criticisms.

(c) There exists a large number of interest-bearing capital-certain assets, such as building society deposits; that is, assets whose value does not vary with the interest rates. Instead, the interest received falls when interest rates change. Those not wishing to hold bonds have no reason to hold money when they could hold these interest-bearing capital-certain assets instead, because they have the advantage of money for the Keynesian speculator and pay interest. Hence, the theory is a theory of demand for (short-term) capital-certain assets rather than a theory of the demand for money.

This leads into a discussion of what is meant by money. It

was pointed out by a reader of this book that this objection would not hold if one took a broad definition of money, for example including liquid capital-certain assets. In fact, there will always be a non-money capital-certain asset about which the objection is valid – perhaps a ninety-day-notice building society account. The argument is an investor fearing a fall in bond or share prices will move into capital-certain assets. Capital-certain assets will be held either as money or in less liquid form according to relative yields etc. – in fact according to a transactions theory. Hence the speculative demand, if it exists, is irrelevant to the demand for money as distinct from the aggregate of capital-certain assets.

(d) Even as a theory of the demand for capital-certain assets the speculative demand as an aggregate theory rests upon a fallacy of composition; that is, while true at an individual level, it is invalid as an aggregate theory. This stems from the rational and efficient market theory but can be derived very simply. The bond stock cannot disappear. Someone must hold bonds. Therefore, at an aggregate level, there cannot be a switch from bonds to money or vice versa. Anyone selling bonds to increase his or her money holdings must be matched by a purchaser of bonds. The bond market will always be in equilibrium, because of low transaction costs, zero storage costs, money transactions, etc. Thus, supply will always equal demand; that is, the price will always be such that the desire to hold bonds is equal to the quantity of bonds in existence. At this price some holders will expect bond prices to fall and others will expect prices to rise. The former will not hold bonds and the latter will. The speculative theory explains who holds money (those who expect bond prices to fall) not the total of bonds held. If expectations change, there will be a change in bond prices – interest rates – not in the quantity of money held.[3] For example, if all the Keynesian speculators awoke believing interest rates would fall, they would all try to buy bonds. None would be available at the former price, so the price would adjust to the level where as many speculators expected interest rates to rise as expected rates to fall. Indeed, because the bond market is in equilibrium, the price is necessarily at this level. In short, the speculative demand for money is a microeconomic theory of the demand for capital-certain assets. At best, to repeat, it explains who holds money, not how much money is held.

Much of the literature has been valuable as pioneering work in the field of portfolio theory but is irrelevant to the objective of this chapter. It is easy to develop an asset demand for money in this context but not clear what it adds to the neoclassical theory.

3.5 Finance demand for money and the buffer stock approach

In addition to his famous trinity, Keynes discussed the finance demand for money (1937). Individuals and companies plan their future expenditure, especially large purchases. At some stage they will need to hold money to pay for these goods and services. They may borrow this but even so are likely to hold money for at least a few days before the bill is paid. These money holdings which precede expenditure were termed the finance demand for money by Keynes. Their role in explaining why income may cause money even though money precedes income was discussed above, p.5. The approach emphasises future or expected expenditure rather than current spending. This emphasis on future expenditure is important and has been echoed by Friedman, who stresses permanent income in his analysis; permanent income is also a forward-looking concept, based upon expectations of future income.

Implicitly, however, by weakening the money–income link many economists regard it as an argument against monetary targets. Although different in concept the buffer stock approach is similar in implication, especially in denying the need for tight monetary targets.

The idea underlying the buffer stock is simple. Given risk and uncertainty not all events are correctly anticipated, so at least one variable must not be equal to its planned value. If one chooses one can arrange one's affairs so that this shock will be in a predetermined variable – the buffer. The idea was pioneered by Bain (1981), for example, although Darby (1972) first used the term – see also Laidler (1984), Goodhart (1989a) and Cuthbertson (1985, pp.130–42).

Bain's concept of money as a 'buffer stock' will be considered first. In his work Bain, like Friedman, seeks to give renewed prominence and formal expression to a traditional view which had previously received little modern attention. The intellectual pedigree of 'bufferism' goes back at least to the famous preamble to the act establishing the US Federal Reserve system, with its stress on the need for an elastic currency. The crucial idea is that economic agents, whether individuals or companies, hold money to insulate themselves against shocks (hence the term 'buffer'). An individual, Alan Brown, with a variable income might well decide to maintain a constant portfolio of assets and an invariant spending pattern and allow his holdings of money to vary so as to enable him to do this. Hence, when his income is below average, his money holdings would fall, and vice versa. This principle can be applied to unexpected or unpredictable as well as expected variations in income. An ice-cream salesman would not wish to abandon a planned night out because it has rained, nor to make his expenditure more generally contingent upon short-term fluctuations in the weather. Similar considerations apply to companies. Bain reasonably concludes from this:

1. Individuals' and companies' holdings of money are likely to fluctuate very substantially.
2. Such fluctuations are likely to be related to the system of credit in force. An alternative to varying money balances is to borrow. If, as in the UK, it is easy for the borrower to adjust the quantity of his or her borrowing (via the overdraft system), then credit will also act as a buffer. If borrowing is inflexible (as for personal borrowers in the US) then money holdings will fluctuate more and money will be the only buffer.

The controversial feature of Bain's analysis is that he aggregates these propositions to a macroeconomic level. He deduces that when the economy is subject to a shock, then the demand for money will respond by shifting, and concludes that the authorities must let the supply of money adjust to this. This is a traditional central banking doctrine in the face of, for example, the 1972 postal strike. However, with the possible exception of such events, which interfere with the workings of the monetary system, monetarists would argue that it was better to hold the money supply constant. The shock must be reflected somewhere, and they prefer to see interest rates or exchange rates absorb the shock. This debate is reviewed later, in Chapter 12.

Buffer stock analysis of the demand for money normally distinguishes between expected and unexpected changes in money holdings, the latter being due to a shock. If my gas bill is £100 instead of an anticipated £150 my bank balance will be £50 higher than expected and I will, it is hypothesised, behave differently than when I receive an anticipated £50 expenses payment. Cuthbertson, a leading advocate of this school, believes that the floor–ceiling approach above may broadly represent the buffer stock approach (1985, p.132). This leads to the main objection to the concept – so what? Some agents will have unexpected positive and others negative balances which net out – as with a cheque delayed in the post – but the aggregate demand for money will be unaffected. Bufferism is most valuable in that it clearly incorporates both realistic assumptions and uncertainly. However, the natural implication of such an approach would be to use a stochastic payments and receipts model such as those analysed by Orr (1970).

3.6 Summary and conclusions

There are two alternative approaches to the demand for money: the neoclassical and the motives approach. Both agree that the demand for money is positively dependent upon prices (with a unitary elasticity), real output (or wealth) and the own rate of interest paid on money and negatively related to the competitive rate of interest paid upon alternatives to holding money. The motives approach purports to derive specific numerical values for these elasticities, but the attempts fail.

Appendix 1: Derivation of the Tobin–Baumol formula

Let: t be the (real) value of income (and transactions) per period;

   r, the rate of interest per period;

   b, the brokerage fee – cost of converting interest-bearing assets into cash – which is assumed to be independent of the size of the transfer;

   K, the (real) value of interest-bearing assets converted into money at each transaction (the individual agent chooses **K**).

The individual (for expositional simplicity assumed to be male), for simplicity, is assumed to start with all his income in interest-bearing form; for example, his salary is paid into a building society. He draws **K** out each time he converts his interest-bearing asset into cash. He spends this at a constant rate until his money balance is 0, when he replenishes his money balance by making another withdrawal. Hence, his money holdings fall from **K** to 0 at a constant rate and rise to **K** again, and so on. Thus, his average money holding is **K**/2. Hence, the interest he foregoes (per period) by holding money is **r**(**K**/2). The individual draws the whole of his income **t** out of the building society over the period, at a rate of **K** per transaction. Hence, he converts interest-bearing assets into money **t**/**K** times. Thus he incurs **b**(**t**/**K**) in brokerage fees.

   The individual maximises utility by choosing **K** to minimise the sum of brokerage fees and interest forgone. Hence, the individual chooses **K** to minimise these costs (*C*):

$$C = r\,\frac{K}{2} + b\,\frac{t}{K}$$

C will be minimised where:

$$\frac{dC}{dK} = 0 \left(\text{and } \frac{d^2C}{dK^2} < 0 \right)$$

$$\frac{dC}{dK} = \frac{r}{2} - \frac{bt}{K^2}$$

so:

$$\frac{dC}{dK} = 0 \text{ when } \frac{r}{2} = \frac{bt}{K^2}$$

that is, when:

$$K^2 = \frac{2bt}{r}$$

so the optimal value of **K** is:

$$K = \sqrt{\frac{2bt}{r}}$$

so average money holding is:

$$\frac{(K)}{2} = \frac{1}{2} \sqrt{\frac{2bt}{r}} = \sqrt{\frac{bt}{2r}}$$

Appendix 2: Interest elasticity of the demand for money

The interest elasticity of the demand for money (E) is approximately:

$$E = \frac{\% \text{ change in quantity demanded } (M)}{\% \text{ change in interest rate } (r)}$$

$$= \frac{\Delta M/M \; 100}{\Delta r/r \; 100} \text{ where } \Delta = \text{'(absolute) change in'}$$

$$= \frac{\Delta M}{\Delta r} \frac{r}{M}$$

However, the exact (point) elasticity can be calculated if M/r is replaced by infinitesimal changes in M and r, so the elasticity is $r/M \; dM/dr$ (dM/dr is the first differential of the demand for money function in calculus notation).

The Tobin–Baumol demand for money function is:

$$M = P \sqrt{\frac{bt}{2r}} \tag{1}$$

$$M = Pb^{1/2}t^{1/2} \frac{1}{\sqrt{2}} r^{-1/2} \tag{2}$$

$$\frac{\mathrm{d}M}{\mathrm{d}r} = -\frac{1}{2}\left(Pb^{1/2}t^{1/2} \frac{1}{\sqrt{2}} \right)r^{3/2}$$

$$E = \frac{\mathrm{d}M}{\mathrm{d}r} \frac{r}{M}$$

$$= -\frac{1}{2}\frac{\left(Pb^{1/2}t^{1/2} \frac{1}{\sqrt{2}} \right)}{M}r^{-1/2}$$

Equation (2) above can be substituted for M:

$$E = -\frac{1}{2}\frac{\left(Pb^{1/2}t^{1/2}\frac{1}{\sqrt{2}} \right)r^{-1/2}}{\left(Pb^{1/2}t^{1/2}\frac{1}{\sqrt{2}} \right)r^{-1/2}}$$

$$E = -\frac{1}{2}$$

Similarly, the transactions elasticity is $+\frac{1}{2}$ and so on. If logs are taken of (1):

$$\log M = \log P + \frac{1}{2} \log b + \frac{1}{2} \log t - \log \frac{1}{2} - \frac{1}{2} \log r$$

This log linear form is the version of the model which is usually tested.

Appendix 3: Bonds, bond prices, and interest rates

A bond is a claim to a stream of income and, if the bond is *redeemable*, eventual repayment. The *coupon rate* is expressed as a percentage per annum. The coupon rate is multiplied by the *nominal*, or *par value*, to give the annual interest payment (thus £100 nominal of a security with a coupon of 15 per cent would give its holder £15 per year). Coupon rate and nominal value never change. The price at which a bond is issued is called the *issue price* and need not be the par value. If the bond is to be redeemed (repaid) the redemption value is also relevant; this is usually but not always par. A bond of £100 nominal value will be traded at a price dependent upon market interest rates. The market price is very rarely either the issue price or the par value. To take an example, a 10 per cent coupon value bond with ten years to mature is currently worth about £80 per £100 nominal. The *flat yield*, or *running yield*, is therefore 12.5 per cent – the result of dividing the income (£10) by the market price. The *redemption yield* is the (internal) rate of return, which will make the net present value of £10 per annum for ten years and £100 in ten years' time equal to the market price.

Yields and bond prices move inversely. This basic principle can best be illustrated by the example of perpetual (or irredeemable) bonds; that is, those with an infinite life. A bond with nominal value £100 and coupon 5 per cent will yield £5 per annum for ever. If the market interest rate is 8.5 per cent, this is worth £50; if the market rate is 20 per cent, £25, and so on. In this case the result is that the price of an infinite bond and its yield are reciprocals of each other. In the case of finite bonds, the relationship is inverse but not reciprocal. Intuitively it is obvious that the attractiveness of a claim to £10 per year for a number of years depends upon interest rates. If building societies pay 10 per cent per annum, one would find this stream of income much less attractive than if this rival investment paid only 5 per cent. Because it would be less attractive, one would pay less for it. Thus, the market value of a bond depends upon interest rates.

Notes

1. *See also* Laidler (1980b, 1982).
2. Arrow (1974, p.103) argues that, given relative risk aversion, this elasticity must at least equal unity.
3. This is not an objection to the original formulation – it reinforces a speculator-determined interest rate. It is an objection to the more moderate versions.

4

IS–LM Model

4.1   A simplified presentation

Since its invention by Hicks (1937), the IS–LM model has
become the most widely taught macroeconomic model in the
Western world and the starting point for much of the more
sophisticated monetary analysis. The model is not without either
its critics or its limitations (see Section 4.8), but it is still
unsurpassed for its power to focus on crucial features of
monetary analysis. At least in its basic form, an essential feature
of the model is an indirect transmission mechanism of monetary
policy. A change in the money supply leads to a change in
interest rates, which in turn leads to a change in income.
Indeed, the model is the epitome of analyses in which the rate
of interest links the two sectors (see p.11). Interest rates are
not the sole determinant of income – the Keynesian 'real' forces
of injections and withdrawals are also crucial. Moreover, these
real forces also help to determine interest rates. Furthermore,
the model is a comparative static one designed to calculate
equilibrium values of interest rates and income rather than to
describe the process of adjustment to a new equilibrium.
Nevertheless, if the main focus of analysis is to investigate the
effectiveness of monetary policy, this rather basic model is
frequently illuminating. The authorities can administer a shock
to the monetary sector by changing the money supply. This will
lead to a change in interest rates which will influence the real

sector. The impact of such a change in the money supply on income will depend upon:

1. How large a change in interest rates is generated by a given change in the money supply.
2. How large a change in the level of aggregate expenditure (demand) is generated by this change in interest rates, that is, how large is the interest elasticity of expenditure.

The effect of a change of the money supply upon aggregate demand (income) will be the combined result of these. Whenever a change in the money supply has only a small effect upon interest rates, or a change in interest rates has only a small effect upon income, monetary policy will be relatively ineffective.

It is possible to analyse the factors which determine the size of these responses. The first – the effect of a change in the money supply on interest rates – depends upon the workings of the monetary sector. The equilibrium condition for the monetary sector is that the demand for money should equal the supply of it. The supply of money is assumed to be exogenously determined by the authorities who can change it as an act of policy: the demand for money, as described in Chapter 3, depends upon the rate of interest – the price of holding money. It is an accurate, if oversimplified, representation of the workings of the IS–LM model to say that this price, the rate of interest, adjusts to equate the quantities of money supplied and demanded. In effect, the authorities shift the inelastic supply curve in the money market, by increasing the quantity of money (Fig. 4.1a).

The response of price to a shift of an inelastic supply curve always depends upon the elasticity of demand. When demand is inelastic (Fig. 4.1b) the change in price is relatively large, whereas when it is elastic (Fig. 4.1c) the effect on price is small. This piece of elementary microeconomic analysis applies just as much in the money market as anywhere else. Thus, the more elastic is the demand for money, the smaller is the change in interest rates for a given change in the money supply. Hence, the more elastic is the demand for money, the less is the effectiveness of monetary policy. Indeed, in the extreme case of a perfectly elastic demand for money (Fig. 4.1d) the rate of interest remains unchanged, and so monetary policy is totally ineffective. This extreme case is known as the liquidity trap. It survives in

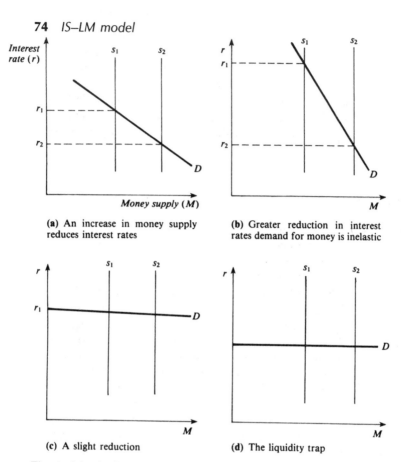

(a) An increase in money supply reduces interest rates

(b) Greater reduction in interest rates demand for money is inelastic

(c) A slight reduction

(d) The liquidity trap

Figure 4.1 A change in the money supply

textbooks to demonstrate the relevance of the elasticity even though both its practical relevance and even its theoretical possibility were denied many years ago. The simplified presentation of the workings of the IS–LM model presented in this section ignores the feedback effects that arise, although it seems Keynes himself may have liked to use this simple version (Keynes, 1971, Vol.XIV). This is Chick's view, see note 3 to Chapter 1. For an example of a feedback effect the change in the rate of interest analysed in the previous paragraph will change income. This change in income will shift the demand for money curve, a higher level of income shifting it rightwards. Thus, the analysis in this section is only partial. Nevertheless, it does capture the spirit of the model. Moreover the basic conclusions continue to hold. Monetary policy is least effective when the demand for money is highly interest elastic and the demand for goods is highly interest inelastic. Monetary policy is most effective when the demand for money is interest inelastic and the demand for goods is highly interest elastic.

4.2　An overview

The model is a two-sector one. The sectors are the goods, or real, sector, and the financial, or monetary, sector. The two sectors are linked by the rate of interest. Any shock to either sector causes the rate of interest to change and so affects the other sector and initiates an interactive process until equilibrium is reattained. The purpose of the IS–LM model is to provide a comparative static framework in which the new equilibrium can be calculated. Equilibrium values are calculated for two variables: nominal income and the rate of interest. In this context 'the rate of interest' is defined as the rate of return on those assets which are direct substitutes for holding money and is a matter of controversy (see p.93). However, in the model there is only one such interest-bearing asset, usually referred to as bonds. The interest rate is relevant, both as the representative price in the financial sector and as the link between the sectors, since it is assumed to influence both expenditure and the demand for money. Nominal income is assumed to be the macroeconomic variable of interest to policy makers. Sometimes prices are taken to be exogenous and the model therefore transformed into a model of output determination. (To determine PQ is to determine Q if P is fixed.) Alternatively, if output were assumed to be fixed, it would be a model of the price level. This, however, is uncommon. It seems best to view the IS–LM model as a model to determine nominal income or aggregate demand and not imply that it is anything else.[1]

The equilibrium condition for the goods sector is that the supply of goods should equal the demand for them; that is, planned output should equal planned expenditure, or planned injections should equal planned withdrawals as in the familiar

Keynesian national income model. The only change from the basic model is that at least some injections and withdrawals are assumed to be interest dependent, especially investment. The model is symmetrical in that the equilibrium condition for the monetary sector is that the demand for money should equal the supply of money. Again, in parallel fashion, the demand for money is assumed to be interest dependent. Hence, the equilibrium value of income can be determined for either sector only if the rate of interest is known. Otherwise, in both sectors, the equilibrium is indeterminate, depending upon the rate of interest. Equilibrium for the system as a whole is only possible when both sectors are in equilibrium. This is determined by finding a rate of interest which would enable both sectors to be in equilibrium with the same level of income.

This, then, is the IS–LM model, which, to recapitulate, has the following key features:

1. A goods sector whose equilibrium condition is that planned injections should equal planned withdrawals.
2. A monetary sector whose equilibrium condition is that the demand for money should equal the supply of money.
3. The rate of interest linking them, whose leverage stems from the expenditure and demand for money functions being interest sensitive.

4.3   The model

As explained above, the IS–LM model is a two-sector model (goods and money). Possible equilibria are calculated for each sector separately. The two sectors are then combined to produce the overall equilibrium for the system as a whole.

(i)   *Goods sector*

The equilibrium condition for the goods, or real, sector is that planned withdrawals (imports, taxation and savings) equal planned injections (investments, exports and government expenditure on currently produced goods and services: government transfer payments (old age pensions, social security, etc.) are

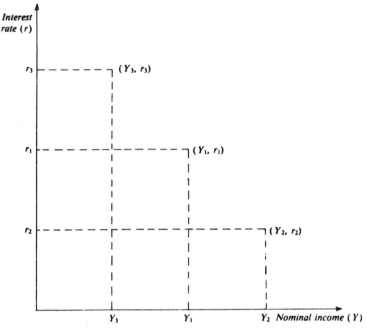

Figure 4.2 Equilibrium in the goods market

treated as negative taxation). Equilibrium values must be calculated for both (nominal) income and interest rates for the reasons explained above. So it is necessary to find all the pairs of values of income and interest rates at which planned injections should be equal to planned withdrawals. These can be seen in Figure 4.2, with interest rates on the vertical and nominal income on the horizontal axis. The range (locus) of possible equilibria can best be derived by starting with a pair of values (Y_1,r_1) which satisfy the equilibrium condition (as no scale is marked, this does not involve any loss of generality as Y_1 and r_1 could be any values). It can then be calculated what interest rate would be necessary if there were to be an equilibrium with income higher than Y_1, say at Y_2 (rather as a demand curve shows what quantities would have to be purchased if consumers were to be in equilibrium at different prices). If income were to be Y_2, planned withdrawals would necessarily be higher because consumers

Income ⇒ *Planned*   ⇒ *Planned* ⇒ *Interest*
Withdrawals *Injections* *Rates*

Figure 4.3 Calculation of equilibrium

would wish both to save more and to spend more on imports and would have to pay more in taxes. Therefore, for the system to be in equilibrium, planned injections would have to be higher. Accordingly, something would have had to be different to have induced a greater desire to invest (or export). Within the model this can only be a lower rate of interest. This would mean that planned investment would be higher. The equilibrium value of interest rate (r_2) corresponding to Y_2 must be such as to induce just enough extra injections to match the extra withdrawals generated by the higher level of income. In schematic form (Fig. 4.3):

1. Each level of income implies a unique level of planned withdrawals.
2. For equilibrium, planned injections must therefore be equal to this value.
3. The equilibrium value of the interest rate corresponding to the initial values of income must be the one at which planned injections are at the necessary level.

It is also possible to derive equilibrium points by starting with the rate of interest. For example, r_3 is higher than r_1. Thus, planned injections would be lower, investment being less profitable. Hence, for equilibrium the planned level of withdrawals would have to be less than when income was equal to Y_1. This implies that the equilibrium level of income corresponding to r_3 must be less than Y_1 – at Y_3, in fact, where the lower level of savings, imports and taxation induced by the lower level of income would exactly offset the fall in injections. By a similar process of induction it is theoretically possible to derive an infinite number of equilibria. These points can be joined together and the resultant curve represents all possible equilibria for the goods market (Fig. 4.4), which will generally slope downwards from left to right. This is called the IS curve because at all points along it planned injections equal planned withdrawals and investment (I) and savings (S) are taken as representative injections and withdrawals respectively – hence IS.

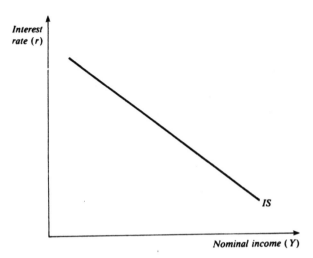

Figure 4.4 The IS curve

(ii) *Money market*

Equilibrium in the financial or monetary sector occurs when the demand for money is equal to the supply of it. The supply of money is taken to be fixed by the authorities as an act of policy and so is exogenous to the model. This means that the search for equilibrium is a search for points where the demand for money is equal to this predetermined quantity (called an isoquantity line in microeconomic analysis). As shown in Chapter 3, the demand for money is largely determined by the rate of interest and level of income. Thus, the equilibrium for the money market will be those pairs of interest rates and income which generate a demand for money equal to the supply. To re-emphasise the crucial point, the demand will be the same at each equilibrium point. These points can be plotted on a diagram, as in Figure 4.5 in which, as before, the interest rate is on the vertical axis and (nominal) income on the horizontal axis.

As for the goods market, the analysis starts by taking an equilibrium pair of values (r_1, Y_1). If income were higher than Y_1 (for example, at Y_3), this would mean that the demand for money would be higher than the supply unless something were to be different to balance this. This can only be a higher rate of interest. Hence, if the demand and supply of money are to be

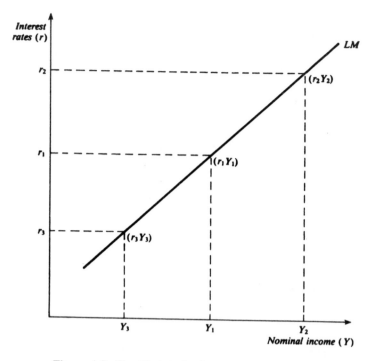

Figure 4.5 Equilibrium in the money market

equal and income to be Y_3, then the interest rate would have to
be r_3. Similarly, if the interest rate were below r_1, so income
would have to be lower by just enough to offset this. Thus, the
equilibrium would be (r_2, Y_2), where the increase in the demand
for money caused by the higher level of income $(Y_2 - Y_1)$ is
exactly balanced by the reduction generated by the higher level
of interest rates $(r_2 - r_1)$. A process of induction can thus
generate an infinite number of money-market equilibria, at each
of which the demand for money is the same. The locus of these
equilibria is called the LM curve, illustrated in Figure 4.5. The
term is derived from L for Liquidity and M for Money; the curve
is dependent upon the demand for money and this was called
liquidity preference by Keynes. LM curves normally slope
upwards from left to right.

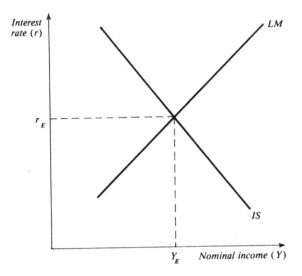

Figure 4.6 Equilibrium in the system

(iii)   *Equilibrium for the system*

The IS and LM curves can be drawn on one diagram, as in Figure 4.6. This makes it possible to determine simultaneously the equilibrium levels of income and the rate of interest. All points along the IS curve are equilibria for the goods market and all points on the LM curves are equilibria for the money market. Therefore, the interaction of the IS and LM curves represents the only point of equilibrium for the system as a whole, since both goods and money markets are in equilibrium at this point and only at this point. Hence, Y_E is the equilibrium level of (nominal) income and r_E the equilibrium rate of interest.

4.4   Application of the model

The apparatus derived in Section 4.3 is most useful when used to calculate a new equilibrium level of income and interest rates in response to a change in an exogenous variable produced by either a shock to the system or an act of government policy. The simplest case is an increase in government spending on goods and services financed so as to leave the money supply unchanged (Fig. 4.7). The original equilibrium is (r_1, Y_1), where IS_1 and LM intersect. The government then decides to increase its spending. This means that at each rate of interest planned injections will be higher than before, so equilibrium income must be higher than before to generate the extra saving, imports and taxation. This means that each equilibrium point will shift to the right; that is, the IS curve will shift from IS_1 to IS_2. The process can be considered in a more detailed fashion at r_1. With the old level of government spending, planned withdrawals and planned injections are equal to each other at (r_1, Y_1). After the increase in government spending, this would no longer be an equilibrium since the increase in public sector injections means that planned withdrawals are now less than planned injections. For there to be equilibrium at r_1, income would have to be sufficiently higher than Y_1 to generate just enough extra (planned) withdrawals to balance the extra government spending (that is, at Y_3). $(Y_3 - Y_1)$ multiplied by the (net) marginal propensity to withdraw generates enough extra withdrawals to match the increase in planned injections (that is, in government spending). The shift can alternatively be regarded as illustrative of the elementary multiplier since the IS curve shifts by the multiplier times the increase in injections. This illustrates the fact that multiplier calculations show what would happen to the equilibrium level of income if the interest rate were held constant; that is, what happens to the IS curve. (Elementary multiplier models assume that interest rate is constant, and are then valid.)

Thus, an increase in government spending can be represented as a rightward shift of the IS curve. This means that the equilibrium level of income rises from Y_1 to Y_2 and the equilibrium rate of interest from r_1 to r_2. This is illustrative of an important point: in the case of a shift of an IS curve, income and interest rates move in the same direction. Figure 4.7 could represent other exogenous changes which directly affect the goods market:

1. An increase in exports – brought about by such exogenous factors as an increase in US income, a change in tastes (for example, Metros became fashionable in France in the late

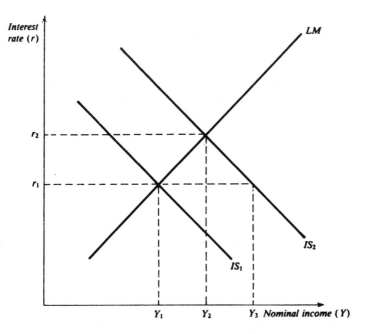

Figure 4.7 An increase in government spending

1980s), a change in the political climate (which produced
an arms order) or the lifting of an embargo.
2. An increase in investment; for example, that following the
discovery of oil – although this has other effects, see p.153.
3. A reduction in taxation or increase in government transfers –
although in this case the slope of the IS curve might change.

In fact, any change in injections and withdrawals can be
represented by a shift of the IS curve so long as it is not caused
by a change in either income or interest rates. Thus, a shift of the
savings function would shift the IS curve, whereas a move along
the existing savings function would also generate a move along
the IS curve.

The IS–LM model is purely a comparative static comparison of
equilibria. This has an advantage in that the analysis is perfectly
symmetrical, so that a shift from IS_2 to IS_1 represents a reduction
in government spending or the exogenous increase in imports

generated by the invention of video recorders, and so on. However, there is the disadvantage of static analysis that one cannot say why income has risen from Y_1 to Y_2. Nevertheless, this deficiency can be remedied by an exercise in (plausible) pseudo-dynamics. The increase in government spending causes income to rise for normal 'multiplier' reasons. The government has, however, borrowed to finance the expenditure, which leads to an increase in interest rates. This reduces private spending (or crowds it out, p.87 below) so that income increases by less than in the elementary multiplier story (that is, to Y_2 instead of Y_3). Such stories are usually told to illustrate diagrams, like Figure 4.7. It is important to realise that they are, strictly speaking, fairy stories, because the model can only be used to calculate equilibria and can say nothing about how or why the economy moves from one to another. Nevertheless, the fairy story is a useful illustration of which process would underlay the IS–LM model if its dynamics were traced.

The money supply was held constant in deriving the model, being fixed as an act of policy. When the money supply changes, the effect is to shift the LM curve – an increase causing a rightward, or downward, shift (Fig. 4.8). The reasoning is straightforward. The supply of money has been increased, therefore the demand must also be higher for equilibrium to be attained. This implies that either interest rates must be lower or income higher or both than when the money supply was lower, since these changes will absorb the extra supply. For example, (r_1, Y_1) was previously an equilibrium point. With the higher money supply this is no longer an equilibrium, because the supply of money exceeds the demand. To restore equilibrium, interest rates would have to fall to r_3; this gives a new equilibrium point (r_3, Y_1). Alternatively, income would have to rise to Y_3 to give a new equilibrium point (r_1, Y_3). Each point along LM_1 will have to shift similarly in either a rightward or downward direction. Both would generate the new LM curve, LM_2.

Hence if the money supply were increased the new equilibrium would be (r_2, Y_2). The higher level of the money supply means that the equilibrium level of income is higher, Y_2 instead of Y_1, but the equilibrium level of interest rates is lower (r_2 instead of r_1). This is a general result: a shift of the LM curve causes income and interest rates to change in opposite directions. This contrast

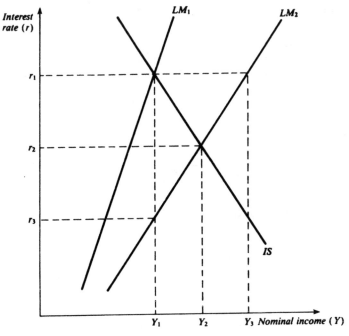

Figure 4.8 An increase in the money supply

with shifts of the IS curve can be used as a diagnostic device. For example, Temin (1976; see also Brunner, 1981b) sought to ascertain the causes of the 1929–33 depression in the USA. Income had fallen, so he argued that if interest rates were higher the cause would have been a shift of the LM curve; but if interest rates were lower, then the cause would have been a shift of the IS curve. He thus hoped to show whether the depression was caused by monetary factors (which would have shifted the LM curve) or goods-market forces, which would have shifted the IS curve.

Normally shifts of the LM curve are produced by changes in the quantity of money supplied. However, they can occur for other reasons. For example, some Keynesians have attributed significance to a change of sentiment which produces a 'bear' mood of great pessimism. Everyone therefore wishes to hold more money than before at each level of income and rate of interest. This shifts the LM curve to the left and so reduces

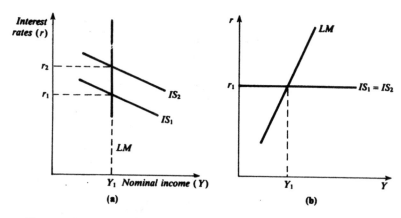

Figure 4.9 Monetarist results: fiscal policy fails

income. Both IS and LM curves can also be shifted by changes in variables which influence spending and the demand for money. The most important of these is wealth, analysed in Chapter 7.

4.5   Monetarist–Keynesian debate

The IS–LM framework has been used for a debate about the effectiveness of 'monetary' and 'fiscal' policy which for many years was the centrepiece of the monetarist–Keynesian debate. Monetary policy for these purposes is defined as an increase in the money supply brought about without any change in injections or withdrawals; that is, by a sale or repurchase of its own securities to or from the non-bank private sector (see p.140). This definition is used so that the change can be represented solely by a shift in the LM curve. Fiscal policy is similarly defined as a change in taxation or government spending which leaves the money supply unchanged; one which produces only a shift of the IS curve. More extensive policy issues are considered in Chapter 6, but this debate focuses on a key issue by isolating the impact of such shifts in the curves.

The extreme monetarist position is to argue that monetary policy is effective but fiscal policy totally ineffective in increasing income (or reducing it if inflation rather than unemployment is

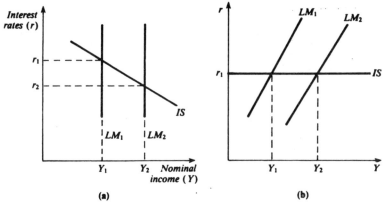

Figure 4.10 Monetarist results: monetary policy succeeds

the policy problem). These results arise if the LM curve is vertical or the IS curve horizontal (Figs 4.9, 4.10). The LM curve is vertical if the interest elasticity of the demand for money is zero, since in this case only one level of income will produce equilibrium in the money market; no change in the rate of interest will have any effect on the demand for money, so there cannot be the counter-balancing effects of interest rates and income which produced the normal slope. The LM would also be vertical if the income elasticity of the demand for money were infinite. This is absurd, but it is worth emphasising that the slope of the LM curve depends upon the income elasticity as well as the interest elasticity of the demand for money. The slope of the IS curve also depends upon the income as well as the interest elasticity. Thus, the IS curve would also be horizontal if the income elasticity of expenditure were equal to zero. In the case in Fig. 4.9a, a shift of the IS curve will change interest rates but not income, whereas a shift of the LM curve does change income (Fig. 4.10a). This case is often referred to as 'crowding-out'. An increase in government spending, holding money constant, leaves total spending unchanged, thus private spending must have fallen by as much as public spending has risen. Thus, public spending has replaced or crowded-out private spending. This is complete or 100 per cent crowding-out. With a steep LM it is possible that private spending may fall but by less than the rise in public

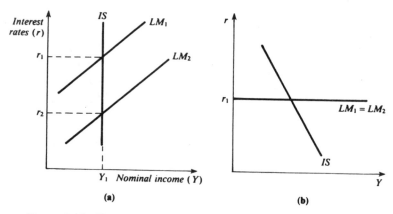

Figure 4.11   Keynesian results: monetary policy fails

spending – hence partial crowding-out. The way IS–LM models are usually presented investment is crowded-out by the higher interest rates that follow an increase in public spending but extra consumption generated by the higher disposable income – 'crowding-in'. Crowding-out is a complex topic because the term has a number of other uses (see Gowland, 1978, p.134). A horizontal IS curve arises when the interest elasticity of investment (or other expenditure) is infinity, such that a very small fall in the rate of interest produces a very large rise in expenditure. In this case the interest rate is pegged at r_1, and when government spending is increased income remains at Y_1 (Fig. 4.9b).

Keynesian results arise from similar extreme values of elasticities. The 'Keynesian' result is that fiscal policy is effective but monetary policy ineffective. Not surprisingly these are the converse of the monetarist cases, a vertical IS curve or a horizontal LM curve. These are illustrated in Figures 4.11 and 4.12. A vertical IS curve is the consequence of interest-inelastic expenditure functions, such that only one level of income produces equilibrium in the goods market, or infinite income elasticity. In this case an increase in the money supply reduces interest rates but leaves income unchanged (Fig. 4.11a), whereas fiscal policy increases income albeit while raising interest rates (Fig. 4.12a). The horizontal LM curve, often called the 'liquidity trap', arises from an infinitely interest-elastic demand for money.

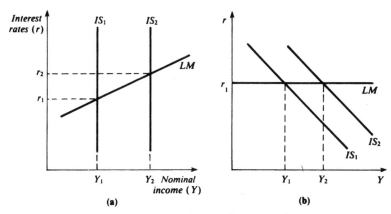

Figure 4.12 Keynesian results: fiscal policy succeeds

A horizontal LM curve would also arise if the income elasticity of the demand for money were zero. This is not inconceivable. Indeed, at a microeconomic level, it has frequently been observed that millionaires have smaller bank balances than the average individual! In this case the LM curve cannot be shifted by changes in the money supply since an infinitesimal change in interest rates suffices to equilibrate the supply and demand for money. As shown in Figure 4.11(b) monetary policy has no effect whatsoever, whereas fiscal policy can alter income without any effect upon interest rates (Fig. 4.12b).

Within this model it is clear that the monetarist–Keynesian debate is an empirical one and that both positions are extreme ones. In fact the purpose of the debate is to illustrate the importance of different values of elasticities rather than to argue that these values are the correct ones – although Keynesians such as Hansen (1953) in the 1950s did seem to believe in the extreme case. The more general view is Friedman's (1969, p.155):

> no fundamental issue . . . hinges on whether the estimated elasticity [of the demand for money with respect to the rate of interest] can for most purposes be approximated by zero or -0.1 or -0.5 or -2.0 provided it is seldom capable of being approximated by $-(\infty)$.

In other words, the monetarists believe in a steep LM curve, not a vertical one, so that the vertical case analysis is a good approximation and vice versa for moderate Keynesians. There are a large number of possible combinations of slopes of IS and LM curves. These, and their implications for economic policy, are set out in the appendix to this chapter (pp.102ff).

The main conclusions derived from this analysis are simple. Monetary policy will be more effective as the interest elasticity of the demand for money is lower and as the interest elasticity of the demand for goods is higher. The intuitive logic of these propositions is clear (pp.73–5).

4.6   An algebraic presentation

The algebraic derivation of the IS and LM curves is straightforward. The IS curve is the locus of all possible equilibria for the goods market. The equilibrium condition for the goods market is that planned injections, J^*, should equal planned withdrawals, W^*:

$$J^* = W^* \tag{1}$$

In a closed economy, there are two injections: government spending (G) and investment (I):

$$J = G + I \tag{2}$$

Government spending is assumed to be fixed exogenously by the government as $\bar{G}$. Planned investments (I^*) is assumed to be negatively related to the rate of interest:

$$G = \bar{G} \tag{3}$$

$$I^* = a - br \tag{4}$$

where b is a parameter measuring the responsiveness of investment to changes in the rate of interest. Thus, combining (2) (3) and (4):

$$J^* = \bar{G} + a - br \tag{5}$$

Withdrawals in a closed economy are savings (S) and taxation (T):

$$W \equiv S + T \tag{6}$$

The simplest possible savings function makes planned savings

(S^*) a constant proportion (s) of income (Y); that is, s is equal to both the average and marginal propensity to save:

$$S^* = sY \tag{7}$$

Taxation depends upon both the level of income and the tax structure. The simplest tax structure is a proportional income tax, with a rate of t (or a general sales tax on all final output at the rate of t). Hence, tax yield would equal this rate of tax multiplied by income:

$$T = tY \tag{8}$$

Combining (6), (7) and (8):

$$W^* = sY + tY$$
$$= (s + t)Y \tag{9}$$

Hence for equilibrium:

$$W^* = J^*$$
$$(s + t)Y = a - br$$

so:

$$Y = \frac{\bar{G} + a - br}{(s + t)} \tag{10}$$

Equation (10) is the equation for the IS curve, since it gives the equilibrium value of income for any value of r.

The slope of the IS curve is $-(s + t)/b$; that is, the slope depends upon b, the parameter measuring the responsiveness of investment of changes in the rate of interest. Thus the IS curve slopes downwards from left to right. As the interest elasticity falls, b falls and the slope becomes steeper. In the extreme case, when investment is not responsive to interest rate changes, b is equal to zero and so the slope is infinite (the IS curve is vertical). Moreover, an increase in G will shift the IS curve by the increase in G times $1/s + t$; the IS curve shifts by the change in exogenous injections times the multiplier. Hence, both the analysis of fiscal policy, based upon increase in government spending ($\bar{G}$) shifting the IS curve (4) and the elasticity analysis of the monetarist–Keynesian debate (5) are simply illustrated.

The LM curve shows the equilibrium for the money market;

that is, where the supply of money (*SM*) and the demand for money (*DM*) are equal:

$$SM = DM \tag{11}$$

The supply of money is assumed to be fixed exogenously by the authorities as $\bar{M}$:

$$SM = \bar{M} \tag{12}$$

The demand for money is positively related to income and negatively to the rate of interest (see Chapter 3). If the responsiveness to changes in income is measured by w and to changes in interest rates by v, the demand for money can be written as:

$$DM = z - vr + wY \tag{13}$$

Combining (11), (12) and (13):

$$\bar{M} = z - vr + wY$$

so:

$$Y = \frac{\bar{M} - z + vr}{w} \tag{14}$$

This is the equation for the LM curve. Its slope is v/w so, as this is positive, the LM curve slopes upwards. When $v = 0$, the equation is:

$$Y = \frac{\bar{M} - z}{w}$$

Thus, the LM curve is vertical at this point. As interest responsiveness of the demand for money rises, that is as v increases, the slope becomes less steep. Ultimately, when the demand for money is infinitely elastic, the LM curve is horizontal. Increasing $\bar{M}$ will shift the LM curve to the right as described above. Usually algebraic presentation of the IS–LM model derives equations for the two curves, that is, (10) and (14), and use the graphical method of illustrating the d etermination of income (Figure 4.6). However, one can solve (1) and (14) by any simultaneous equations method to derive equations for Y and r, as for example Laidler (1985) does. In this case:

$$Y = \frac{vG + av + b\bar{M} - bz}{(s + t)(v + bw)} \qquad (15)$$

It can thus be seen that income will normally rise when either G or M increases. However, when the demand for money is interest inelastic, and $v = 0$, then fiscal policy is ineffective. Similarly, when the demand for investment is interest inelastic, and b equals zero, changes in the money supply have no effect on income. Indeed, (15) then collapses to the multiplier equation, autonomous expenditure (that is, $\bar{G} + a$) divided by the net marginal propensity to withdraw $(s + t)$.

The principal advantage of the algebraic method of presentation of the IS–LM curve is that it facilitates the addition of extra variables to the system. For example, the average and marginal propensities to consume may not be equal. In which case, if the function is written:

$$S = S_0 + S_1 Y \qquad (16)$$

S_1 is the marginal propensity to save. When S_0 is positive, the APS will always exceed the MPS, and vice versa when S_0 is negative. The previous formulation then becomes a special case, where $S_0 = 0$. Similarly, savings are often argued to be a function of after-tax income, disposable income $(Y - T)$. Consumers choose, it is argued, whether to save or spend only their disposable income. On the other hand, it is argued that the most sensible interpretation of the Keynesian absolute income hypothesis (that is, linking saving to current income) is that it represents pension contributions which do depend upon pre-tax income. Both hypotheses can be incorporated easily by writing a function in which saving depends upon both pre- and post-tax income. Furthermore, it is usually argued that a higher level of wealth (W) will lead to a higher level of consumption and so a lower level of saving at each level of income. Incorporating all these implies a savings function of the following form:

$$S = S_0 + S_1 Y + S_2(Y - T) - S_3 W \qquad (17)$$

Similarly, it is straightforward to incorporate sophisticated demand for money relationships. This flexibility is impossible in geometric derivations because only two-dimensional diagrams can be drawn, and is very clumsy in inductive derivations.

4.7 A geometric analysis

The geometric presentation of the IS–LM model has been relegated to last because it is neither as rigorous or flexible as the algebraic presentation, nor as simple as the inductive presentation. Figure 4.13 shows the derivation of the IS curve by means of a four-quadrant diagram, in which:

(b) This quadrant shows the goods-market equilibrium (in the simplest case, illustrated here, planned saving equals planned

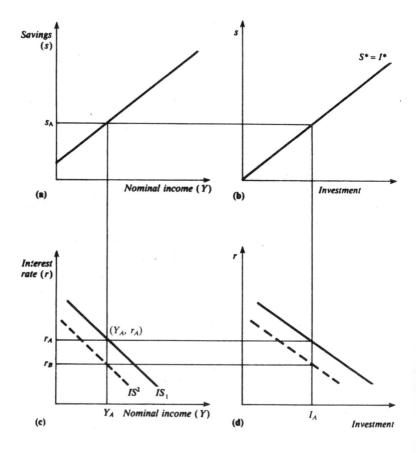

Figure 4.13 The IS curve: a geometric derivation ((Y_A, r_A) is equilibrium for the goods market)

investment). Planned saving is shown on the vertical and planned investment on the horizontal axis. Thus this equilibrium condition is a 45° line.

(a) This quadrant shows the savings function, with planned saving on the vertical and income on the horizontal axis. If the function passes through the origin, the marginal and average propensities to save are equal. When the average propensity to save is greater, the intercept on the vertical axis is positive (and, vice versa, a negative intercept implies that the marginal propensity to save is larger).

(c) This quadrant shows the IS curve.

(d) This quadrant shows the investment function. The interest rate is on the horizontal axis and the level of desired investment on the vertical so this function slopes downwards.

The IS curve is derived as follows:

1. Select a level of income (for example, Y_A) in quadrant (c).
2. Move to quadrant (a) to read off the level of planned saving S_A.
3. Move to quadrant (b) to ascertain the level of planned investment therefore necessary for equilibrium I_A (which of course is equal to S_A).
4. Move to quadrant (d) to read what level of interest rate would have generated I_A; this is r_A.
5. Move back to quadrant (c) and mark (Y_A, r_A) as a point on the IS curve.
6. Repeat for all possible values of Y.

The main virtue of this method is that it is easy to see how a change in either behavioural function – quadrants (a) and (c) – causes the IS curve to shift. If, for example, a loss of confidence caused an inward shift of the investment function to the dotted line shown in quadrant (d), the equilibrium rate of interest would be r_B. The IS curve would then shift inwards to the dashed line shown in quadrant (c), so that it encompassed (Y_1, r_B) and all the other points derived by repeating steps 1 to 6 above.

A four-quadrant derivation of the LM curve is possible only if the demand for money is partitioned into an income-inelastic and interest-elastic sub-function and an interest-inelastic and income-elastic sub-function. As this contradicts both versions of the

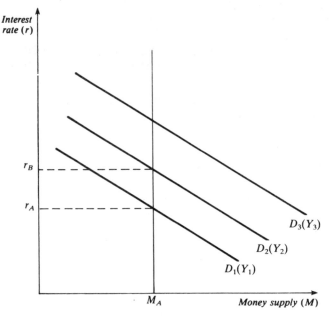

Figure 4.14 The LM curve

demand for money it seems undesirable to derive the functions in
this manner although it is frequently done. As a result, the
baroque seven-quadrant diagram of Ackley (1961, p.379)[2] is
omitted. Instead, a conventional demand diagram is shown (Fig.
4.14), with price and quantity on the axes – in this case, of
course, interest rates and money supply. As usual a different
demand curve exists for each level of income, because for all
normal (superior) goods a rise in income causes the demand
curve to shift rightwards. The LM curve can be derived by
drawing a vertical line at the given exogenous money supply (for
example, M_A). The LM curve is derived by combining the
interest rate at which this line intersects each demand curve with
the level of income which generated the curve, for example
$(Y_1,r_A)(Y_2,r_B)$. It is then easy to see why the LM curve normally
shifts if the money supply changes (a new vertical line is drawn)
or any other variable (such as wealth) changes, since every
demand curve shifts.

4.8   Beyond IS–LM

In the IS–LM model the effectiveness of monetary policy depends upon the interest elasticities of expenditure and of the demand for money. Nevertheless, despite the ubiquity of the IS–LM model, it either assumes away or cloaks a number of crucial issues which have divided monetarists and Keynesians. These include the following.

(i)   *Exogeneity and controllability of money*

The IS–LM model is based on the assumption that the authorities determine the supply of money. This assumes that it is both independent of income and controllable. This would be denied by many Keynesians (for example, Kaldor, 1982). This issue is considered further in Chapter 6 (see Section 6.5).

(ii)   *Nature of the transmission mechanism*

In the IS–LM model the transmission mechanism of monetary policy is via its effect upon interest rates; a change in the money supply leads to a change in interest rates, which leads to a change in the demand for goods. This is an *indirect* transmission mechanism, whereas Friedman and his disciples have argued for a *direct* transmission mechanism. This was illustrated as Friedman's restatement of the quantity theory (see pp.32ff) and is analysed more fully in Chapter 5. Alternatively one may argue that as the model is a comparative static one, there is no way of saying what the transmission mechanism is and that it is only convention to interpret IS–LM as the indirect transmission mechanism. Even so, IS–LM allows one to say nothing about which transmission mechanism is correct.

(iii)   *Interest rate or money supply targets*

In the IS–LM model there is no difference between a policy whose target is expressed in terms of money and one expressed in

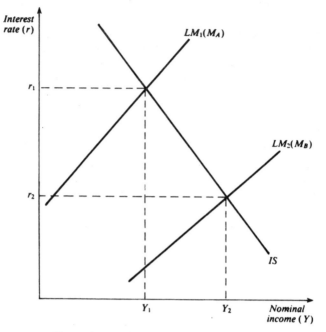

Figure 4.15 The equivalence of money and interest rate targets

terms of interest rates (Fig. 4.15). The authorities wish to increase income from Y_1 to Y_2. They might increase the money supply from M_A to M_B and so shift the LM curve from LM_1 to LM_2. This achieves their objective and in doing so reduces interest rates from r_1 to r_2. Instead they might reduce interest rates from r_1 to r_2 and move along the IS curve from Y_1 to Y_2. This also achieves their aim. The open-market operations necessary to achieve this would necessarily shift the LM curve to LM_2, otherwise the money market would not be in equilibrium. Hence, Figure 4.15 illustrates both policies and distinguishing them is purely a question of semantics.

However, this distinction is central to the entire monetarist–Keynesian debate (see the Cagan quote on p.195 of Eatwell *et al* (1989)). It certainly seems to be the major practical difference between Keynes' contemporary analyses of the causes of the depression and Friedman's subsequent one (Keynes, 1971, Vols. XII, XXI; Friedman and Schwartz, 1963). Friedman and Keynes agreed that a major cause was errors by the US Federal Reserve system, which ran US monetary policy. Keynes criticised the Federal Reserve for allowing interest rates to rise (and for failing to reduce them) and Friedman for allowing the money supply to fall sharply. Qualitatively, the criticisms are identical, since Keynes' preferred policy would have led to a higher money supply and Friedman's to a lower level of interest rates. The differences arise in describing and quantifying the correct alternative policy – stable rates or stable money supply. The IS–LM model can throw no light on this or similar problems. This issue can be analysed using Tobin's model, discussed in the next chapter, or Poole's model, discussed in Chapter 12 (see Section 12.2).

(iv)   *Opportunity cost of money*

The 'rate of interest' is the opportunity cost of holding money; that is, the rate of return on those assets which are direct alternatives to holding money. However, in a formal model no consideration can be given to exactly what this means in the real world: Keynesians and monetarists have very different views about the demand for money (see Chapter 3), which in turn imply radically different views about the meaning of 'r'. These in turn imply very different opinions about the potency of monetary policy.

Keynesians argue that only a very narrow range of short-term financial assets are perceived of as being direct alternatives to holding money. Thus 'r' is the rate of interest paid upon these and so is the rate of return on building society deposits, treasury bills and some similar securities. Hence, Keynesians seek to find out how sensitive expenditure on goods is to variations in these. A Keynesian's IS curve is thus a measure of the responsiveness of expenditure only to changes in short-term interest rates.

A monetarist, on the other hand, believes that *all* other assets are direct alternatives to holding money. Hence, the monetarist's 'r' measures the implicit or explicit rate of return on all of these – houses, land, factories, dishwashers, cars, shares and so on –

besides the short-term financial assets. A monetarist would also include longer-term financial assets (bonds), but there is less controversy here since many Keynesians would agree and in any case long-term and short-term interest rates usually move together closely. Any increase in asset prices means that the rate of return on them falls, either explicitly, as in the case of bonds and shares, or implicitly, for owner-occupied houses and consumer durables. The owner of a house receives *inter alia*, say, 156 bedroom weeks per year from a 3 bedroom house. This is part of the return on owning a house. If this is divided by the price of a house one has a rate of return on houses, called the house rate of interest by Keynes, see Turvey in Hahn and Brechling (1965, pp.164–72). If house prices double this rate of return is halved. More generally, the implicit rate of return on the asset is the (subjective) value of the services derived from the asset (v), less depreciation (d), divided by its market value (M):

$$\text{rate of return} = \frac{v - d}{M}$$

An increase in the market value must reduce the rate of return on the asset, given that the value of the services derived from an asset is invariant with respect to its price. It is standard to think of the interest rate as the inverse of the price of bonds, p.70 above. Monetarist analysis suggests that it is the inverse of the price of all assets.

For the monetarist the opportunity cost of holding money is therefore affected by any change in asset price, as well as by changes in the interest rate paid on short-term financial assets. Hence, the monetarist's IS curve measures the responsiveness of expenditure to changes in all of these. This means that monetarists and Keynesians would represent the same expenditure function by different IS curves. If industrial investment depended only upon share prices, and house building depended only upon house prices, as in valuation ratio models (see pp.43 and 117), Keynesians would regard this as evidence for a vertical IS curve because expenditure was not responsive to short-term interest rates – in their view, the opportunity cost of holding money. Monetarists, on the contrary, would regard it as evidence for an elastic IS curve because expenditure was responsive to interest rates using their analysis of the opportunity cost of holding money. These consequences reflect intuitively obvious points. If houses are direct substitutes for money, a change in the money supply will cause a change in house prices, and it is reasonable to attribute any consequent change in economic activity to the increase in the money supply, see Spencer (1990) and Spencer and Muellbauer (1990). Thus, the monetarist view about the demand for money implies the transmission mechanism encapsulated in the monetarist IS curve. If houses are not direct substitutes for money, the Keynesian view follows. This analysis is another way of stating the point made on page 36. Monetarist analysis emphasises adjustment through asset markets. In the case of the UK (and US) economy, this means the housing market, the stock exchange and the market in consumer durables.

More general criticisms of IS–LM have been made – not least by its inventor, Hicks (1983). The precise logical status of IS–LM is subject to much criticism but not its utility in a few limited but important cases.

4.9 Summary and conclusions

The IS–LM model is a two-sector model: goods, or real, sector and financial, or monetary, sector. Equilibrium levels of income and interest rates can be calculated simultaneously within the model. Goods-market shocks produce movements in income and interest rates in the same direction; so, for example, an increase in government spending leads to a rise in both income and interest rates. Money-market shocks produce changes in these variable in opposite directions; so, for example, a rise in the money supply causes interest rates to fall whereas income rises. Extreme values of interest elasticities of either spending (0) and the demand for money (∞) lead to the 'Keynesian case' when the monetary policy is incapable of changing incomes. The monetarist case is similarly the consequence of either an infinitely interest-elastic demand for goods or a perfectly inelastic demand for money (or in both cases, extreme income elasticities). In this case 'fiscal policy' cannot influence income but only influences the rate of interest.

Appendix: A taxonomy of IS–LM curves and the generation of perverse curves

The IS curve can take four possible slopes:

(A) Downward sloping. The 'normal' slope arises when the interest elasticity of the demand for goods (the interest elasticity of the demand for investment plus that for other categories of expenditure) takes a value between -0 and $-\infty$

(B) Vertical. The IS curve is vertical whenever the demand for goods is perfectly interest inelastic, or infinitely income elastic

(C) Horizontal. The IS curve is horizontal if the demand for goods is infinitely interest elastic, or has a zero income elasticity

(D) Upward sloping. The IS curves can be upward sloping in certain so-called 'perverse' situations.

There is in fact nothing perverse about these cases of upward-sloping curves. For example, in the case of an accelerator model in which the desired levels of certain categories of investment are partially income determined, both stock building and fixed investment may be income sensitive (see Austin in Gowland, 1979). This IS curve is upward sloping whenever the marginal propensity to invest is greater than the sum of the marginal propensity to withdraw.

Second, an upward-sloping IS curve arises when saving is *positively* related to the level of interest rates. This can occur because a change in interest rates has both an income and a substitution effect on saving (see pp.172ff; also Gowland, 1990, Chapter 10). These effects are in opposite directions, so that a rise in interest rates has a positive substitution and a negative income effect on desired saving (and vice versa for a fall in interest rates). When the income effect is the larger the elasticity of saving is positive. This may merely tend to produce a more inelastic IS curve, but if the effect is sufficiently large to offset any investment generated, the IS curve is upward sloping.

However, while either of these may produce an upward-sloping IS curve, the combination may not. Using a linear model for simplicity and the simplest case of a closed economy without government

$$S = aY + br$$

$$I = cY - dr$$

so

$$Y = \frac{(b + d)}{(c - a)} r$$

IS curve will be upward sloping when

$$\frac{(b + d)}{(c - a)} > 0$$

that is if $(c - a)$ and $(b + d)$ are both negative or both positive.

'c' (the accelerator coefficient) and 'a' (the MPS) are both usually assumed to be non-negative – it is hard to rationalise negative values. $(c - a)$ will be positive if and only if c (the accelerator coefficient) exceeds a (the MPS) and negative whenever $a > c$.

The interest sensitivity of investment is assumed to be non-positive – anything else is bizarre. Hence 'd' is positive (or 0). Thus $(b + d)$ will be positive unless d is both negative *and* of greater absolute size than 'd'. This would occur if the interest sensitivity of saving is both negative and absolutely larger than that of investment. This means that the income effect of changes in interest rates on savings exceeds the sum of the substitution effect and the interest sensitivity of investment, as above.[3] In principle an IS curve could be upward sloping for part of its length and downward for part, thereby producing multiple equilibrium.

The LM curve can be:

(A) Upward sloping. This cases arises if the interest elasticity of the demand for money is between $(-)0$ and $(-)\infty$

(B) Vertical. This case arises if the interest elasticity of the demand for money is equal to zero, or the income elasticity is infinite

(C) Horizontal. This, the liquidity trap, arises when the demand for money is infinitely interest elastic, or has a zero income elasticity

(D) Downward sloping. This case arises when the demand for money is positively related to interest rates.

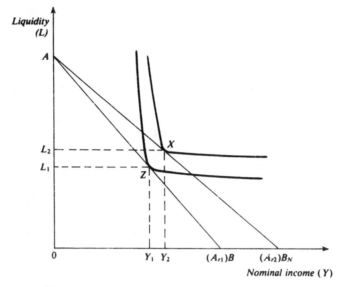

Figure 4.16 The LM curve may be upward sloping

A downward-sloping LM curve can arise in three different cases. First, through an income effect, when an investor disposes of his or her portfolio to gain both liquidity from money and income from interest-bearing assets. A rise in interest rates may be presented as an outward shift of a budget line (Fig. 4.16). When only money is held, A represents zero income and maximum liquidity. For simplicity, liquidity services are defined as 1 per unit of A. When only interest-bearing assets are held B represents zero liquidity and maximum income equal to rA (where r is the interest rate and A the portfolio's size). AB is the investor's budget line. A rational investor will select a point such as z, where he or she receives a Y_1 income and L_1 liquidity. When interest rates rise, the budget line pivots to AB_N, where $B_N = Ar_2$, where r_2 is the new higher rate of interest. The substitution effect will tend to reduce optimal money holdings and the income effect to increase them. There is no reason why X should not be selected when the income effect is the larger, so the optimal level of money holdings rises when interest rates rise.

Table 4.1 Taxonomy of IS and LM curves

Case	Goods Market Elasticity	IS Curve	Money Market Elasticity	LM Curve	Conclusion
A1	$0 > \epsilon > -\infty$	Normal	$0 > \epsilon > -\infty$	Normal	Both monetary and fiscal policy work
A2	$0 > \epsilon > -\infty$	Normal	0	Vertical	Only monetary policy works (monetarist case)
A3	$0 > \epsilon > -\infty$	Normal	$-\infty$	Horizontal	Only fiscal policy works (Keynesian case)
B1		Vertical	$0 > \epsilon > -\infty$	Normal	Only fiscal policy works (Keynesian case)
B2	0	Vertical	0	Vertical	Fiscal and monetary policy must be used in conjunction with each other
B3	0	Vertical	$-\infty$	Horizontal	Only fiscal policy works (ultra-Keynesian case)
C1	$-\infty$	Horizontal	$0 > \epsilon > -\infty$	Normal	Only monetarist policy works (monetarist case)
C2	$-\infty$	Horizontal	0	Vertical	Only monetary policy works (ultra-monetarist case)
C3	$-\infty$	Horizontal	$-\infty$	Horizontal	Neither monetary nor fiscal policy works
D1	positive	Upward sloping	$0 < \epsilon < -\infty$	Normal	Perverse results possible
D2	positive	Upward sloping	0	Vertical	Perverse fiscal policy effects
D3	positive	Upward sloping	$-\infty$	Horizontal	Fiscal policy works, monetary policy does not
A4	$0 > \epsilon > -\infty$	Normal	Positive	Downward sloping	Perverse cases possible
B4	0	Vertical	Positive	Downward sloping	Perverse interest rate effects
C4	$-\infty$	Horizontal	Positive	Downward sloping	as C1
D4	positive	Upward sloping	Positive	Downward sloping	Perverse interest rates effect

Note: 'Elasticity' is with respect to interest rate. Income elasticities are also relevant. For example, the IS curve is horizontal if the income elasticity of expenditure is zero as well as if the interest elasticity is zero. Either extreme value is sufficient. Normal slopes require that both elasticities should lie between zero and infinity (ignoring sign).

Second, a downward-sloping LM curve can occur when there are extrapolative expectations in the bond market. The speculative demand for money (see pp.62–5) rests on an assumption that expectations are regressive, so that a rise in interest rates generates expectations of a fall in the figure. Extrapolative expectations are that investors believe that a rise (fall in bond prices) makes a further rise likely. UK experience suggests this is so (Gowland, 1982). In this case the microeconomic demand for capital-certain assets is a positive function of interest rates, because a rise in interest rates leads those investors who fear a further rise (fall in bond prices) to sell bonds. There are the same problems as with the speculative demand for money in converting this to an aggregate demand for money relationship, but it is still a more probable outcome than that case.

Third, a downward slope occurs when money pays interest. This feature is particularly relevant when attention is paid to the various possible interest rates which might comprise the '*r*' of the model. If, contrary to normal use, the interest rate chosen was that which influences expenditure it might be the price of bank credit (that is, the rate banks charge on loans). The rate paid on bank deposits, the 'own rate', is linked to this. In the latter case, the LM curve is upward sloping. Certainly this model is a variant of IS–LM which is arguably relevant to the UK.

There are sixteen possible pairs of IS–LM, which are explained below. These are presented in five groups: (i) normal IS curves, (ii) vertical IS curves, (iii) horizontal IS curves, (iv) upward-sloping IS curves and (v) downward-sloping LM curves (Table 4.1).

(i) Normal IS curves

Case A1

The IS and LM curves are both normally sloped (see Figs 4.7, 4.8). Either fiscal policy (a shift of the IS curve) and monetary policy (a shift of the LM curve) suffice to change income.

Case A2

In this case the IS curve is normally (downward) sloped, and the LM curve vertical. This is the standard monetarist case (see Figs 4.9, 4.10) in which fiscal policy crowds out private expenditure such that it is unable to influence income. Monetary policy does, however, work.

Case A3

This combination of a horizontal LM curve and a downward-sloping IS curve is one of the standard Keynesian cases (see Figs 4.11, 4.12). The horizontal LM curve, the 'liquidity trap', is unaffected by changes in the money supply, so no change in the money supply influences income, whereas shifts of the IS curve change income without even changing interest rates.

(ii)   *Vertical IS curves*

Case B1

A vertical IS curve and an upward-sloping LM curve comprise the other standard Keynesian case illustrated in the text (Figs 4.11, 4.12). A shift of the IS curve causes income to change, whereas a shift of the LM curve generates only a change in interest rates, so fiscal policy works but monetary policy is ineffective.

Case B2

In this case both IS and LM curves are vertical. Either the two curves overlap in which case income is determined but interest rates indeterminate or they do not in which case the economy is in disequilibrium. The authorities should use monetary and fiscal policy in conjunction with each other such that the curves are coincident at the desired level of income. Interest rates are indeterminate, however. This is not a surprising result since interest rates do not influence either spending or the demand for money; so it is not surprising that neither goods- nor money-market forces nor both are sufficient to make it determinate.

Case B3

This combination of a vertical IS and a horizontal LM curve produces an ultra-Keynesian special case (see Fig. 4.17). No increase in the money supply shifts the LM curve, so it cannot influence either interest rates or income. On the other hand, fiscal policy influences income through its effect on the IS curve; a rise in government spending from G_A to G_B causes the IS curve

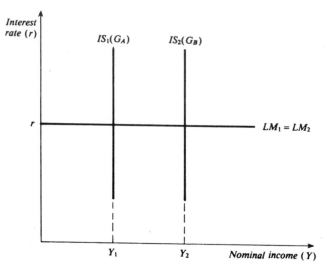

Figure 4.17 An ultra-Keynesian case

to shift from IS_1 to IS_2 and so income rises from Y_1 to Y_2. This case is in fact the elementary multiplier model and, as in this case, the level of income is known without knowledge of the rate of interest.

(iii) *Horizontal IS curves*

Case C1

A horizontal IS curve in conjunction with an upward-sloping LM curve is one of the standard monetarist cases, where monetary policy can influence income but fiscal policy has no effect on either income or interest rates (see Figs 4.11, 4.12).

Case C2

A vertical LM curve in conjunction with a horizontal IS curve produces an ultra-monetarist model. Nothing shifts the IS curve, whereas changing the money supply shifts the LM curve and

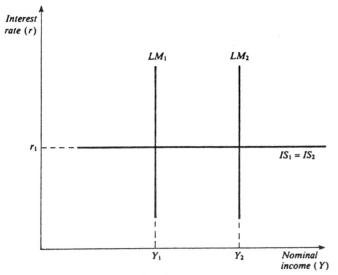

Figure 4.18 The quantity theory case

changes income (Fig. 4.18). As income is determined solely by monetary forces, this model is the elementary quantity theory.

Case C3

When both IS and LM curves are horizontal, the model is called degenerate. Neither curve ever shifts, so two cases must be analysed. In the first the curves are not coincident, so no equilibrium is possible. In the other the curves are coincident, so there is a determinate equilibrium level of interest rates. Any level of income is an equilibrium, however, so income is indeterminate.

(iv) Upward-sloping IS curves

Case D1

The simplest model involving an upward-sloping IS curve involves its interaction with a horizontal LM curve. In this case normal results prevail (Fig. 4.19a). The outward shift of the IS curve leads to a rise in income. Monetary policy is ineffective of course.

Case D2

A vertical LM curve and an upward-sloping IS curve produce simple but paradoxical results. A rise in the money supply from M_A to M_B causes the LM curve to shift rightwards, but while the level of income rises, the rate of interest also rises (Fig. 4.19b). A shift in the IS curve, generated by the rise in government spending from G_A to G_B, is illustrated in Figure 4.19(c). This model is unstable.

Case D3

When both curves are upward sloping the results depend upon which is the steeper. When the IS curve is steeper, a rise in government spending causes both income and interest rates to rise (Fig. 4.19d). A rise in the money supply causes income and interest rates to fall (Fig. 4.19e). When the LM curve is steeper, then a rise in the money supply causes income and interest rates to rise, whereas a rise in government spending causes a fall in both income and interest rates. This case is not illustrated because it is an extension of case D2.

(v) *Downward-sloping LM curves*

(The derivation of these results is left as an exercise for the reader.)

Case C4

A downward-sloping LM curve and a horizontal IS curve generate conventional results, as in Case C1.

Case B4

A vertical IS curve and a downward-sloping LM curve produce normal results insofar as income is concerned but the interest rate effects are perverse; that is, increasing the money supply raises interest rates as well as leaving income unchanged, whereas

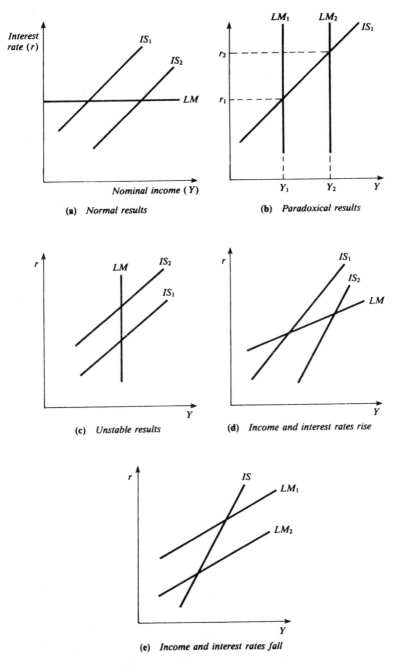

Figure 4.19 Upward-sloping IS curves

higher government spending *reduces* interest rates besides increasing income.

Case A4

When both curves slope downwards, the results depend on the relative slopes of the two curves. When IS has the steeper slope:

1. Increasing the money supply reduces income and increases interest rates.
2. Increasing government spending increases income and reduces interest rates.
3. The model is unstable.

When the LM curve has the steeper slope:

1. Increasing the money supply increases income and reduces interest rates.
2. Increasing government spending raises interest rates and reduces income.

Case D4

Whilst Ackley's (1961) seven-quadrant diagram represents the baroque extreme of IS–LM curves, the spirit of the rococco is well captured by this doubly perverse world of an IS curve which slopes upwards and an LM curve which slopes downwards. The results are relatively classical, however. The effects on income are conventional, but interest rate effects are perverse; that is, interest rates rise when the money supply is increased and fall when government spending rises.

Notes

1. Modigliani (1963) pointed out that the nominal income model is only possible if the real-income elasticity of demand for money equals the price elasticity. As the price elasticity equals unity, the real-income elasticity must also equal unity. The real-income elasticity of demand for goods is also taken to be unitary. Such assumptions do not seem unduly restrictive in a macroeconomic model designed to illustrate the workings of the economy. Indeed, compared to the assumptions implicit in the aggregation necessary to produce any macroeconomic

model, they are trivial. Moreover, the assumptions are in effect assumed in much advanced microeconomic analysis as 'homothetic tastes'. Another problem concerns the nature of the investment function, but in no version of the model is it theoretically rigorous. Friedman (1974; in Gordon, 1974) and Brittan (1981) take a similar approach. A modern variation, for example Hillier (1986, p.72), is to 'derive' an aggregate demand (*AD*) curve. In this case ouput is calculated for varying price levels with a fixed nominal money supply – the result being the *AD* curve. This illustrates rather than solves the problem; only a multi-equation algebraic system of equations can resolve it.

2. Ackley has revised his text, but the citation to the first edition is given because this outstanding text best preserves the spirit of the Keynesian high noon.

3. Paul Turner of Southampton drew my attention to an error in my presentation of this point in the first edition.

5

Tobin's Model

5.1 General equilibrium approach to monetary policy

Friedman's restatement of the quantity theory was introduced on p.34 as the first of the models to incorporate the concept of portfolio balance. The portfolio approach was then described more generally (see p.43), and it was finally shown how the IS–LM model could be interpreted as a three-asset portfolio model (see p.75). Both Friedman's approach, at least as presented above, and the IS–LM model incorporate very restrictive assumptions. To derive a proportional relationship between money and income, the new quantity theory has to assume that the private sector wishes to hold constant the ratio of its money balances to its expenditure and to its holdings of assets other than money. The IS–LM approach is even more restrictive in that it simultaneously assumes one crucial aspect of the monetarist case, the exogeneity of money, and one of the Keynesian's *vis-à-vis* the nature of the transmission mechanism. There is no way in the IS–LM model that a Keynesian can argue that the money supply is determined solely, or even largely, by income. Equally there is no way that a monetarist could argue that changes in the money supply have a direct effect upon spending rather than an indirect one through the effect upon the rate of interest.[1] This does not render either model useless, but it does emphasise that both have been produced for a specific purpose: to elucidate crucial features of the monetary system.

There is, however, an obvious case for a more general approach which does not rely upon these special assumptions. This is provided by the general equilibrium approach to monetary theory, the essence of which is encapsulated in Tobin's (1969) model. Perhaps the most important feature of this approach is the light it throws upon the transmission mechanism of monetary policy. Nevertheless, it is almost as important that it acts as a general framework which makes clear how the other models fit together and are interrelated. In this way it is rather like a map of a country, whereas the models considered elsewhere, IS–LM, flow-of-funds and quantity theory alike, are like town plans which focus on a specific issue or issues.

General equilibrium theory was developed so that conventional microeconomics could be based on valid theoretical foundations (see Arrow and Hahn 1970).[2] It also provides a rigorous framework in which the interrelationships between different markets can be analysed. Both of these are relevant to monetary theory. The monetary theorist seeks to analyse the interactions between different markets, real and financial. Moreover, the use of general equilibrium theory also ensures that monetary theory has a rigorous underpinning based on a coherent theory of individual behaviour. In this sense the monetary theorist is following Hicks' (1935) famous simplifying advice. The individual is assumed to allocate his or her wealth across a range of assets so as to maximise his or her utility. Thus, an economic agent simultaneously determines his or her holdings of money, of financial assets and of various kinds of real assets. In response to a shock, such as a change in money holdings induced by official policy, the agent will calculate his or her new equilibrium and adjust to it at the optimal speed as in Friedman's analysis. No prior restrictions are imposed on the nature of the new equilibrium; the agent is not presumed to be restricted to respond only to certain stimuli (as with interest rates for IS–LM) nor to be intent on maintaining some fixed ratio, as in the elementary Friedmanite quantity theory. Anything is allowed as a possible response save only that the economic agent cannot violate his or her budget constraint nor can he or she behave inconsistently. The consequence of this is that at a macro-economic level, the economist is interested in the substitutability of every asset for every other asset, whereas in IS–LM there are only three assets and so only two substitutions: money for interest-bearing assets and interest-bearing assets for real capital. This information can best be represented in the form of a matrix showing (partial) elasticities of substitution (see Table 5.1).

Hence, the effects of monetary policy on this asset would depend upon a much richer range of effects and require a much wider range of knowledge. This, and the complexity of the matrix, give rise to the simplifications presented in Sections 5.2 and 5.3 below.

One of the most important and interesting of the effects of monetary policy brought out by this approach is that of the *valuation ratio* upon investment, sometimes known as Tobin's q. The valuation ratio in this context is the ratio of the market price of an asset to its replacement cost (the term is also used in Marris' (1964) theory of the firm where the formal meaning is identical but otherwise the usage is totally different). Its meaning and role in influencing investment are most clearly seen in the case of housing. The market value of a house is clear, since houses are traded actively. Its replacement cost is the cost of rebuilding it. This comprises the cost of acquiring the site (that is, the value of the site), the cost of 100,000 bricks, so many windows, the cost of hiring bricklayers, and so on. This would involve complex calculations, but the concept is simple. This figure is, in principle, of interest to two parties: a potential house

Table 5.1 A Keynesian general equilibrium model: partial elasticities of substitution

A_1 Cash	A_2 Bank deposit	A_3 Building society share	A_4 Bond	A_5 Equity	A_6 Lathe	A_7 Washing machine
A_1	high	zero	zero	zero	zero	zero
A_2		high	zero	zero	zero	zero
A_3			high	zero	zero	zero
A_4				high	zero	zero
A_5					high	zero
A_6						high

buyer and a speculative builder. A potential house buyer should compare the replacement cost of a house with market price. If the market price exceeds the replacement cost this person should consider having a house built rather than buying a currently existing one. If the margin of market cost over replacement price is sufficiently high to cover the inconvenience of having a house built, the purchaser will have a house built. Hence this decision will increase investment, since housebuilding is a form of investment, a Keynesian injection. Hence, a rise in the market price of houses, the valuation ratio, could persuade some potential purchasers of existing houses to have a house built instead. In practice the calculations are made by speculative builders (of whom in the UK Barratts are probably the best known) who build houses and offer them for sale. They know that they can sell the houses they build at the market price, so this determines their revenue. Their costs are the replacement cost of building houses. Thus, a rise in the valuation ratio means that it is more attractive to build houses, so they build more. More formally, a rise in the valuation ratio means that the marginal revenue curve shifts outwards relative to marginal cost, so equilibrium output rises. This mechanism can easily be extended. An oil company such as BP would like to increase its holdings of oil-bearing land, drilling rights, etc. It can explore and try to discover new fields or it can buy existing oil fields, through buying the companies which own them. It can therefore calculate the relative cost of acquiring oil reserves in these two ways. This leads to a valuation ratio comparison – a replacement cost (explore etc.) or a market price (buy existing reserves). This market price is determined by the share price of the companies which owned them. Hence when share prices collapsed in October 1987 it became much more attractive for oil majors, like BP, to buy reserve-rich companies like Britoil.

A similar mechanism applies in the case of investment in plant and machinery, since companies can expand in two ways. They may invest in plant and machinery (internal growth) or they may acquire another company (external growth). Put differently, a company can buy a new factory (that is, invest) or it can buy a second-hand factory by buying a company which owns one. The market value of a company is the value of its ordinary shares plus the value of its debts, since to own it one would have to buy all of the shares in the company and assume responsibility for its debts. The replacement cost is the physical cost of replacing its assets (that is, the cost of buying lathes, land, etc., plus any 'good will'). A rise in the valuation ratio can occur if there is either a rise in market value (that is, share prices) or a fall in replacement cost. Such a rise will make it more attractive to invest in new plant and machinery and less attractive to purchase existing companies. Like so many other subsequent developments in economics, the origin of this concept can be found in Keynes:

> *the daily* revaluations of the Stock Exchange inevitably exert a decisive influence on the rate of current investment.
> For there is no sense in building up a new enterprise at a cost greater than that at which a similar existing enterprise can be purchased whilst there is an inducement to spend on a new project that may seem an extravagant sum if it can be floated off on the Stock Exchange at an immediate profit. (Keynes, 1936, p.151)

The advocates of this model, Tobin and Fleming, argue that the ratio is the main determinant of investment. It is illuminating to compare their model with the orthodox neoclassical theory of investment. This argues that firms compare the economic value of an investment with its cost and invest if the former is greater. Economic value is the net present value of the stream of benefits from the project, that is, the discounted stream of quasi-rents it produces. Cost in this approach is the same as the replacement cost in the Tobin–Fleming approach. Fleming calculates economic value directly by ascertaining the market value of the project. If capital and asset markets are perfect, market value and net present value are equal. In disequilibrium, the two may not be equal and an estimate of economic value based upon market prices is preferable. Net present value calculations are a means of calculating economic value, not an end in themselves; so, if a better method of calculation is available, it should be used.

Keynes rightly emphasises the dual influence of asset prices – on both the potential user of the asset (the house purchaser in the first example) and those building for resale: the speculative builder. In a footnote to the above passage Keynes, referring to his earlier *Treatise* (1930, Vol.ii, p.195), stresses that this reinforces the more traditional argument.

> When a company's share (price is high) it can raise more capital by issuing more shares on favourable terms (so) this has the same effect as if it could borrow at a low rate of interest. (Keynes, 1936, p.151, note 1)

The valuation ratio model thus gives prominence to share and house prices as determinants of investment. The importance of this is that the money supply may have a direct impact upon shares and house prices, so there is an additional means by which monetary policy can influence the economy. This approach, of course, is similar in spirit to the emphasis on asset market adjustment in the monetarist approach. In the UK the policy community seems to feel that these affects are reinforced by the impact on the cash flow of mortgagees of changes in mortgage rates. This seems prima facie implausible for a number of reasons. The payments on most mortgages are adjusted annually, rather than whenever interest rates change. Mortgage interest is a transfer payment which is paid out to the holders of building society deposits, etc. A substantial proportion of these are held by the retired who depend upon them for their income. One would expect their spending to be at least as influenced by short-term variations in interest rates as mortgagees. The policy community's view may well be right, but it probably rests more upon psychology than elementary economics. Much empirical work sought to identify the effects of money supply on asset prices.[3] It has not been particulary conclusive, but nevertheless, the mechanism is generally accepted by economists. However, the focus of empirical work has shifted in the light of the rational expectations revolution, see p.287 below. In effect there is agreement that the relationships exist but have not been fully delineated. Indeed, many moderate Keynesians would accept that their models should include, as a transmission mechanism of monetary policy, the effects of money supply on asset and share prices. The consequent argument that monetary policy should be used to generate stability in asset markets is one which appeals both to monetarists and to many Keynesians, especially Tobin, and almost certainly would have appealed to Keynes. The difference is that monetarists would expect that this would be achieved by stability of monetary growth, while Keynesians would expect that it would be necessary to offset changes in market sentiment by fluctuations in the rate of monetary growth.

There are a number of other means whereby the housing market can be affected by monetary policy besides this asset-price mechanism, so it is not surprising that, especially in the USA, it is generally accepted that housebuilding will be the type of economic activity most (and most immediately) affected by monetary policy. The attractiveness of property construction, residential and commercial, is more affected by changes in interest rates than is any other form of fixed investment, because the nature of net present value calculation is such that a change in interest rates has more effect on the desirability of projects the longer-lasting they are – and property is the most durable form of fixed investment. If the discount rate rises from 10 to 20 per cent, the value of a £1 return in one year's time falls by 11 per cent, from 90p to 80p. The value of £1 in ten year's time falls by 69 per cent, from 35p to 11p. In general, the further into the future a return is, the more its value changes, and of course the longer lived a project is, the more its returns are in the further distant future. Hence, the longer lived a project is, the more its net present value changes as interest rates alter.

Most property, moreover, is purchased with borrowed money, and the loans are long term in most cases (for example, fifteen- to thirty-five-year mortgages from banks or building societies for most houses). Most builders and developers rely on borrowed money to finance the construction of offices and houses, so in all ways the housing market is most affected by changes in credit and money-market conditions. This gives further leverage to monetary policy and some complex transmission mechanisms, especially as there are specialist housing finance bodies, such as building societies in the UK and to a decreasing extent Savings and Loans Associations in the USA. These bodies have very liquid liabilities which are quite substitutable for bank deposits, so changes in monetary policy affect them rapidly. These effects have sometimes been intensified by the traditionally inefficient and rigid structure of these bodies. In fact, so potent is the effect of monetary policy on the housing market that it is frequently a constraint upon monetary policy. The adjustments forced upon builders, house buyers and, especially, those repaying mortgages, may be so large that the costs exceed the benefits in terms of economic management – especially as, rightly or wrongly, mortgage rates are perceived to be of key political importance. This issue is discussed in Gowland 1990. At first sight it is paradoxical that high mortgage rates are unpopular. A rise in the mortgage rate increases the disposable income of depositors. This group is larger than mortgagees. In particular, high interest rates benefit senior citizens living on investment income. It is not obvious that their votes are of less importance than those of the younger mortgagees. The resolution of the paradox may lie in the symbolic importance of interest rates, rather than their direct material impact. Low interest rates are traditionally viewed as being a symbol of economic success.

The Tobin approach is not without its limitations. The major omission within the model is any meaningful role for credit markets. In a formal sense Tobinite economic agents can choose to borrow since any debt is a negative asset. An agent distributes his or her portfolio among both positive assets and negative ones subject to the constraint that the sum of these positive and negative assets equals the agent's net worth. It fails to capture many of the crucial elements of borrowing, see the discussion of credit rationing, pp.243ff. Hence, as this mode of analysis is both formalistic and inadequate, it is more accurate to say that the model does not incorporate borrowing as an option for agents.

5.2   Neo-Keynesian model

A general equilibrium model is necessarily very complex, even when only a small number of assets are included – and in the real world, there are many thousands of assets. Thus, it is necessary to simplify the model so that it can be used. Moreover, it is even more important to show what assumptions are necessary in order to derive the neo–Keynesian and monetarist models. In this way it is possible to show exactly what has to be assumed, so as to derive the key propositions of the two models.

Neo–Keynesian results can be derived if it is assumed that assets can be arranged along a liquidity spectrum (Fig. 5.1), with

$A_1 \longleftrightarrow A_2 \longleftrightarrow A_3 \longleftrightarrow A_4 \longleftrightarrow A_5 \longleftrightarrow A_6 \longleftrightarrow A_7$

| Cash | Bank deposits | Building society shares | Bonds | Equity | Lathes | Washing machines |

Figure 5.1   The neo-Keynesian model: a liquidity spectrum

the most liquid asset on the left and the least liquid on the right (this is done for seven assets, taken as representative of the various types of asset). Crucially, it is assumed that each asset is a direct substitute only for its immediate neighbours. Hence, the (partial) elasticity of substitution for every asset with any non-adjacent asset can be taken to be zero (Table 5.1).

An immediate consequence of this assumption is that money does not exist in the economist's sense; no asset has any special characteristic which distinguishes it from all others. In a general equilibrium model the existence of money is an empirical question, the conditions for which are given in the next section. Hence, one can test a key monetarist assumption which is incorporated without question into the models analysed elsewhere in this book.

The transmission mechanism of financial policy is also clear-cut (the term 'monetary policy' seems inappropriate in a model without money). For example, suppose that the authorities increase the quantity of cash and so throw private sector portfolios into disequilibrium. The effect will be to cause a switch into bank deposits, the neighbouring asset. This should increase the 'price' of this asset (that is, lower its rate of return). As a higher quantity of bank deposits is held than before, paying a lower rate of interest, there will be a switch into the next asset, building society shares. This sequence will be repeated again and again until eventually real assets are reached (in the example used here, after five intermediate steps). The increase in the demand for real assets (for example, lathes and washing machines) will lead to an increase in their prices or the quantity produced. Nevertheless, the effect is indirect and diffuse. This transmission mechanism has often been compared to throwing a stone into a pond, so creating ripples which eventually reach the shore. A better metaphor perhaps is to compare it with models of migration, whereby there is a switch in population from, say, Newcastle to London without anyone moving more than twenty miles: some people move from Newcastle to Durham, others from Durham to Darlington, and so on; finally, some move from Stevenage to London. This indirect transmission mechanism is, of course, a generalisation of that presumed by the basic IS–LM models. Its unmonetarist character is, however, much clearer in this more general model.

This indirect transmission mechanism means that a change in the conventionally measured money supply does affect price and output but that the effect may be small, slow and unpredictable. Moreover, it is inadvisable to use the money supply as a target because it is so far removed from the real end of the spectrum. Rather, the authorities should observe some variable closer to real assets (that is, bonds or equities). Monetary policy will only have any effect insofar as it influences these variables, and it is therefore better to use them as intermediate targets. Tobin, who uses a similar simplification of his own model, for example, regards the rate of return on equities as the best target for financial policy. This introduces another implication of the model, a tendency to prefer price targets, such as interest rates, to quantity targets, such as the money supply.

Many self-styled Keynesians would modify this model to incorporate a range of direct substitutions amongst long-term financial assets and real assets. Nevertheless, the 'liquidity spectrum' and the nature of the substitutions it describes are the core of (neo-)Keynesian models of the financial sector. If 'near money' or some very liquid asset exists such that it is both a close and the only substitute for money, the Keynesian results follow; namely, the indirect transmission mechanism and the inappropriateness of the money supply as a policy target.

5.3 Monetarist model

To derive monetarist results within a general equilibrium framework, an equally drastic set of simplifying assumptions is

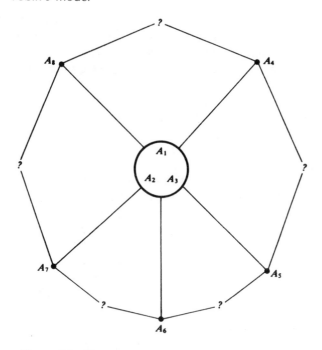

Figure 5.2 The monetarist model: money and other assets

necessary. These imply that in neo–Keynesian terms there is a clean break in the liquidity spectrum such that all the assets to the left of the break are (almost) perfect substitutes for each other. Thus, to use the example shown in Figure 5.2 and Table 5.2, assets A_1, A_2 and A_3 are almost perfect substitutes for each

Table 5.2 A monetarist general equilibrium model: partial elasticities of substitution

	A_1	A_2	A_3	A_4	A_5	A_6	A_7
A_1		Very high	Very high		All		
A_2			Very high		significantly greater than 0 but		
					significantly less than ∞		
A_3							
A_4							
A_5							
A_6							

other but A_3 and A_4 are not very close substitutes. This 'clean break' defines money, money being all the assets to the left of the break (that is, cash and those assets which are almost perfect substitutes for it). This means that the existence of money has been rendered into a testable proposition, and numerous studies have sought to show that it does or does not exist (summarised in Goodhart, 1975). None of these has proved very conclusive, so Goodhart (1975) has suggested an alternative means of testing for a 'clean break' by using turnover data; that is, the average number of times each asset changes hands per period. Money would have a much higher turnover than any other asset and turnover may be taken as a proxy for liquidity. Hence, if the neo–Keynesians were right, there would be a gently declining turnover ratio as one moved rightwards along the liquidity spectrum, whereas if the monetarists are right, the left-hand assets would have very high turnovers followed by a precipitate drop as one reached the assets which were not money. Turnover data is not easy to acquire, but it seems to uphold the monetarist case.[4]

The other monetarist hypothesis is that all the assets beyond the clean break are equally good or bad substitutes for money (Fig. 5.2, Table 5.2). The matrix of substitution has only two values. There is an almost infinite value for the different types of money for each other and a significant but lower value for the elasticity between money and each of the other assets. In the example shown in Figure 5.2 and Table 5.2 money is defined as assets A_1, A_2 and A_3 and all other assets are direct substitutes for money. This pattern of substitution can be illustrated by a radial diagram which replaces the liquidity spectrum (Fig. 5.2). The other assets may be good or bad substitutes for each other; the monetarist case is independent of this. In fact, the substitutability of the other assets for each other is likely to be a consequence of their definition; if, for example, radios and cassette players are defined as separate assets, there will be much higher elasticities of substitution than if they are grouped as electronic music makers, and the elasticity of substitution between this and cars calculated. It is worth noting, however, that if all the other assets are very close substitutes for each other, they may be regarded as a single asset. Hence, the result would be a two-asset model:

money and other assets. In other words, a high elasticity of substitution between all the assets which are not money produces the world of the elementary quantity theory. However, monetarist results can be derived whatever the value of this elasticity.

The consequences of the monetarist pattern of substitutes can be seen when the consequences of an increase in the money supply are examined. The private sector's portfolio is thrown into disequilibrium, but the response is to switch funds to all other assets rather than to a limited range of liquid assets as in the neo-Keynesian models. There is, therefore, an immediate increase in the demand for all other assets and so an increase in their price or quantity, depending as ever upon the elasticity of supply. Thus, the effect of an increase in the money supply is direct and likely to be quicker and more predictable than in the neo–Keynesian version – though Friedman at least would deny that monetary policy is either quick or totally predictable in its effect. In these circumstances the money supply is clearly the most appropriate target for monetary policy. In brief, the validity of the monetarist case, as compared to the Keynesian one, depends upon which assets are direct substitutes for money.

5.4 Summary and conclusions

The Tobin model is a general equilibrium analysis of the financial sector. Its main implications are that the monetarist–Keynesian debate is an empirical one. The major propositions of both camps can be derived as special cases within the model. Emphasis is laid not on the size of elasticities but on what is a substitute for money. Monetarists' conclusions follow from money being a substitute for all other assets, not just a few short-term, highly liquid financial assets. This is an extension of the debate about the nature of 'the interest rate' in IS–LM models (see p.99). Indeed, monetarists frequently claim that a fundamental Keynesian heresy is to say that (financial) interest rates are the price of money (see p.22). Instead, they are the price of credit, being determined by the desire to borrow and lend. The 'price of money' includes all the costs of holding it (that is, including the inflation rate). Keynesian results follow from the assumption that only a limited range of financial assets are substitutes for holding 'money'. In this, the world of the liquidity spectrum, monetary targets are not desirable. Moreover, in effect there is nothing distinctive about money (strictly it does not exist). It is merely an extremely liquid asset which is slightly different from a range of very liquid assets which themselves are not too dissimilar from other liquid assets. Thus the main conclusion of the analysis in this chapter is that the impact of monetary policy depends upon what is a substitute for money. This impact, crucially, will in any case be observed in asset (especially housing) markets.

In fact the value of the Tobin (1969) approach is that it highlights the critical policy issues:

1. direct and indirect transmission mechanism;
2. what is a substitute for money; and
3. monetary policy involves asset market adjustment where assets are housing, consumer durables, shares and corporate holdings of inventories.

Notes

1. The monetarist might try recourse to incorporating wealth effects, so that an increase in the supply of money increased wealth and so consumption. However, while this introduces a direct transmission mechanism, it is then impossible to tell whether the effects on income are direct or indirect. Indeed, in comparative static models the whole debate is moot. The spirit of IS–LM is of an indirect transmission mechanism. More recent work has concentrated on the role of expectations in this process, see the survey in Gowland (1990, Chapter 5).
2. Hahn in Surrey (1976) offers some interesting thoughts on the problems of a theoretically rigorous monetary theory in the course of an onslaught on Friedman. See also Hahn (1982).
3. See Gowland (1975) and the superb, if slightly dated, summary in Goodhart (1975), regrettably omitted in Goodhart (1989).
4. See Percival (1982) and Fisher (1989), pp.14–30 especially pp.22–8.

6

Flow of Funds

6.1   Flow-of-funds approach

The flow of funds, as its name implies, describes the funds which are transferred (that is, flow) from one economic agent to another as a result of those financial transactions which take place within a given period, such as a year. This emphasis on flows means that the model complements the analysis of stocks on which portfolio models lay stress. These funds are often presented in the form of a matrix such as Table 6.1. This shows the transactions amongst three individuals: *A* borrowed £100 from *B* and £200 from *C*, while *B* borrowed £20 from *C*. The final row and column show the net effects of these transactions. *A* borrowed a total of £300 (so he or she lent –£300; borrowing is negative lending). *C* lent £220 while *B* was a net lender of £80, the gross lending of £100 less his or her borrowing of £20. Usually such matrices are drawn up for the entire world. In this case the transactions of many agents are combined into one entry and one of the cells represents the rest of the world. Hence, for example, if the matrix in Table 6.1 had been drawn up by someone interested in a particular village, *A* might be the farmers who live in Trumpton, *B* the other residents and *C* the rest of the world. The groups presented in such a matrix would depend upon the purposes of the analyst. Flow-of-funds matrices are usually much

Table 6.1 A flow-of-funds matrix

		Borrowing by		
		A	*B*	*C*	Total lending
Loans by	*A*	0	− 100	− 200	− 300
(£s)	*B*	+ 100	0	− 20	80
	C	+ 200	+ 20	0	220
Total borrowing (£s)		300	− 80	− 220	

more complex than in Table 6.1. The forms of borrowing may be distinguished by subdivisions of the cells of the matrix. For example, *C*'s loans to *B* may consist of £100 of a conventional loan and the purchase of a financial asset from *B*. This financial asset could be a bill, bond, mortgage or some other security wherein *B* acknowledged his or her debt and set out the terms of it. Moreover, *B* might sell to *C* some asset he or she already owned. He or she might for example have sold C a claim on *A*. This would then be entered twice, as a repayment of a loan by *B* to *A* and as a loan by *C* to *A*. The Bank of England's flow-of-funds matrix distinguished between fifty-two types of financial asset and comprises six groups of economic agents: the public sector, the banks, other financial institutions, industrial and commercial companies, the personal sector and the overseas sector (that is, the rest of the world). For some purposes the UK public sector is divided into either two groups (general government and other) or three (central government, nationalised industries and local authorities). Similar distinctions are used in Japan and most of continental Europe. In Australia and the USA the distinction is usually between the Federal government and state and municipal authorities.

The other formal tool of flow-of-funds analysis is a source-and-uses-of-funds statement, as shown for an imaginary John Doe in Table 6.2; this is also called a cash flow statement but in general it is not the same as sources-and-applications-of-funds statement, although in this case the two could be identical. The individual's sources of funds are his income (£10,000), the reduction in his assets (£3,000 – the shares and deposit) and his borrowing from various sources (£13,000). Besides current living expenses, he has purchased a house and a car and increased the size of his bank deposit, as well as having lent £200 to the government. The individual's net acquisition of financial assets can be calculated. His gross assets have risen by £500 (*A* and *B*) but have also fallen by £3,000 (*C* and *D*). Hence, his assets have fallen by £2,500. In addition, he has increased his liabilities by £13,000 (*E* and *F* and *G*). Hence his financial deficit is £15,500 or, alternatively, his net acquisition of financial assets is –£15,500.

The value and purpose of flow-of-funds analysis lies not so much in these formal tools – useful though they may be as a summary of an individual's activities or the financial system – as in a number of simple relationships that arise in their construction. Some of these are derived from accounting, some from economics and some are so basic that it is difficult to regard them as other than common sense – but then economics has frequently been defined by its devotees as applied common sense. The most basic of all the relationships is that *A*'s loans to *B* must equal *B*'s indebtedness to *A*. This follows from the meaning of the words loan and indebtedness. The relationship is equally true in changes, that is, flows; that is, if *A* lends £100 to *B*, it follows that *B* must have borrowed £100 from *A*. This was used in constructing Table 6.1.

Table 6.2 Sources and uses of funds

Source of Funds	£s	Use of Funds	£s
Income	10,000	Expenditure on current goods and services	7,000(*J*)
Sale of shares	2,000(*C*)	Purchase of house	17,000
Reduction in building society deposit	1,000(*D*)	Purchase of car	1,500(*H*)
Mortgage	10,000(*E*)	Increase in bank deposit	300(*A*)
Borrowing from parents	2,000(*F*)	Purchase of Savings Certificates	200(*B*)
Borrowing from bank	1,000(*G*)		
	26,000		26,000
Net acquisition of financial assets = –£15,500			

Table 6.2 illustrates another basic relationship: for any group the sources and uses of funds must balance. This is again self-evident, once it has been pointed out. Another relationship that is very similar is the accounting convention that assets must equal liabilities, or that the change in assets must equal the change in liabilities. Another truism is that the purchase of an asset must equal the sales of it. Alternatively, the purchase of an asset less the sales of it must be zero, or that the sum of net acquisitions (that is, net of sales) must be zero. If A, B and C together have purchased £10,000 of asset x, someone must have sold it to them. Thus, in a four-agent model (A, B, C and rest of world) it is true that the rest of the world's sales of asset x are £10,000.

From these relationships it follows that the sum of the financial surpluses of the agents or groups shown within a matrix must be zero (so long as one group is the rest of the world). A financial surplus shows the net acquisition of each of the financial assets by an individual or group. The sum of financial surpluses is the sum of the sum of the net acquisitions of each financial asset. As each of the sum of the net acquisitions of assets is zero, so is the sum of these sums. A simple example illustrates this, for two agents, A and the rest of the world, B, and two assets, x and y:

A's financial surplus = A's net acquisition of x and
$\qquad\qquad\qquad\qquad$ A's net acquisition of y

B's financial surplus = B's net acquisition of x and
$\qquad\qquad\qquad\qquad$ B's net acquisition of y

so:

and $\qquad$ $\begin{array}{l} A\text{'s financial surplus} = \\ B\text{'s financial surplus} \end{array}$ $\left(\begin{array}{l} A\text{'s net acquisition of } x \text{ and} \\ B\text{'s net acquisition of } x \end{array} \right)$

$$+$$

$\qquad\qquad\qquad\qquad$ $\left(\begin{array}{l} A\text{'s net acquisition of } y \text{ and} \\ B\text{'s net acquisition of } y \end{array} \right)$

As the terms within each bracket sum to zero, it follows that A's financial surplus plus B's financial surplus equals zero.

All these relationships imply constraints upon the relationship between the cells of a matrix. Usually it is possible to derive any of the entries from knowledge of the others. An example of this

Table 6.3 A flow-of-funds matrix

	by A	by B	
net acquisition of x	AX	BX	0
net acquisition of y	AY	BY	0
financial surplus	AS	BS	0

is provided in Table 6.3, utilising the two-person (A and B), two-asset (x and y) world used in the preceding example. A's net acquisition of asset x is called AX, his or her surplus AS and so on. If only A's net acquisition of $x(AX)$ and B's financial surplus (BS) are known, the entire matrix can be constructed. For example, if AX were 100 and BS 200, as AX is 100, BX is -100 because $AX + BX = 0$. As $BS = BX + BY = 200$, therefore BY is equal to 300. Hence, AY is equal to -300, because $AY + BY = 0$. Hence, a researcher interested in finding out the size of AY can do so from knowledge of AX and BS. In the example, a financial forecaster might derive forecasts of A's behaviour and of B's by independent means. The forecaster could then check whether these independent forecasts of AX, AY, BX and BY were consistent (see Hewitt, 1977). Indeed, the forecaster could also check the consistency of the components of his or her forecast if he or she had separate forecasts of AX and AY on the one hand and AS on the other. Such consistency checks and methods of deriving unknown figures are invaluable in constructing historical data. Most current economic data is inaccurate to some degree or other, see for example, Johnson (1989). This is true in nearly all countries besides the UK. For example, world exports should be equal to world imports for obvious reasons. Nevertheless, according to the data, world imports exceed world exports by about 5%. Such discrepancies can only be discovered and analysed by use of the consistency checks provided by flow-of-funds analysis and Keynesian national income analysis.

The most important and useful independent check on the consistency of the forecast is that some of the items in it can be derived from a forecast of the real sector of the economy. A person's financial surplus necessarily equals his or her savings less his or her investment less any acquisition of existing real assets. This follows from the equality of sources and uses of funds.

Certain uses and sources can be combined. For example, savings equals income (a source) less consumers' expenditure (a use). In Table 6.2 one could deduct items *H* and *J* from income and enter savings £1,500 instead of the three items income, *H* and *J*. The relationship would still be valid. Grouping the seven items which comprise the individuals' financial surplus, the remaining items would be:

> saving (£1,500) − purchase of existing house (£17,000)
> = financial surplus (−£15,500)

This interrelationship with Keynesian variables is also crucial in flow-of-funds analysis as a link between the financial and real sectors. The value of flow-of-funds analysis lies in the consistency which is forced upon forecasters or other analysts and in the links between transactions which are highlighted, both within the financial sector and between the financial sectors. Examples of this using government finance and money supply identities are given later in this chapter but a very simple example; a three-sector model (Public Sector Financial Surplus + UK Private Sector Financial Surplus + Overseas Sector Financial Surplus = 0) reveals one of the many economic misjudgements of the 1970–4 Heath government. In the 1972 budget the government forecast a very large public sector deficit, about £4,000m. They also forecast an economic boom that meant that investment would rise and that saving would fall. Thus, the private sector's financial surplus would not be very large; in fact, it was about £1,000m. Necessarily, therefore, the forecasts implied an overseas sector financial surplus of £3,000m. This is, in effect, a balance of payments deficit of £3,000m. Nevertheless, the government appeared to be amazed when a deficit of this magnitude emerged in 1973. The authorities had apparently produced, and believed, an inconsistent forecast. Very elementary flow-of-funds analysis would have averted the error. A similar point applies to the analysis of countries with large balance of payments deficits such as the USA in the 1980s or the UK (1988–). A balance of payments deficit can only be eliminated if either the public sector or domestic private sector financial position improves, since if the overseas sector's surplus declines there must be a corresponding change elsewhere. Hence exchange rate changes or other improvements in competitiveness cannot eliminate a balance of payments deficit without a macroeconomic adjustment, that is a rise in private sector net saving or a fall in the budget deficit. Indeed an improvement in competitiveness can produce a worsening of the balance of payments. Higher exports generate higher income which leads to higher imports. Either the rise in exports or in imports can be larger, Gowland (1983a, p.82), depending on the size of the marginal propensity to import and multiplier.

6.2   The flow-of-funds model and the monetarist–Keynesian debate

The two most crucial flow-of-funds relationships are the government finance equation and the money supply identity, also called the bank balance sheet equation or, simply, the flow-of-funds equation (the latter term is used elsewhere in this book). The basic government finance equation is that the amount that government borrows must equal the amount lent to it (various more complex versions of this equation are given towards the end of this section after the money supply equation has been derived). In a closed economy:

$$
\begin{aligned}
PSBR = \ & \Delta \ \text{Currency held by the non-bank private sector } (C_p) \\
& + \ \Delta \ \text{Non-bank private sector loans to the public sector} \\
& \qquad (PLG) \\
& + \ \Delta \ \text{Bank loans to the public sector } (BLG) \qquad \textbf{(1)}
\end{aligned}
$$

(Δ *means 'change in'*)

The *PSBR* represents the amount that must be borrowed, and in a closed economy this must be lent by either the non-bank private sector or the banking sector. This is a pure identity that is always true. Borrowing by A must equal lending to A, and lending to A must equal lending to A by C plus lending to A by non-C (that is, everyone who is not C). It is more convenient to express this lending as a change in the (nominal) stock of loans outstanding, hence the use of 'Δ loans'. Lending by the non-bank private sector can take two forms: currency (C_p) and more orthodox loans, such as gilt-edged securities, national savings certificates, etc. (PLG): G is used as an abbreviation (for government) for the public sector. Currency is a peculiar form of non-bank loan to the public sector, but it is a loan nevertheless. Its peculiar features are that it bears no interest and in practice need never be repaid. It is a prerogative of sovereign governments to borrow in this way; indeed, a definition of sovereignty is the right to issue currency in this way. Nevertheless, a bank note is a government IOU as the famous wording on the English notes makes clear ('I promise to pay the bearer on demand . . .'). Bank loans to the public sector need not be distinguished in the same way, so there are the three forms of lending to the public sector: ΔC_p ΔPLG, ΔBLG. The equation would still be valid if there were a surplus (*PSDR*) although in this case the PSBR would be negative and so would the sum of the three right-hand-side variables.

Money can be defined in various ways (see pp.23–6). The one used here is a broad definition comprising all bank deposits plus non-bank private sector holding of currency. As bank can be defined at will, various real-world definitions of money are covered by this formal definition; the former M_3 or £M_3 in the UK if a bank is conventionally defined, or M_4 if building societies are also regarded as banks:

$$\text{Money supply } (M) \equiv C_p + \text{Bank deposits} \tag{2}$$

However, deposits are bank liabilities, and it is convenient to ignore the very small total of non-deposit liabilities. In this case:

$$\text{Bank deposits} = \text{Bank liabilities} \tag{3}$$

If (3) is substituted into (2):

$$M = C_p + \text{Bank liabilities} \tag{4}$$

Moreover, by the balance sheet convention (see p.131):

$$\text{Bank assets} = \text{Bank liabilities} \tag{5}$$

Equation (5), in turn, can be substituted into (4) so:

$$M = C_p + \text{Bank assets} \tag{6}$$

Bank assets take various forms: loans, premises, computers, and so on. However, all but loans can be ignored as were non-deposit liabilities (see Gowland, 1982, p.49 for a relaxation of both assumptions), so:

$$\text{Bank assets} = \text{Bank loans} \tag{7}$$

If (7) is substituted into (6):

$$M = C_p + \text{Bank loans} \tag{8}$$

Bank loans can be subdivided so long as the categories are exhaustive, that is, include all possible borrowers. The categories used here are the public sector and the non-bank private sector (everyone else). Hence:

$$\begin{aligned}\text{Bank loans} = \ &\text{Bank loans to the public sector } (BLG)\\ &+ \text{Bank loans to the non-bank private}\\ &\text{sector } (BLP)\end{aligned}$$

$$\tag{9}$$

Substituting (8) into (9):

$$M = C_p + BLG + BLP \tag{10}$$

Equation (10) can be rewritten in changes; if a relationship is true in levels, it is necessarily true in changes:

$$\Delta M = \Delta C_p + \Delta BLG + \Delta BLP \tag{11}$$

The government finance equation (1) can be rewritten as:

$$\Delta BLG = PSBR - \Delta C_p - \Delta PLG \tag{12}$$

This is the proposition that lending by banks to the public sector is equal to total borrowing by the public sector less lending to the public sector by non-banks: an obvious if contorted identity.

Equation (12) can be substituted into (11):

$$\Delta M = \Delta C_p + (PSBR - \Delta C_p - \Delta PLG) + \Delta BLP \tag{13}$$

As ΔC_p appears twice, once as a negative and once as a positive, then it can be omitted. This is a consequence of the fact that to change the money supply currency must be put into circulation and all the ways of putting currency into (or out of) circulation already appear as the remaining items in (13). Hence, to include currency as well as the other items would be double counting. Hence:

$$\Delta M = PSBR + \Delta BLP - \Delta PLG \tag{14}$$

Equation (14) is the flow-of-funds equation or money supply

identity for a closed economy. As shown above (pp.14–20), it is also the money-creation equation. The right-hand-side variables are often called supply-side counterparts. It is easy to derive the more complex form for an open economy, which merely adds the overseas impact on the money supply to the right-hand side (OV); the other three items being called domestic credit expansion (DCE). Thus:

$$\Delta M = PSBR + \Delta BLP - \Delta PLG + OV \tag{14a}$$

or:

$$\Delta M = DCE + OV \tag{14b}$$

This relationship has many uses and highlights many important issues in economics. Its role in formulating rules for membership of exchange rate systems such as the ERM of the EMS is discussed on p.20. The function that will be highlighted here is its role in the monetarist–Keynesian debate. A monetarist argues that the size of (nominal) income depends only upon the size of the money supply. The monetarist has therefore to argue that the effect of a change in the money supply is independent of how it is created, or of which right-hand-side variable (in 14 or 14a) changes at the same time (see Friedman, 1969). This proposition, that the effect of a change in the supply of money does not depend upon what happens to banks' balance sheets, is challenged by all non-monetarists. They would argue that the size of the money multiplier does depend upon which right-hand-side variable changes. This debate is explored in the next section.

A similar debate concerns the method of financing the budget deficit (1), here written with the terms in an altered order:

$$PSBR = \Delta C_p + \Delta BLG + \Delta PLG \tag{1a}$$

ΔC_p obviously involves a change in the money supply and so does ΔBLG (because of the indirect method by which BLG occurs). Thus (1a) reflects the fact that government deficits can be financed by money creation or by borrowing from the non-bank private sector. If this change in the money supply covered by government-induced money creation is called ΔGMC:

$$PSBR = \Delta GMC + \Delta PLG \tag{15}$$

Equation (15) is also crucial to the monetarist–Keynesian debate.

An extreme Keynesian argues that the effect of a change in the *PSBR* on income is independent of how it is financed, of whether *GMC* or *PLG* change. A moderate Keynesian argues that there may be a difference between the effects but only insofar as the rate of interest is different if the *PSBR* is financed by money creation rather than by a change in *PLG*, usually called bond finance. A monetarist obviously believes that the difference is crucial, since by one means money is created but not by the other.

This question can be rephrased by asking: does it matter how government expenditure (implicitly, on current goods and services) is financed? This involves going back to the definition of the *PSBR*:

> *PSBR* = Public sector (government) spending on current goods and services (*G*)
> + Public sector (government) transfers to other sectors
> + Public sector acquisition of assets
> + Δ Public sector loans to other sectors
> − Taxation (*T*)
> − Asset sales by public sector

Thus, if *G* changes, there can be a change in either the *PSBR* or an offsetting change in one of the other items which make up the *PSBR*. Usually for simplicity all but *T* are held constant. (This is not unreasonable; a reduction in transfers is equivalent to an increase in taxation and the offsetting changes in the other three are equivalent to an increase in *PLG*.) Hence, an increase in *G* can be financed by an increase in taxation as well as by changes in *GMC* or *PLG*. These debates are also analysed in the next section.

Some analysts call the government finance equation the 'budget-constraint' or 'budget-restraint equation': usually these analysts wish to distinguish those public sector transfer payments which are payments of interest on the National Debt from all other public sector transfers. Thus, here the 'budget constraint' is reserved for analyses which rely upon the effect of interest payments (see p.199). Frequently in this literature it is assumed that the only source of money creation is government spending, so (15) is written as:

$$PSBR = \Delta M + \Delta PLG \qquad (15a)$$

Strictly, of course, the relationship is (from 14):

$$PSBR = \Delta M - \Delta BLP + \Delta PLG$$

Hence, in some of these models, ΔBLP is assumed to be zero or alternatively to bear a fixed relationship to ΔGMC, that is a credit multiplier model. As $\Delta M = GMC + \Delta BLP$, so if ΔBLP is $k\Delta GMC$, $\Delta M = (k + 1) \Delta GMC$ and so ΔM can be substituted for ΔGMC in (15). Recently this has been reversed and the full version used – see Blinder (1989).

Thus, flow-of-funds analysis suggests that the monetarist–Keynesian debate is an argument about the answers to two questions:

1. Does it matter what the supply-side counterpart to a change in the money supply is? As Friedman (1969) once put it, 'The crucial issue [for macroeconomic policy] is whether knowledge of the sources of the change in money permits an economically and statistically significant improvement in predictions of the future course of income'.
2. Does it matter how the *PSBR* (or government) spending is financed?

This restatement of the debate stresses that the argument is empirical and, moreover, that a moderate position is plausible. To answer 'Yes, Yes' seems *a priori* at least as probable as the 'No, Yes' of the monetarist or the 'Yes, No', of the Keynesian.

6.3   Flow-of-funds analysis of economic policy

Flow-of-funds analysis of economic policy is based upon the implications of the two key relationships:

$$\Delta M = PSBR + \Delta BLP - \Delta PLG \qquad (14)$$

$$PSBR = \Delta GMC + \Delta PLG \qquad (15)$$

The first point that emerges is that a simple comparison of monetary and fiscal policy is not particularly relevant. A change in the money supply must be accompanied by a change in one of three right-hand-side variables. The first, the *PSBR*, is a measure of the impact of fiscal policy. There has been a long debate about which is the best of the alternative indicators of the impact of fiscal policy.[2] From the debate it has emerged that, while the *PSBR* would not be a Keynesian's first choice, it is still a valid measure of fiscal policy. *PLG* is a measure of interest rate policy, since to increase this quantity it will usually be necessary to offer a higher rate of interest. Hence, an act of monetary policy must be accompanied by an act of fiscal, credit or interest rate policy. All of the latter are determinants of income in elementary Keynesian models. Hence, when analysing real-world policy actions, the monetarist–Keynesian debate concerns why an action changes income and by how much, rather than whether it will change. For example, if the government induces a rise in *BLP*, the Keynesian analysis is that because credit is more readily available, saving is lower and investment higher at each level of income; hence, by the usual 'multiplier' argument income must rise (borrowing to finance consumers' expenditure is negative saving). The monetarist argument is that because *BLP* is higher, the money supply has necessarily risen, so income must rise. Hence, the analyses agree qualitatively but not quantitatively; nor do they agree about the process whereby they achieve their results. A similar conclusion follows from analysis of the *PSBR* equation: an increase in the *PSBR* (fiscal policy) must be accompanied by a change in either *GMC* (monetary policy) or by an increase in interest rates, to induce a higher *PLG* (interest rate policy). Thus, fiscal policy must have a financial counterpart. Hence, monetary and fiscal policy are not independent, but are interdependent, as illustrated by the two equations. Moreover, the two policies considered in Chapter 4 were only a small selection from the menu available. In effect they were an increase in the *PSBR* financed by a higher level of *PLG* ('fiscal policy') and an increase in the money supply achieved by a reduction in *PLG* (open-market operation) – 'monetary policy'. There are obviously many other policies to be considered, see below.

The flow-of-funds equation (14) may be regarded as the surrogate supply function of money – surrogate because it stands in place of the factors which determine these variables and so the money supply. As the money supply is defined as being the sum of deposits (*D*) and currency holdings of the non-bank private sector (C_p), by use of both relationships it is possible to derive the equilibrium condition for the monetary system, that the supply of money should equal the demand. This is achieved when actual holdings of money $(D + C_p)$ equal their desired level and when the three right-hand-side variables are also equal to their equilibrium levels. Hence by use of $(D + C_p)$ to represent the demand for money and the flow-of-funds equation to represent the change in the supply of it, equilibrium can be derived. Like all equilibrium conditions in economics it is an identity with the words 'desired' or 'planned' inserted into it.

The flow-of-funds relationship can also be used as a consistency check upon the predictions of either the real or financial sector and so ensure that the overall forecast is consistent. The forecast of the *PSBR* inserted into the money-creation equation must be consistent with the values of G and T in the real forecast. Similarly, the values of *BLP* and *PLG* must be consistent with the values of S and I. $(S - I)$ is the private sector's financial surplus and is therefore equal to its net acquisition of financial assets (that is, to $\Delta M + \Delta PLG - \Delta BLP$). As stated above, the Heath government seems to have ignored this, as it was apparently surprised by the explosion of monetary growth in 1972–3 that was implicit in its forecasts of real variables (T, G, S and I). Moreover, these relationships act as a link between the financial and real sectors in the flow-of-funds model. The values of T, G, S and I (and X and M in the open economy version) imply values of the financial variables, and vice versa. For example, a rise in *PLG* must imply more saving, less investment or a disposal of other assets to satisfy the private sector's source-and-uses-of-funds relationships. Hence, one has a transmission mechanism of monetary policy. The rise in *PLG* (and fall in M) must be consistent with the private sector's source and uses being at equilibrium levels. If this relationship is disturbed, the consequent readjustment will alter income. Indeed, this flow-of-funds link between the sectors is the flow analogue to the stock relationship analysed in portfolio models. The two analyses should complement each other.

The comparison of alternative supply-side counterparts to an increase in the money supply is shown in Figure 6.1 by using the IS–LM model. The original equilibrium, at Y_0, is determined by the intersection of IS_1 and LM_1. The case of the money supply

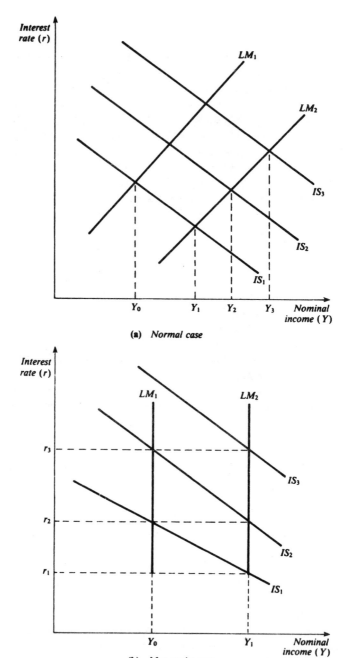

(a) *Normal case*

(b) *Monetarist case*

Figure 6.1 Alternative supply-side counterparts

increase accompanied by a fall in *PLG* was shown in Chapter 4 (p.85). This involved a shift of the LM curve. Thus, the equilibrium will be at Y_1 where IS_1 and LM_2 intersect. If the increase in the money supply is matched by a rise in the *PSBR*, the LM curve still shifts to LM_2 (because the comparison is of changes of equal size in the money supply). However, the IS curve will also shift, because injections are higher and/or withdrawals lower at each level of income. In the simplest case – where the increase in the *PSBR* is an increase in current government spending on domestically produced goods and services (G) – the shift is by ΔGk, where k is the Keynesian multiplier. This shift is exactly that described for the 'fiscal policy' case on page 82. Hence, in the case of a *PSBR*-generated rise in the money supply the IS curve shifts to IS_3 and the LM curve to LM_2. Thus, income rises to Y_3. The final case, where *BLP* rises, is the most complex. The LM curve shifts to LM_2 as before. The shift in the IS curve depends upon what the borrowers do with the funds. If it were all spent on investment goods or consumers' expenditure, there would be a net injection at each level of income of exactly the same amount as if there had been an increase in G and so a shift of the IS curve to IS_3. On the other hand, if the funds were held with banks or used to buy financial assets or existing real assets, there would be no shift of the IS curve, because the level of injections and withdrawals would be unaltered at each level of income. It seems reasonable to assume that some of the funds are spent in each fashion, so there would be a shift of the IS curve to IS_2 and a rise in income to Y_2.

This also illustrates any change in the money supply, whose counterpart is a change in some item in the *PSBR* other than G. If the change is in government lending or the sale or the acquisition of assets, the IS curve does not shift, and the analysis is exactly as for a change in *PLG*. If there is a change in taxation or any other government transfer, the IS curve shifts but not as far as if the change is in G. This shift may be larger or smaller than in the case where *BLP* is the counterpart, but for simplicity can be taken to be the same, so Y_2 is also the effect of a money supply increase matched by a tax cut or a rise in transfers. Hence, in the normal case, the effect of the alternative supply-side counterparts is such that, for a given change in the money supply, the effect on income is largest when the counterpart is the *PSBR*, smallest for *PLG* and intermediate for *BLP*. The monetarist case where all three have the same effect can only be derived within the IS–LM framework by having either a horizontal IS curve or a vertical LM curve. (In the former case the IS curve never shifts, so the intersection of LM_2 is always with the same IS curve (see Fig. 4.6).) The IS curve shifts in Figure 6.1(b) to IS_2 (for *BLP*) and IS_3 (*PSBR*) but remains at IS_1 (for *PLG*). However, income is Y_1 in all three cases. The effect of the different methods of finance is to alter the rate of interest and the composition of income but not its size. For example, with a *PSBR*-matched increase in the money supply there is a rise in the interest rate to r_3 to crowd out enough private spending (compared to the other methods which also generate Y_1) to offset the higher level of public expenditure. To conclude, it should be stressed that the IS–LM model is a moderate Keynesian vehicle in its treatment of this issue, so it is not surprising that the monetarist result is a special case. Nevertheless, the general result still holds. The effect on income of an increase in the money supply matched by a rise in the *PSBR*, especially in *G*, is always at least as large as for any other counterpart and is normally larger than any alternative at least in the short term (p.196).

The potency of this result, that an increase in the money supply carries the biggest punch when the supply-side counterpart is *G*, is increased in significance because this policy could equally have been called an increase in *G* financed by money creation. The effect is the same whether one puts the emphasis on the change in *G* (by calling it *G* financed by *M*) or on the change in *M* (matched by a rise in *G*). Hence, the analysis in Figure 6.1 for the normal case also reveals the effect of a change in *G* when this is financed by a change in *M*. This part of Figure 6.1(a) is reproduced in Figure 6.2. The economy was originally in equilibrium at Y_0. The effect of an increase in government spending financed by money creation is to shift the LM curve to LM_2 and the IS curve to IS_3, so the equilibrium level of income is Y_3.

If instead the increase in *G* were financed by *PLG*, the IS curve still shifts to IS_3 but the LM curve remains at LM_1, because the money supply has not changed. This is, in fact, the 'fiscal policy' case mentioned before (p.82). Hence, income will rise to Y_5. (Y_5 may be bigger or less than Y_2 on Figure 6.1a, because

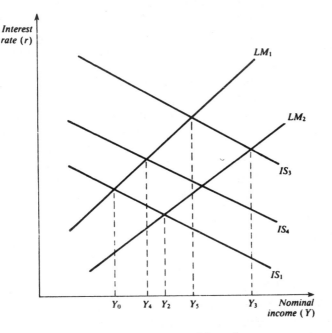

Figure 6.2 Alternative means of financing government expenditure

their relative magnitude depends upon the slopes of IS and LM.) Y_5 must be less than Y_3.

If the increase in G is financed by an increase in taxation, there is no change in the *PSBR* and, accordingly, no change in the money supply. However, the IS curve does shift, because of the balanced budget multiplier, but only to IS_4; that is, well to the left of IS_3. (The reason that the IS curve shifts at all is that part of the increase in taxation is financed by a fall in saving; the basis of the balanced budget multiplier.) Thus, the increase in withdrawals at each level of income is less than in injections, so there is a (small) net injection at each level of income. (For example, if G and T both rise by £100m and saving falls by £10m, there is a net injection of £10m, because injections are £100m higher and withdrawals only £90m higher at each level of income. Thus, if G is financed by a rise in taxation, income only rises to

Y_4.) The rise in income is thus largest when G is financed by money creation. To summarise, income rises to Y_3 for money-financed expenditure, to Y_5 for (PLG) bond-financed expenditure but only to Y_4 for tax-financed expenditure. Y_5 must be greater than Y_3, and Y_3 greater than Y_4. This result holds in the monetarist extreme case, but in the extreme Keynesian cases money- and PLG-financed expenditure have the same effect. These results can be combined with the earlier one about supply-side counterparts. The joint implication is that the best way to change income will be to change both G and M, irrespective of whether this is termed money-financed government expenditure or money supply increase, where supply-side counterpart is government expenditure. This is because:

1. In the normal case it will have a bigger effect on income than any alternative policy.
2. It will still influence in the extreme cases; that is, a shift of IS *and* LM curves changes income even when the curves are vertical or horizontal (unless both are horizontal; see p.109).

This result has proved enormously influential in that governments, especially in the UK but also elsewhere, have usually followed its precepts and sought to change income in this fashion. This was very marked, for example, in the deflationary period of the 1974–9 Labour governments. It seemed, moreover, by 1973 to have settled the theoretical debate about the impact of alternative counterparts to money creation and methods of financing the *PSBR*. The remaining questions were empirical, in particular, the relative impacts of bond *PLG*-financed public expenditure and credit *BLP*-matched money creation. This concept was to be challenged by Blinder and Solow's (1973) budget-constraint result (see p.194). However, it was to be reinforced by a point made by Friedman (in Gordon, 1974, p.141). He accepted that the above analysis was valid in the short term but emphasised that it was not in the long term because government spending is a flow and money a stock. This means that a shift of the LM curve is permanent and a shift of the IS curve only temporary. For example, if government spending is increased by £100m, the IS curve shifts out for one period and then returns to its previous level (because in the following period injections have returned to their previous level). If this is financed by money creation the money supply is always £100m higher, so the LM curve shifts for ever. Alternatively, if the shift of the IS curve is made permanent by an increase of £100m per year in public spending then the LM curve will shift every year, because the money supply will rise by £100m in each year because the extra expenditure has to be financed each year. This point can be seen very easily by looking at the equations at the start of this chapter. Indeed, Friedman's point is one of the most effective uses ever made of these equations. This point means that in general either there is a 'one-shot' temporary shift of the IS curve but a permanent shift of the LM curve, or a permanent shift of the IS curve and a continual outward movement of the LM curve. The effect of this simple and irrefutable point is devastating. Its implications for any IS–LM model comparison of alternative policies is profound and, of course, has the effect of increasing the case for emphasis on the money supply and monetarist analysis. More generally it emphasizes the importance of stock analysis as opposed to flow analysis. In the analysis presented above it would reduce the importance of examining alternative supply-side counterparts. In Figure 6.1(a) the analysis above is valid in the short run, but in the next period the IS curve shifts back to IS_1 for both the *PLG* and *BLP* cases, so the effect of all three counterparts on income is the same. On the other hand, the greater efficacy of money compared to bond *PLG*-financed expenditure is reinforced. The IS curve in all cases shifts back to IS_1 in the second period. Thus, tax- and bond-financed expenditure have no long-run effect on income, whereas money-financed expenditure leaves income permanently higher at Y_1.[3]

6.4 Summary and conclusions

Flow-of-funds analysis puts monetary analysis within a rigorous framework. The two crucial equations are:

(1) $PSBR = $ Δ Currency held by non-bank private sector
       + Δ Bank loans to public sector
       + Δ Non-bank private sector loans to public sector
          (government finance equation)

In an open economy an extra term is necessary, adding

government net purchases of foreign currency to the left-hand side (in which case *PSBR* is replaced by domestic borrowing requirement) or net sales to the right-hand side (in which case the misleadingly labelled 'overseas loans to public sector' term is added).

(2) Δ Money supply =   *PSBR*
+ Δ Bank loans to non-bank private sector
− Δ Non-bank private sector loans to public sector
+ Overseas effect on money supply

Both equations can be used to analyse macroeconomic policy.

Analysis of the alternative effect on income of alternative supply-side counterparts to the money supply reveals that it may matter which of the four right-hand-side variables changes when the money supply changes. Similarly, it is likely to matter how a budget deficit is financed. In general, money-financed government expenditure (or, if the term is preferred, *PSBR*-generated increases in the money supply) seems likely to have the biggest effect on income.

Notes

1. Throughout this section problems caused by changes in the value of existing securities are ignored. However, this is the reason why the flow (*PSBR*) is used rather than a change in a stock (such as Δ National Debt).
2. See, for example, Caves (1968, p.30); Ward and Neild (1978), Chouraqui *et al* (1990), Blanchard (1990), Gramlich (1990).
3. Brian Hillier has drawn my attention to frequent misuses of this passage in Friedman by various authors, including Blinder and Solow (1973). Mine seems the correct interpretation, however; Stein (1982, pp.11–23) also cites the passage in the sense in the text.

7

Inflation and Unemployment (I): The Mainstream Debate

7.1   Introduction

From the early 1950s the major issue in macroeconomic theory concerned the possible role in eliminating unemployment of a balanced deflation, that is a reduction in wages and prices of equal magnitude. (Deflation is often used to describe policies designed to achieve this goal. Here it is used to refer only to a change in the price level.) In particular it was argued that the full employment level of output could always be generated by a sufficiently large balanced deflation. This debate often seemed arid and rather abstract but was very important for both theoretical and policy reasons. The debate served to introduce wealth effects into macroeconomics and thereby removed a major weakness of IS–LM (wealth effects are considered in Section 7.2). Moreover, the debate proved to be crucial to the UK in the 1970s and 1980s. Many politicians, notably Mrs Thatcher and her successive Chancellors, as well as economists, argued that inflation was a major cause of unemployment in the UK. This argument was based upon the inverse of the above theoretical proposition since, if a balanced deflation reduces unemployment, (a balanced) inflation would increase it. Thatcherites also argued that a reduction in inflation is at least necessary, and perhaps sufficient, for the reduction of unemployment. This is a more sophisticated variant upon the theme that a balanced deflation is sufficient to eliminate unemployment, being cast in terms of the rate of change of the price level rather than the absolute level of prices. Thus, after the theoretical debate has been analysed in Sections 7.3, 7.4 and 7.5, its relevance to the UK and some related issues are discussed.

7.2 Wealth effects

In the basic IS–LM model presented in Chapter 4 both the demand for money and expenditure functions included only income and interest rates. In fact, they are likely to depend as well upon other factors, of which wealth is the most important.[1] Irrespective of the approach to the demand for money employed, wealth should be positively related to the demand for money, that is, *ceteris paribus*, an increase in wealth should lead to an increase in the demand for money. In many cases a change in wealth will be associated with a change in income, but analytically one should examine first a change in wealth, holding income constant (because the more complex case involves summing the effects of a change in income, holding wealth constant and of a change in wealth, holding income constant). However, examples of an exogenous change in wealth that does not affect income (significantly) are not difficult to find, for example the discovery of an oil field in the period until oil is extracted or, of crucial significance in the UK, a rise in house prices or share prices. Such an exogenous increase in wealth means that more money will be demanded than before at each combination of income and interest rates. Holding the money supply constant, as usual to derive the LM curve, there will be an excess of the demand for money over the supply of it at the values of income and interest rates that were previously equilibria for the money market. Hence, to restore equilibrium the LM curve must shift to the left. To take a specific example, illustrated in Figure 7.1(a), (r_1, Y_1) was previously an equilibrium pair of values such that the demand for money equalled the supply of it. After there is an exogenous increase in wealth, the demand for money at (r_1, Y_1) rises so there would be an excess demand for money. If income remains at Y_1, this can only be eliminated by a rise in interest rates (to r_3), and if the interest rate remains at r_1,

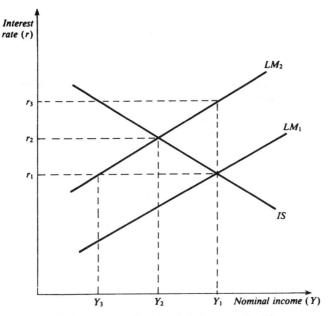

(a) *Increase in wealth shifts the LM curve to the left*

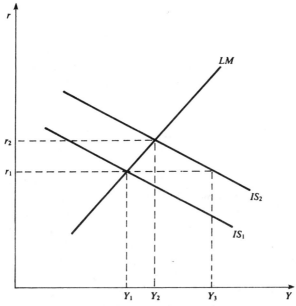

(b) *Increase in wealth shifts the IS curve to the right*

Figure 7.1 Wealth effects

it can only be eliminated by a fall in income (to Y_3); that is, the LM curve must shift leftwards (or upwards). Hence, *the effect of an increase in wealth is equivalent to that of a fall in the money supply.* As in Figure 7.1(a), if the IS curve were unchanged, an increase in wealth would cause income to fall (from Y_1 to Y_2) and interest rates to rise (from r_1 to r_2).

Less paradoxically, an exogenous increase in wealth normally causes the IS curve to shift rightwards. An increase in wealth means that more is spent at each level of income, so less is saved. This means that planned withdrawals are less at each level of income (if wealth leads to an increase in taxes paid or to a taste for imported goods, this need not hold). Accordingly, for any given interest rate and, therefore, level of planned injections, a higher level of income is necessary to generate an equal quantity of planned withdrawals, so the IS curve must shift rightwards. For example, in Figure 7.1(b) (r_1, Y_1) was previously in equilibrium; that is, planned injections were equal to planned withdrawals. As a result of the exogenous increase in wealth, planned withdrawals are less than before and so less than planned injections. It would take an increase in income to Y_3 to generate enough extra withdrawals to restore equilibrium at r_1; that is, the IS curve shifts rightwards by this amount; $(Y_3 - Y_1)$ is the increase in income predicted by the elementary multiplier. Thus, an exogenous increase in wealth would cause both income and interest rates to rise, to Y_2 and r_2 respectively, if the LM curve did not shift (Fig. 7.1b).

Combining the two analyses, the overall effect of an exogenous increase in wealth is to raise interest rates, but the effect on income is ambiguous. This follows because the wealth holders dispose of part of their wealth (that is, they sell assets) to acquire both consumer goods and money. The latter depresses asset prices, and so by definition it raises interest rates. This rise, and the fall in asset prices, reduces the output of capital goods. Hence, the effect on income depends upon whether the increase in the demand for consumer goods is more or less than the reduction in the demand for capital goods, and upon the supply curves for the industries. If the change in wealth is a change in the money supply, there is no ambiguity (because there is a switch from money to both goods and non-money assets, asset prices do not fall). In fact, the conventional movement of the LM curve in response to a change in the money supply already includes any wealth effect which it generates. In general, moreover, wealth-generated movements of LM curves seem to be so trivial that they can be ignored.

The wealth effect analysed above is one of the five macro-economic effects of the discovery of oil as in the UK in the 1970s. Another, an exogenous shift in investment, was discussed earlier (p.83). The others are:

1. The effect on public sector finances – that is, a fall in the *PSBR* – which, *ceteris paribus*, would shift the LM curve to the left (by reducing the money supply) and the IS curve to the left (by increasing the level of planned withdrawals at each level of income).
2. The effect on the balance of payments (on the IS curve via the foreign trade multiplier and on the LM curve via the overseas impact on the money supply).
3. The effect on sectoral allocation of output (see p.179), the monetarist perspective on 'deindustrialisation'.

If North Sea oil were to be exhausted, one could analyse the effects on the UK economy by reversing the above analysis. The analysis might also need to incorporate any impact of oil on the exchange rate using the tools presented above, p.38.

One wealth effect is the so-called 'Keynes windfall effect', to which Leijonhufvud gave great prominence (1968, p.324).[2] The Keynes windfall effect is the change in spending at each level of income which is caused by changes in the market value of bonds, which, in turn, is the inverse of the change in interest rates. Hence, a rise in interest rates implies a fall in wealth which increases savings and reduces consumers' expenditure at each level of income. In other words, it shifts the IS curve leftwards compared to the IS curve drawn assuming that saving is a function only of income. In effect this is a proposition that every move along an IS curve necessarily generates a shift of it. This is confusing so it is easier to regard the Keynes windfall effect as a reason for a more elastic IS curve; an IS curve would be drawn for a given nominal bond stock, the market value of which varies with interest rates. The standard elementary IS curve rather inconsistently assumes this market value to be constant (or assumes government debt to be in capital-certain form or that

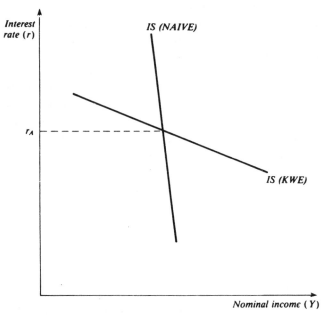

Figure 7.2 The Keynes windfall effect (KWE)

wealth does not affect consumption). The IS curve which allows for the Keynes windfall effect will coincide with the elementary one at some point (where the market value of bonds equals the implicit assumed value). At all higher interest rates the IS curve will be to the left of this because of the negative form of the Keynes windfall effect described above. At all lower interest rates the IS curve will be to the right of the naive one because of the extra spending generated by the higher capital value of government bonds. In brief, the Keynes windfall effect means that the IS curve pivots around, as in Figure 7.2, compared to the naive one.

7.3 Real balance effects

If IS and LM curves have normal slopes, the effect of a balanced deflation is to increase output and so reduce unemployment. A sufficiently large balanced deflation would therefore eliminate unemployment. This is illustrated in alternative ways in Figure 7.3. In Figure 7.3(a) real output (Q) is on the horizontal axis, price being exogenous. In this version of the IS–LM model, the LM curve is drawn for a given real money supply. Hence, a balanced deflation, holding the nominal money supply constant, will increase the real value of the money supply (M/P increases, if P is reduced) and so shift the LM curve rightwards. Output rises and interest rates fall. In Figure 7.3(b), nominal income is on the horizontal axis. A balanced deflation leaves the LM curve unchanged (since it is drawn for a given nominal money supply) but shifts the IS curve inwards by the amount of the reduction in prices. In this case both nominal income and interest rates fall to Y_2 and r_2, respectively. If Y had fallen to Y_3, nominal income would have fallen by as much as price (that is, the amount by which the IS curve shifted). As Y_2 is greater than Y_3, nominal income (PQ) has fallen by less than the price level (P) so output (Q) must have risen.

This result, however, is not valid in the extreme Keynesian liquidity trap case (Fig. 7.4). Figure 7.4(a) reproduces Figure 7.3(a), except that the LM curve is horizontal. In this case the increase in the real value of the money supply does not shift the LM curve; LM_1 is the same as LM_2 (see p.88). Hence, real income is unchanged. Similarly, in Figure 7.4(b), which is Figure 7.3(b) with a horizontal LM curve, the fall in nominal income (PQ) is as great as the fall in prices (P); that is, it is equal to the full amount by which the IS curve shifted – Y_2 and Y_3 are now coincident. Hence, the rules of arithmetic dictate that real output (Q) is unchanged. It is not clear whether Keynes actually regarded that as a valid argument against deflation although Friedman (1974; in Gordon, 1974, p.175) argued convincingly that he did. Alternatively, he may have been concerned about the problems of disequilibrium, of what happened while prices were falling, rather than objecting to the comparative static equilibrium argument about the impact of a lower level of prices. Moreover, he pointed out that one could achieve the same effect on nominal income by increasing the money supply, which would shift the LM curve outwards relative to the IS curve (Keynes, 1936, p.266). (These objections do not apply to Mrs Thatcher's variant concerning the level of inflation rather than of prices.) In

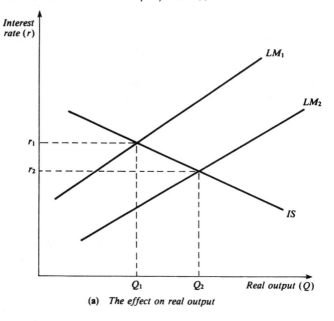

(a) *The effect on real output*

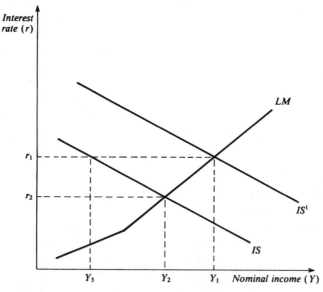

(b) *The effect upon nominal income is less than the fall in prices*

Figure 7.3 Balanced deflation

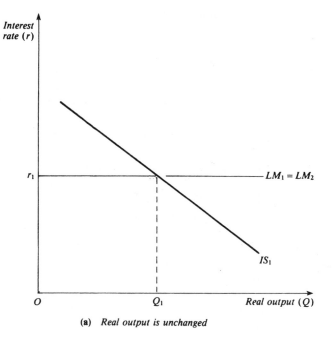

(a) *Real output is unchanged*

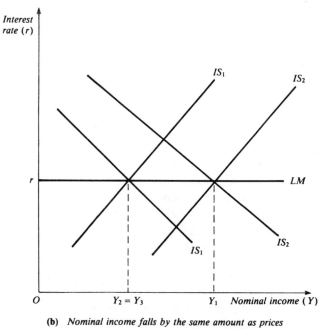

(b) *Nominal income falls by the same amount as prices*

Figure 7.4 Balanced deflation: the liquidity trap case

any case, it was accepted in the 1950s that the liquidity trap was the Keynesian orthodoxy.

Patinkin (1956, 1959) pointed out the logical fallacy of this position by arguing that a fall in prices would cause an outward movement of the IS curve. The increase in the real value of the money supply meant that real wealth had risen, so the IS curve would shift rightwards as the (wealthier) holders of money spent more than before at each level of income. The rightward movement of the IS curve from IS_1 in Figure 7.4(a) and IS_2 in Figure 7.4(b) would necessarily cause real income to rise, irrespective of the elasticity of the LM curve. This effect was called the real balance effect, for obvious reasons, or the Pigou effect, although Pigou's analysis had probably (in the language of the IS–LM model) only dealt with the effect on the LM curve.[3] It quickly became fashionable to discover variants of the real balance effect by applying the same principle to other financial assets. In fact, the principle could be applied to any asset denominated in money terms. Hence it is not surprising that, by 1968, Leijonhufvud could list fourteen variants of the real financial effect.

7.4   Inside and outside assets

A belief that balanced deflation would necessarily cure un-employment was never a canon of the monetarist creed, but denial of it was a basic Keynesian tenet. The real balance effect seemed to act as a stabilising force in an economy and so to reduce, if not to eliminate, the need for an activist 'Keynesian' demand-management policy. Thus, the counter-attack against Patinkin's position was launched by two prominent Keynesians: Gurley and Shaw (1960). Gurley and Shaw's basic point was simple.[4] The wealth effect induced by a fall in prices can have a negative effect upon spending and shift the IS curve inwards. This is because a fall in prices increases the real value of debts and other liabilities as well as assets. A debtor finding that the real value of his or her debts has risen should reduce his or her expenditure. Moreover, many financial assets were another person's financial liability and a change in prices would make the debtor poorer, just as it would make the creditor better off. Gurley and Shaw divided financial assets into inside assets, those matched by liabilities, and outside assets, those not matched by liabilities. The wealth effect used by Patinkin could only work on an outside asset since in the case of an inside asset there is both a positive and a negative wealth effect, on lender and borrower respectively. There was no reason to assume that either wealth effect was bigger. The consequences of such a massive redistribution of wealth would be hard to calculate, but Leijonhufvud is right to criticise economists for ignoring such distributional effects (see also Gowland, 1983b). A rise in the value of debt might cause debt deflation; Kalecki (1944). When the value of a debt rises there will necessarily be an increase in the risk of default by the borrower. If such defaults (bankruptcy) occur then the expenditure of both borrower and lender is reduced; this deflationary impact was the focus of Kalecki's attention. In the neoclassical spirit of Patinkin, it is worth pointing out that the effect could occur without any bankruptcy occurring. When the risk of default increases the lender should reduce his or her assessment of the value of the security. This would generate a negative wealth effect. Hence it may be that once one allows for possible default the net wealth effect of a change in the value of inside assets is negative. In the 1980s this analysis became topical because of the debt mountain in the USA, see Kaufman (1986) and Friedman (1988). In post-Keynesian models the vulnerability of an economy to debt deflation is termed financial fragility.

The work of Gurley and Shaw, therefore, put the focus of the debate on to the existence of outside financial assets. In a gold-standard world, gold was an outside asset, but this was clearly of no relevance to modern economies. All financial institutions' assets were matched by liabilities and so were the assets of those who lent to the institutions (for example, building society deposits and mortgages). In fact, the only possible outside assets, it appeared, were:

1. Bank deposits matched by public sector obligations to banks.
2. Government debt both in the form of currency and of securities, either national savings or bonds such as gilt-edged stocks, etc.

Both of these could be outside assets, and very substantial ones so long as government obligations were perceived as net wealth by the private sector and also so long as governments do not change their spending plans when there is an increase in the real value of their debt. The latter is undeniable, but the former – that government obligations could be a form of net wealth – had already been denied by some economists. The view that claims on the government are not net wealth is the so-called Chicago doctrine, later revived as the Ricardian doctrine; Barro, 1974. Some of Barro's new classical associates regard this as a special case – for example, Sargent (1979). Barro (for example, 1989, pp.178–236) still defends it both cogently and vigorously. If there were a counterbalancing liability to currency and government bonds, these would also be inside assets, and there would be no outside assets at all. The foundation of the Chicago doctrine was that individuals take note of future tax liabilities in determining their consumption plans. Government bonds and currency and all other forms of public sector debt will have to be serviced and ultimately repaid. So their existence implies that taxation will have to be levied in the future. Accordingly, rational individuals will plan their consumption on the basis of their contingent tax liability to redeem the National Debt. If the real value of the National Debt changes, so does this contingent tax liability. Any real balance effect will therefore be offset exactly by reductions in spending to finance the extra burden of future taxation.

There are a number of distinct objections to this Chicago doctrine that individuals discount their future tax liabilities and that, therefore, changes in the real value of government debt are not perceived by the personal sector as changes in its wealth. One objection is that the Chicago argument is pure fantasy as nearly all consumers are unaware of changes in the real value of the National Debt and do not take its size into account when deciding whether to make purchases. This could obviously be tested, but the Chicago proposition seems highly implausible.[5] Moreover, even if they did consider it, the change in the value of the National Debt represents an extremely illiquid liability to the taxpayer, whereas the change in the value of currency and bonds represents an increase in liquid assets. Hence, even if real net wealth is unchanged, liquidity is higher and so spending will rise (that is, the IS curve will shift as postulated by Patinkin).[6] To deny this liquidity effect it is necessary to assume that no individual's borrowing is ever constrained. Tobin (1980) adds further to the list of implausible assumptions necessary for this Ricardian/Chicago doctrine. Tobin pointed out the implications of the fact that individuals do not live for ever. The future tax liability in many cases will be paid by future tax payers not present ones. Thus, the Ricardian hypothesis is that people reduce their spending so that their savings will be sufficient to pay any increase in their heir's tax bill – not a very plausible theory. This – the bequest motive – is central to much modern analysis, see the references in note 5. To negate the Ricardian doctrine, see also the references cited in the notes, it is sufficient to show that at least some economic agents do not increase their saving sufficiently to offset fully the positive effect of a rise in the value of the debt. Barro (1989, pp.178–236) is in a small minority in defending his position but, of course, minority views can be right. His most persuasive piece of evidence is that private sector saving in practice often falls when budget deficits fall or disappear, as in the UK in the 1980s. In all the other cases he cites other explanations are available which seem more convincing to me. (For empirical evidence, see Nicoletti, 1988.) Hence by application of Occam's razor, it is reasonable to assume the Ricardian doctrine inoperative.

Hence, in summary, Gurley and Shaw had reduced the scope of wealth effects but not destroyed Patinkin's case. Changes in the price level would lead to large movements of the IS curve, as the 1970s were to demonstrate in the UK. Moreover, Pesek and Saving (1967) demonstrated the existence of another outside asset and so concluded this area of the debate in favour of the proposition that balanced deflation could always cure unemployment. This 'new' outside asset was the shares of banks and other financial intermediaries. These represented a claim on the assets and profits of these institutions. A part of their profits consisted of the difference between the interest rate at which they lent and that at which they borrowed. On existing contacts, at least, this was fixed and was, moreover, fixed in money terms. If a bank had a £1m deposit for five years at 5 per cent and a £1m loan for five years at 6 per cent, then it had an asset equal to the net present value of £10,000 per annum for five years. This asset was not matched by any liability and was an outside asset.[7] Much ink has been spilled over this effect, see Sweeney (1988, pp.149–223).

It has been argued that in competitive equilibrium the profits and market value of a bank should be zero. This is wrong. As Chick (1973) pointed out, the Pesek–Saving argument was undeniable since no one would set up a bank if they did not thereby create net worth. The argument should be:

(a) In competitive equilibrium the market value of a bank should equal the opportunity cost of the resources embarked in it.

(b) When there is a once-and-for-all unanticipated change in the price level, this value changes as per Pesek and Saving. If the change were anticipated correctly with certainty this effect would already be incorporated into the market value. If it were anticipated correctly but without certainty (the more realistic case) the Pesek–Saving effect would operate but be smaller than in the unanticipated case.

Reductio ad absurdum, a balanced deflation would make bank shareholders sufficiently wealthy to ensure full employment. More practically, the area of portfolio analysis had been extended and the effect of monetary growth and inflation on bank profits emphasised (not without relevance to the 1970s and 1980s). The underlying message of the analysis presented so far in this chapter is that financial factors matter and are usually much more complex than is allowed for in simple models.

7.5 Economics of Thatcherism

Since 1979 the Conservative government in the UK has pursued economic policies which, in certain key areas, mark a radical departure from the approach adopted by all previous post-war governments. Moreover, these policies seem to be based on a distinctive and extremely interesting approach to economic theory. This analysis is certainly not, for example, orthodox Friedmanite monetarism – hence the epithet 'economics of Thatcherism'. The most important element of this approach is the proposition that inflation *causes* unemployment; a view also advanced by Mrs Thatcher's successor John Major. This is in marked contrast to the 'orthodox' argument that inflation is the *alternative* to unemployment (the Phillips curve). If inflation does indeed cause unemployment a number of implications allegedly follow. Inflation becomes 'public enemy number one', which must be eliminated both for its own sake and because it is a cause of unemployment. Moreover, reflation is doomed to fail and unemployment can only be permanently reduced if inflation is eliminated, or at least reduced to low levels. Finally, much greater force is given to the view that loss of output and jobs is the most important cost of inflation (Gowland, 1989; Gowland, 1990, Chapters 5 and 7).

The analytical underpinnings of the proposition that inflation causes unemployment are examined in this section for a number of reasons. Besides its intrinsic theoretical interest and practical relevance to the UK, the analysis is also important because it demonstrates that wealth effects and, in particular, real financial effects are not just theoretical curiosities, *pace* the conventional wisdom of the 1960s (for example, Ackley, 1961, pp.269–73).

It is most convenient to begin the analysis by presenting the post-war orthodoxy analysis of demand management in the framework of an aggregate demand/aggregate supply model (Fig. 7.5). The aggregate supply curve is taken to be given AS. The government can determine the position of the aggregate demand curve by fiscal (or monetary or exchange rate) policy. For example, it might choose either aggregate demand curve AD_1 or, alternatively, AD_2, AD_2 being achieved by increasing government spending and the money supply. If the government were to choose AD_1, the price level would be P_1 and aggregate output would be Q_1. If, instead, AD_2 were chosen, both the price level and the aggregate output would be higher, at P_2 and Q_2 respectively. Hence, inflation would be higher and unemployment lower, because more workers would be required to produce the higher level of output. Thus, the government would have to choose between a higher level of inflation at (P_2, Q_2) and a higher level of unemployment at (P_1, Q_1). Governments were thus placed in a dilemma – hence, the model was often called the 'dilemma model'. In choosing the most appropriate level of aggregate demand the government had to choose between unemployment and inflation, so the model was often called the 'trade-off model'. To complete the analysis which underlay

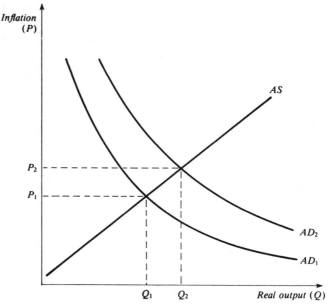

Figure 7.5 Orthodox analysis

'orthodox' economic policy, it is necessary only to add that every UK government from 1947 to 1979 at least once introduced an incomes policy in the belief that it would shift the aggregate supply curve to the right and so facilitate both more employment and lower prices. This was always something of a pious hope in that no convincing evidence was ever produced to substantiate this belief – although it has to be said that no evidence has ever definitely refuted the possibility.

Mrs Thatcher's critique of the orthodox approach would start by denying the possibility of producing a beneficent shift of the aggregate supply curve by an incomes policy. (Indeed, those who support her have argued that any effect would be upwards. Their argument is that incomes policy weakens market forces, and anything which weakens market forces reduces efficiency and so shifts aggregate supply upwards.) More crucially she would argue that post-war governments of both parties were mistaken to concentrate on short-term demand management, whereas they should have concentrated on long-term supply policy. This mistake was especially serious because the effect of pursuing an aggregate demand policy was to cause the aggregate supply curve to shift upwards. There are a number of reasons for this. A major reason is the effect of inflationary expectations, discussed below. Nevertheless, of considerable importance was the effect on both trade unions and firms of a belief in full employment, induced by faith in aggregate-demand-management policy. Keynesians welcomed such a belief because it was likely to be self-fulfilling (see p.273). Unfortunately, the belief also meant that trade union leaders (and their underlying apparatchiki) ceased to believe that excessive wage claims could price their members out of jobs. Firms tended to develop 'X-inefficiency' insofar as they believed that they could sell whatever they produced irrespective of quality or cost. Both effects would shift the aggregate supply curve upwards. In consequence, the real trade-off is not that between inflation and unemployment in any one period but is instead a trade-off over time. Low short-term unemployment can be bought but only at a cost of not only higher inflation but also of higher unemployment in the long term.

The analysis underlying this view is shown in Figure 7.6. As in Figure 7.5, the government can choose the level of aggregate demand. If it selects AD_2 the short-term result – more output and less unemployment – is the same as in the orthodox case. However, in the longer term this result is reversed because the aggregate supply curve shifts upwards (leftwards) in response to the higher inflation engendered by the increase in aggregate demand. Ultimately, when the aggregate supply curve is at AS_2, output at Q_3 is lower than it was originally and consequently unemployment is higher. Hence, the cost of a short-term reduction in unemployment is a long-term increase in unemployment. Similarly, a short-term increase in unemployment may be the cost of a long-term reduction. There are many reasons why this shift of the AS curve may occur. In practice the effects of a belief in full employment may be the most important. In particular this belief implies that sales will be high in future so managers tend to become complacent and put less emphasis on quality, reliability, etc, see Gowland (1990, Chapter 5). A reduction in efficiency shifts any supply curve inwards. In theoretical analysis, however, the most important is a variation of

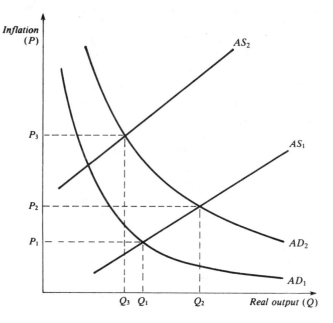

Figure 7.6 'Economics of Thatcherism'

Friedman's (1968a) analysis of the relationship between inflation and unemployment, pioneered in his seminal work.

Friedman's analysis has been incorporated into virtually all subsequent analyses of inflation whether 'Keynesian', 'monetarist', 'neoclassical' or whatever. Friedman's proposition is that if everyone expects prices to rise, then everyone will change their behaviour such that they do. This can be seen in a very simple case. Suppose that everyone wakes up believing that prices will be 10 per cent higher than the day before. The demand curve for any product depends upon the price of all other goods. However, the relevant 'other prices' are those that consumers believe to be the prevailing ones. Hence, in this simplistic example, all demand curves shift rightwards. Each consumer entering a shop believes that prices are higher elsewhere than they were yesterday and so is prepared to pay more for each good in that shop than he or she was yesterday. An analogous argument explains why supply curves shift upwards – as supply also depends on the prices perceived to be charged for other goods (producers' marginal revenue curves shift when they perceive prices to be higher elsewhere). Similar arguments apply in the labour market: real wages are perceived to be lower, so workers react, while the demand for labour shifts rightwards. The latter is a 'derived demand', being equal to marginal value product so it shifts because product demand curves have shifted rightwards. Thus, to an equal extent, demand curves shift rightwards and supply curves leftwards in response to higher inflationary expectations. Hence, prices rise. Friedman also demonstrated that, in the absence of money illusion, the shifts would be such that the expectations would be fulfilled. At a macroeconomic level, these changes in behaviour cause the aggregate supply curve to shift upwards. Clearly the most important point in any model incorporating such expectational effects is what determines the expected rate of inflation. So long as it is accepted that when actual inflation rises, the effect is that expectations of future inflation are higher, it is straightforward to provide the missing link in the Thatcherite analysis. An outward shift of the aggregate demand curve causes a higher rate of inflation and so, through the effect on inflationary expectations, an upward shift of aggregate supply.

Friedman's own analysis can be summarised as saying that inflation is equal to the sum of demand inflation and expected inflation. Expected inflation, in turn, would depend upon the previous period's inflation and can be assumed equal to it; that is:

Inflation = expected inflation + demand inflation
Expected inflation = last year's inflation

The conclusion is obvious:

Inflation = last year's inflation + demand inflation

Friedman accepted a trade-off between unemployment and *demand* inflation (not total inflation, as in the orthodox analysis). Lower unemployment would cause demand inflation. This means that a lower level of unemployment would necessarily imply that inflation exceeded last year's level (that is, that it accelerated). In Sir Geoffrey Howe's graphic simile, inflation is like an addictive drug: the more you have, the more you need and the more harm it does to the system. Friedman's analysis is shown in Figure 7.7

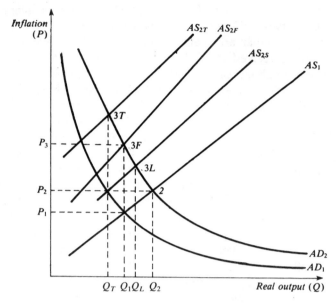

Figure 7.7   Three stories of reflation

in terms of aggregate supply and demand curves. This diagram
presents three alternative 'stories of reflation'. One is Friedman's, the others represent the views put forward by the
Conservative government and the Labour opposition in the 1983
and 1987 general elections in the UK. The 1983 general election
has been described as a referendum on economic theory, so it
gives an additional point to this theoretical analysis by showing its
policy relevance (P_1, Q_1), the intersection of AD_1 and AS_1
represents the UK in 1987 with an inflation rate of P_1, and an
output level of Q_1. If the Labour Party had won the election it
was committed to a policy of reflation. All stories agree that this
would have shifted the aggregate demand curve to AD_2 such that
in 1988 the economy would have been at point 2, such that output would
have risen to Q_2 and inflation to P_2. Moreover, all three accounts
agree that this higher level of inflation would have increased
inflationary expectations such that the aggregate supply curve
would have shifted upwards. The divergence between the three
accounts – Friedmanite, Labour Party (modified orthodox) and

Thatcherite – stem from how far the aggregate supply curve shifts upwards. Friedman would argue that the aggregate supply curve would shift exactly to AS_{2F}, so that in 1988 the economy would be at point $3F$ where output would have fallen to its original level, Q_1, but inflation would be permanently higher, at P_3. The extent of the shift of the aggregate supply curve depends upon how much inflationary expectations rise in response to the rise in inflation (from P_1 to P_2). Friedman's assumption that expected inflation rises by exactly the same amount as the rise in inflation is both sufficient and necessary to ensure that the aggregate supply curve shifts by just enough to reduce output to its original level, Q_1. The result of Friedman's analysis is that the levels of inflation and unemployment are independent of each other – a *short-term* reduction in unemployment (the workers needed to produce $Q_2 - Q_1$) can be bought but only at a cost of an acceleration in inflation. The modified orthodox analysis, by contrast, preserves a permanent trade-off between inflation and unemployment. The Labour Party accepted this view, at least if Labour's other policies were adopted. The aggregate supply curve would shift by less than in Friedman's analysis such that in 1985 it would be at AS_{2L} and the economy would be at point $3L$. The level of output would be permanently higher (at Q_{2L}) and so unemployment would be permanently lower. Thus, the orthodox trade-off remains. This is the case so long as inflationary expectations are less than the rise in inflation – defensible by reference to econometric evidence. Mrs Thatcher's analysis diverges from Friedman's in the other direction. The aggregate supply curve shifts by more than in Friedman's analysis – to AS_{2T}. This means that output in 1989 would be lower, at Q_3T, than in 1987. Thus, the temporary fall in unemployment and rise in inflation would have caused a longer-term rise in unemployment. This view of the aggregate supply curve is valid so long as a rise of x per cent in inflation generates a more than x per cent rise in the expected rate of inflation. This view is highly plausible if economic agents look at the change as well as the level of inflation – such that, for example, if inflation were 6 per cent in Year 1 and 5 per cent in Year 2, the expected level in Year 3 would be 4 per cent, whereas if inflation has been 4 and 5 per cent respectively, the expected rate would be 6 per cent in Year 3. To complete the analysis of politics in the 1980s, the then

SDP–Liberal Alliance analysis would seem to be that of the Labour Party if an incomes policy were in force, but the Conservative one otherwise. Hence, to return to the main theme, different views about aggregate supply can be generated by different views about inflationary expectations. These different views about aggregate supply can justify an orthodox trade-off between inflation and unemployment, or Friedman's denial of the trade-off, or the Thatcherite 'perverse' trade-off. Such a trade-off can also be used to justify a short-term reduction in aggregate demand (as in 1980–1 or 1989–90) to produce a longer-term rise in employment. This argument, based on aggregate supply analysis, is reinforced by an aggregate demand argument, whereby it is claimed that inflation causes unemployment. This argument rests upon the proposition that, at least in the UK, there is a positive relationship between inflation and saving. In consequence, a rise in inflation causes both the savings ratio (average propensity to save) and marginal propensity to save to rise. This leads to a fall in income, and so a rise in unemployment, by a process which in its implicit form is that Keynesian chestnut the 'paradox of thrift'. A rise in the savings propensities is likely to lead to a fall in output and possibly to no rise in saving. For example, if

> Planned saving = 0.1
> Income and investment = 10

the equilibrium level of income is 100 (and saving = 10).

If the private sector chooses to save more, say 0.2 income, the equilibrium level of incomes falls to 50 (and saving remains = 10). This process, it is argued, is a major reason why UK unemployment rose in the mid-1970s and early 1980s, and why output rose after 1982–83. In 1973–5 and 1979–80 a rapid acceleration in inflation led on each occasion to a very marked rise in the savings ratio. Similarly, in 1982–3 a fall in the rate of inflation seems to have triggered off a consumers' boom in the UK in which consumers' real spending rose by over 7 per cent, whilst real personal disposable incomes rose by about 1 per cent. Empirically, therefore, the inflation–savings nexus is very marked in the UK. It is important to analyse the theoretical underpinnings of this relationship. There are a number of reasons why a rise in inflation should lead to a rise in the savings ratio

(Gowland, 1990, Chapter 10). The most important reasons are as follows.

(i)   A Wealth Effect

An exogenous rise in wealth will lead to a rise in consumers' expenditure, *ceteris paribus*; that is, it will lead to an increase in the level of spending at each level of income. Hence, it will lead to a fall in the savings ratio, since saving is defined as 'income less consumers' expenditure'. By the same reasoning, a fall in wealth will lead to a rise in the savings ratio (and so to a fall in output, other things being equal). This fall in wealth is engendered by inflation because most personal sector wealth is in money-denominated forms – so a rise in prices reduces the real value of these assets and so of wealth. This process is, of course, the real financial effect discussed above in Section 7.3. Real financial effects have thus proved to be of major relevance to policy makers in the UK.

(ii)   A liquidity effect

In many cases, as Gurley and Shaw pointed out, financial assets are matched by liabilities; that is, they are 'inside assets'. In these cases a fall in inflation reduces the real value of both assets and liabilities. In some cases these may be owned and owed by the same person; for example, a building society mortgagee with a deposit will see the real value of both fall at a time of inflation. In other cases the creditor and debtor are different people. Nevertheless, at an aggregate level, the fall in the real value of both assets and liabilities necessarily reduces liquidity. This is partly because the debts destroyed are more illiquid than the assets. In addition, however, a fall in the value of both assets and liabilities reduces liquidity by definition. A person with a building society deposit of £5,000 and a mortgage of £5,000 is more liquid than a person with neither. In consequence, he or she is much more easily able to undertake additional expenditure if plans are changed. For this reason, a rise in liquidity has always been regarded as a sufficient reason for a rise in consumers' expenditure, even if wealth and income were unchanged. Equally, therefore, the reduction in liquidity engendered by inflation will lead to a fall in spending and a rise in the savings ratio.

(iii) *The real interest-rate effect*

Economic popularisers used to argue that inflation would lead to a *fall* in saving because 'saving would not pay'. Indeed, they often derided theoreticians who argued the converse. It is, therefore, necessary to analyse their argument. It is essentially a price theory argument, which holds that spending would occur now instead of the future because expected future prices had risen. Thus, a rise in the relative cost of future goods would reduce spending on them. The argument could be cast in terms of either the opportunity cost of present and future consumption or the real rate of interest; a rise in (expected) inflation reduces the real rate of interest and the return on saving. As the populariser's argument is about the impact of prices on behaviour it is analysed using the normal apparatus of choice theory; namely, indifference curves and budget lines. This analysis is presented in Figure 7.8 for the simplest possible case: an individual receiving income in only the first period and spending it over two. This is not unrealistic if the periods are taken to be 'working life' and 'retirement' respectively, but in any case the analysis is easily generalisable to cover more periods: borrowing, receipt of income in every period and other complications (see Gowland, 1990). The individual is interested in two things, consumption in Period 1 (that is, C_t) and in Period 2 (that is, $C_{t + 1}$); so these are the axes on the choice diagram. The maximum consumption in Period 1 is the income received in this period, marked as OA. Maximum consumption in Period 2 is income plus interest received less an allowance for inflation (income not spent in Period 1 is invested, but its purchasing power is reduced by inflation). Formally, maximum consumption in Period 2 is income in Period 1 times $(1 + r)$, where r is the real rate of interest. This is marked as OB. AB is therefore the budget line facing the individual, whose slope is the relative price of present consumption in terms of future consumption. He or she chooses

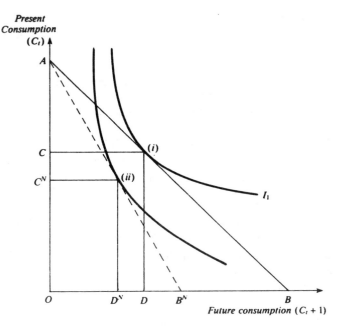

Figure 7.8 Real interest rates and saving

Point (i) and consumes OC in Period 1 and OD in Period 2, (i) being where the appropriate indifference curve is tangential to AB. However, as OA is income in Period 1 and OC consumers' expenditure, AC is therefore saving in Period 1. Hence, the diagram represents the optimal choice of consumption and saving with a given real interest rate. When inflation rises, and the real interest rate falls,the budget line pivots inwards to AB^N. Point (ii) reflects a perfectly rational response to the new choice opportunities, with consumption in both periods being reduced to OC^N and OD^N respectively. However, saving has *risen* to AC^N in consequence of the rise in inflation. This is clearly rational – the substitution effect (whereby a fall in real interest rate reduces saving) has been offset by an income effect (working to increase saving). Either may predominate – in the USA the substitution effect seems the larger, whereas in the UK the income effect (reinforced by the wealth and liquidity effects) is clearly greater.

The inflation–saving link seems strong, although it need not lead to 'Thatcherite' conclusions. At a minimum it is clear that the orthodoxy of 1970 – that consumers' expenditure depended only on current (and lagged) income – is no longer valid. Variations in consumers' spending are at least as likely to be caused by 'other factors' (in Keynesian terms, the consumption function is unstable). Of these credit is perhaps the most important, see Chapter 8. Finally, it is worth emphasising that indexation of personal savings (by eliminating the relationship) may stabilise the economy. Thus, the 'creeping indexation' introduced by UK governments between 1975 and 1982 may very well dampen down future instability in the economy.

7.6 Summary and conclusions

An important ingredient missing from the basic IS–LM model is wealth. Exogenous changes in wealth are likely to shift both the IS and the LM curve. The effects of endogenous changes in wealth, such as the Keynes windfall effect, should be incorporated into the slope (and position) of the curves.

Wealth effects have been most discussed in the context of the effects of a change in the real value of financial assets caused by a change in the price level, especially of the money supply.[8] Their importance was debated in the context of a debate about whether a 'balanced deflation' increased output. Keynesians argued that this would not occur in the 'liquidity trap' case. Patinkin argued that the consequent increase in the real value of the stock of financial assets would shift the IS curve by generating extra consumption at each level of income, and so guarantee a rise in output irrespective of the slope of the LM curve (other than in the pathological case where both curves are horizontal). Gurley and Shaw argued that financial assets had to be divided into inside and outside ones, according to whether there was a matching liability. Patinkin's real wealth effects would be negated in the case of inside assets by negative wealth effects upon debtors. Thus the effect of a balanced deflation upon output depends upon the existence of outside assets. *Pace* the Ricardian doctrine, public sector debt and shares in banks are outside assets, so financial real wealth effects do operate. Besides their crucial theoretical relevance, these effects are an essential element of the Thatcherite view that inflation causes unemployment.

Notes

1. Sweeney (1988) provides a brilliant survey and critique of the material presented in Sections 7.2–7.4. He emphasises the Hicksian micro-foundations of the analysis.
2. This is sometimes referred to as simply the Keynes effect. However, as this is also used to describe other effects, I follow Leijonhufvud's usage of 'Keynes windfall'.
3. See Pigou (1943). It is a matter of debate exactly what Pigou meant. See, for example, Gilbert (1982). Leijonhufvud (1968, p.108) and Pesek and Saving (1967) both argue that Keynes (1936, p.92) incorporated this price-induced real wealth effect.
4. Kalecki (1944) may have anticipated them; the meaning of this very short comment on Pigou is also disputed.
5. Some empirical work has purported to justify the doctrine indirectly, see the survey in Tobin (1980). However, following Tobin, I feel that these results actually support the permanent income hypothesis. Barro (1989, pp.178–236) cites more recent evidence concerning budget deficits. This debate is closely related to the debate about the burden of the National Debt, see Hillier's survey in Creedy (1990). Incisive critiques of the Ricardian doctrine have been provided by Buiter (1990, pp.183–251).
6. Gurley and Shaw recognised this as a portfolio effect.
7. Pesek and Saving (1967) sometimes stated their argument in terms of the capitalised value of bank profits as on p.222, but usually used alternative methods of exposition. Later authors reformulated their ideas, starting with Metzler (1969).
8. The real value of the money supply can also change when its nominal value changes. However, (a) this is usually not relevant to the monetarist–Keynesian debate. For example, it is irrelevant in comparing the effects of bond- and money-financed government spending since wealth changes by the same amount in both cases, albeit in different forms; (b) the nominal value of the money stock can change without a change in the nominal value of wealth, for example in the case of open-market operations, which reduce private sector holdings of public debt by the same amount as the increase in money holdings.

8

Inflation and Unemployment (II): The Nature of a Monetary Economy

8.1   An unstable economy

By the late 1970s the mainstream debate concerning inflation and unemployment had apparently been settled in favour of the proposition that a balanced deflation could cure unemployment. Clower (1965; reprinted in Clower, 1969) and Leijonhufvud (1968, 1969) argued that this debate was misplaced. They accepted the role of wealth effects but stressed that these could be destabilising. In Chapter 7, wealth effects were in general stabilising. Inflation led to unemployment. Presumably unemployment tends to dampen inflation. Instead, wealth effects could cause inflation to rise to hyperinflationary levels or depression to persist. These ideas can be found in both post-Keynesian analysis (especially Minsky, 1982) and in more formal orthodox analysis, see Blanchard and Fischer (1989, Chapter 5 on bubbles, multiple equilibria and stability). Clower's and Leijon-hufvud's main hypothesis, however, was that the nature of a monetary economy was such that it was prone to certain kinds of instability that could not occur in a barter economy. The point of this, of course, was not to argue that a barter economy was preferable but rather that an active interventionist macro-economic stabilisation policy should be pursued by governments. In particular, they wished to demonstrate the fallacy of conventional arguments about the self-righting nature of eco-nomies by showing that these rested upon the (implicit) assumption of a barter economy. These ideas are analysed in Sections 8.2 and 8.3 respectively, with Leijonhufvud's ideas being presented first for analytical convenience, although Clower's work preceded his.

Clower, Leijonhufvud and others claimed that they were re-affirming the 'economics of Keynes', as opposed to the 'Keynesian economics', conventionally presented. They argued that the Keynesian models presented above were not a true representation of Keynes' ideas but instead were based on a mechanistic model produced by Hansen and Hicks which failed to capture Keynes' essential insights. They derided the orthodox Keynesians as 'hydraulic Keynesians' (Coddington, 1983) because of this allegedly excessive reliance upon mechanistic analysis. In point of fact, both sides of the exegetical debate seem to be right in that both capture certain aspects of Keynes' multifacetal and complex thought.[1] Nevertheless, the reinterpretation of Keynes is much less important than the richness and interest of the ideas introduced by Clower and Leijonhufvud. These ideas were partially derived from the 'fundamentalist Keynesians'; for example, Shackle (1968), who laid great stress upon Keynes' analysis of uncertainty which was set out in Chapter 12 of *The General Theory* (1936). Both the 'fundamentalist' and 'Clower–Leijonhufvud' schools of Keynesians are closely related to the 'post–Keynesian' analysis presented in Section 8.4. Bain and others who emphasise the role of money as a buffer stock are also discussed in this section because they also derive non-monetarist conclusions from the monetarist postulate that money matters.

All of the authors analysed in this chapter have criticised the aggregation implicitly assumed in the monetarist model, and the orthodox Keynesian one as well. The conventional macro-economic models treat output as a single good, or implicitly assume that resources can easily be switched from one sector to another. Indeed, Mayer (1978) regarded the 'irrelevance of allocative detail' as being one of the fourteen tenets which defined monetarism. In practice, orthodox Keynesians are just as addicted to this very useful simplification. It is, therefore, of interest to see how the quantity theorist would analyse structural shocks to an economy to elucidate the flaws and merits of his approach. Two such shocks are examined: an exogenous change in relative prices, such as an oil price increase, and the discovery of North Sea oil. The analysis of the OPEC price rise starts by assuming that the world money supply is fixed; an assumption relaxed later. If the world money supply is fixed, in a monetarist model world expenditure is also fixed (that is, world output, Q, times world prices, P). This can be subdivided into expenditure on oil (P_0Q_0) and expenditure on all other goods (P_RQ_R) – some actual goods being divided between the two; for example, about 60 per cent of the expenditure on tomatoes is expenditure on oil because of the quantities of oil needed to heat greenhouses. In algebraic form this is:

$$M = \bar{M} \tag{1}$$
$$PQ = KM \quad (K \text{ is the money multiplier}) \tag{2}$$
$$PQ = P_0Q_0 + P_RQ_R \tag{3}$$

So, if either P_0Q_0 or P_RQ_R changes, the other will be affected, not PQ. If there is an increase in the relative price of oil, as in 1973–4, 1978–9 and 1990, the outcome depends upon the price elasticity of demand for oil. If this were elastic, expenditure on oil would fall. If, as is generally taken to be the case, the demand is inelastic, expenditure on oil would rise. Necessarily, therefore, (P_RQ_R) expenditure on everything else must fall. This fall in the demand for everything else should (depending upon supply elasticities) cause both a fall in output (Q_R) and a reduction in the (relative) price on non-oil goods (strictly their price will be lower than it otherwise would be). As the price of oil is higher but the price of everything else lower than it otherwise would be, the effect of OPEC on inflation is therefore indeterminate. The effect on output and employment is clear-cut because the output of both oil (Q_0) and non-oil goods (Q_R) fall. Therefore, the OPEC price rise should have caused a rise in unemployment but need not have had any clear-cut effect on inflation. This is consistent with the evidence (see Gowland, 1983a, p.114). Moreover, if one relaxes the assumption about a fixed world money supply, the conclusion is strengthened. Deficits by OECD countries have a bigger negative impact on the world money supply than OPEC surpluses have a positive impact. This seems to have more than offset any action by policy makers to offset the rise in unemployment between 1974 and 1975, and in any case many of them were more worried about inflation.

The analysis of the discovery of North Sea oil is very similar. The effect of a much higher level of output of oil must be to reduce expenditure in the rest of the economy if the money supply is unchanged. Hence, the output or price level or both of the non-oil sector of the economy must fall (the monetarist version of 'deindustrialisation'). This may be deplored, as it is by some, or viewed as an essential adjustment to the discovery of oil. According to this position, an attempt to offset the effect by expansionary monetary policy would have been to cause enough inflation to offset exactly this effect on expenditure via wealth effects (see p.154). It is also almost certainly the case that the role of the North Sea in causing unemployment has been overstated relative to other factors, especially the long-run structural defects of many industries. Nevertheless, the monetarist analysis of how this occurs is at least as persuasive as any other version of deindustrialisation. The critic could justly say, however, that aggregate analysis assumes an implausibly high degree of smooth adjustment by markets. This and the neglect of institutional detail would be the starting point of new Keynesian and post–Keynesian critiques.

8.2 Leijonhufvud's analysis

Leijonhufvud (1968) sought to show that the main features of the Keynesian model – the multiplier, the marginal propensity to consume and the divorce of saving from investment – were caused by the absence of a futures market in labour and by the existence of money, which interfered with the signalling mechanism of a market economy. Before explaining how he demonstrated this, it is necessary to explain Leijonhufvud's objective. He sought to show that the persistence of mass unemployment could be caused by forms of market failure which were inevitable in a monetary economy. In other words, he sought to refute Say's law, that in a market economy there would always be full employment so long as prices were free to adjust to clear markets. Leijonhufvud wanted to prove that the advocates of Say's law were implicitly assuming a barter economy. If he succeeded in proving that the existence of money led to forms of market failure which meant that unemployment could persist, he could claim to have refuted the view that the economy is necessarily self-righting and so have demonstrated the need for an active macroeconomic policy. He would also have countered the arguments about a balanced deflation being necessarily able to cure unemployment (see Chapter 7). Leijonhufvud's analysis is then cast in the form of a contrast of a monetary and barter economy because Leijonhufvud argued that a barter economy was implicitly assumed by classical economists (and by the orthodox school in the 1960s): Keynes' real exchange economy (see p.27).

The most widely known of Keynesian ideas is the multiplier; that is, an initial shock to the economy will be magnified. In particular, the oft-told 'Keynesian' story is that an initial fall in output and/or employment will lead to a further fall in output or employment. The argument is contingent upon the proposition that the initial shock leads to a fall in current income, which leads to a fall in consumers' expenditure. This fall in expenditure leads to a further fall in output, and so on. This process is analysed in elementary Keynesian models in terms of the marginal propensity to consume. The fall in the equilibrium level of income generated by an initial shock is equal to the shock (the change in net injections) times the multiplier. The size of the multiplier depends upon the size of the marginal propensity to consume, such that when the MPC equals zero the multiplier is equal to one and there is no magnification (the formula for the multiplier is that it equals the inverse of the marginal propensity to withdraw less the marginal propensity to inject).

Leijonhufvud argued that 'the multiplier was an illiquidity phenomenon', that the downward spiral of contraction in income caused by an initial shock was caused by the forced reduction in consumption by the initially unemployed. If they had been able to borrow in unlimited amounts against future income, or to sell their labour forward, then there would be no slumps. This proposition is best understood by analysis of a simple example. This concerns a thirty-year-old male building worker who earns and spends £200 per week. One week, because of bad weather, his earnings fall to £100. This is the epitome of a Keynesian shock, albeit on a small scale. According to neoclassical analysis he would calculate his optimal strategy given this shock. This would be to spend £199.80 in the current and each subsequent week. He could do this if he borrowed £99.80 and repaid it with interest over the remainder of his working life at 20p per week. This would be optimal because the shock has had a minuscule effect on his permanent income, wealth and lifetime income, and so on his consumption plans. In fact, this policy is optimal so long as there is diminishing marginal utility of consumption (which implies that a smooth pattern of consumption is desirable). Thus, orthodox analysis implies no magnification of the shock since the expenditure of the worker is virtually unaffected. In other words, the marginal propensity to consume is zero. Indeed, it is a basic result of both the life cycle and permanent income hypothesis that this is so (see Gowland, 1990, Chapter 10). Leijonhufvud's argument is that because of 'liquidity constraints' the worker is forced to reduce his expenditure to £100 because he cannot borrow the £99.80 necessary so that he can spend £199.80. That this is so is a technical failure in the capital market but is inevitable and certainly implies no defects in the practices of financial institutions. Hence, the marginal propensity to consume is high, rather than zero as in the orthodox analysis. Consequently, a shock is multiplied because the worker's reduced expenditure causes someone else to suffer a reduction in income, and so on. In the theoretical world of general equilibrium the constraint, called a 'realised income constraint' by Clower, could be broken by a forward sale of labour; in order to finance current consumption, a worker sells to someone else the right to his or her labour in, say, ten years' time. Such a transaction is both impracticable and illegal (as slavery). Even if this form of a market in human capital were legal, virtually every form of market failure would exist in it. Leijonhufvud argued that the absence of a futures market in labour was the reason why unemployment could exist in an otherwise frictionless, perfectly competitive economy. This was related to the work of Arrow and Debreu (1954), who had shown that the existence of competitive general equilibrium depended upon the presence of a complete set of futures markets and contingent markets; that is, not merely could one sell or buy any product in a future market but the transaction could be conditional. For example, one could sell 50 bushels of wheat for delivery in the year 2010, conditional upon rainfall in the UK of at least 20 inches in that year. In this way Leijonhufvud started the process whereby macroeconomic and microeconomic theory became more closely related. The application of microeconomic theory by Leijonhufvud was simple. If the unemployed could sell their future labour, they would buy goods which would create a demand for their labour. Hence, there was an excess supply of labour and an excess demand for goods but no way in which the two could be removed. In practice, of course, the worker may be able to borrow but can never sell future labour. Hence it is better to concentrate on this possibility. In this case the 'multiplier is an illiquidity phenomenon'; the reason spending may fall when income does is the fact that individuals cannot borrow in unlimited quantities, that is, there is credit rationing, pp.243ff.

Clower (1965) had preceded Leijonhufvud (1968) in his resurrection of the marginal propensity to consume. The account given concerning the building worker captures exactly the reasons why Clower believed that 'realised income' would influence consumers' expenditure. Similarly, companies might face a 'realised sales constraint'; they could not hire the labour they wanted because they had no money to pay them. Clower distinguished between 'notional' and 'effective' demand for both goods and labour. Notional demand is what the consumer wishes to do and would do if capital markets were perfect (spending £199.80 per week, in the example above). Effective demand is what the consumer can do given the liquidity constraint he or she faces (£100, in the same example) stemming from credit rationing. Clower argued that unemployment arose and persisted because effective demands fell short of notional ones. If all notional demands were operative, Say's law would be valid, and only an excessive real wage could cause unemployment. Given quantity constraints, unemployment could persist. This Clower–Leijonhufvud approach provides a theoretical underpinning for the availability doctrine (p.244).

Other conclusions follow. One is that there is an efficiency case for unemployment pay to correct market failure in the credit market, as well as the more familiar equity case. If the building worker received unemployment pay he would not have to reduce his spending (or at least by a lesser amount). Another is the 'corridor theory'. Leijonhufvud argued that economic agents would have sufficient savings and borrowing opportunities to cushion small shocks but not large ones. Hence, the government needed to intervene to deal with large shocks but could let market forces cope with small ones. (This was called the corridor theory because of an analogy with someone returning home in an intoxicated state.) Leijonhufvud had thus provided a justification for limited government intervention rather than fine tuning. In general Leijonhufvud sought to justify moderate social-democrat interventionist policies based on free-market assumptions, a task that is obviously relevant to the 1990s.

Leijonhufvud's most interesting theoretical proposition was to explain that the fundamental Keynesian proposition that planned savings and investment might diverge arose from the existence of a monetary economy. The divorce of savings and investment is the most crucial of all Keynesian ideas. In classical models a decision to save is a decision to consume in the future instead of the present, and the analysis of the effects of it is the same as a switch from, say, drinking beer to drinking wine. Keynes accepted the validity of the market analysis in the case of a switch from one good to another but not from consumption in one period to another. This is often said to be because those making the decision about the level of saving are not the same as those making the decision to invest. This is not a satisfactory reason for the Keynesian emphasis on saving and investment as the same is true of beer drinkers and wine producers; moreover, Keynes used it in his early writings, especially the *Treatise* (1971, Vols. V, VI) but not in the *General Theory* (1936). The neoclassical analysis of the effect of a switch from the demand for one good to another is straightforward. If a lot of people buy wine instead of beer, this acts as a signal through the price mechanism for brewers to produce less and wine growers more. Labour is reallocated by the inward shift of the demand for brewery workers and outward shift of the demand for wine workers. Classical analysis postulates a similar chain of events in the case of a decision to save (that is, to consume in the future rather than now). Investment will rise by an amount equal to the fall in current consumption because the extra future demand makes it profitable to do so. In other words, the price mechanism should work to ensure full employment when there is a switch from present to future consumption, just as it does when there is a switch from one sort of present consumption to another.

Leijonhufvud argued that the key difference was that no signal was transmitted in the case of saving in a monetary economy. In a barter economy an individual could only save by purchasing a claim to specific goods at a specific time. (Of course, this agent could also buy and store goods, but it is obvious that in this case the demand for currently produced goods cannot fall.) So, to trace an example, an individual increases his or her savings. He or she reduces his or her purchases of currently (1991) produced baked beans and buys a certificate entitling him to a washing machine in 1992. There is a reduced demand for baked beans for immediate delivery and an increased demand for future washing machines. This changes relative prices, so there is an incentive for Hotpoint to hire redundant baked-bean production workers to build a factory to produce the washing machine for delivery in 1992. The price mechanism can ensure that a decision to save automatically produces a decision to invest. The decision to save involves a decision to purchase a specific item at a known future date. Relative price changes signal that it is profitable to supply this good (that is, to invest so as to be able to do so). Hence, in a barter economy what is usually called Say's law would apply, and there would automatically be full employment.

In a monetary economy, however, saving takes a monetary form and is therefore not specific, so no signal is transmitted about which good will be purchased and when. This generality of money is one of its principal attractions, because savers do not want to commit themselves to a specific item or to a specific date of future purchase. Indeed, in many cases savers have no idea when they will wish to spend their savings or what they will purchase; they are just saving for a rainy day. The existence of money allows savers to save in a non-specific form, and in consequence, no signal is transmitted. Hence, there is no incentive to invest. Those who believe in Say's law had traditionally believed that the price mechanism worked through interest rates – more saving would lower interest rates and make investment more attractive. Leijonhufvud would not dispute the role of interest rates as an intertemporal signalling device but would claim that they were necessarily imperfect, because of the generality of money.

Indeed, Leijonhufvud's whole analysis was based upon imperfect responses of the system. He did not argue that no signal was transmitted but only that it was not necessarily perfect.

Similarly, past savings or borrowing would reduce the impact of liquidity constraints but not eliminate them. Leijonhufvud (1981) has subsequently suggested that economies are therefore likely to be self-righting in response to small but not large shocks for the obvious reason that the bigger the adjustment needed the more likely imperfect signals and available liquidity are to be inadequate; that is, the corridor theory above.

8.3 Clower's analysis

The 'dual decision' or 'sequential markets' hypothesis was Clower's main conclusion from his adage that 'money buys goods and goods buy money but goods do not buy goods' (Clower, 1969, p.207–8). Workers must sell their labour before they can buy goods; the two transactions do not take place simultaneously as is implicitly assumed in Walrasian general equilibrium. As a consequence, the (full employment) equilibrium may be unattainable. If the unemployed workers were to be employed by firms, they would buy the goods which would make it profitable for the firms to employ them. However, no firm can or will employ more workers, because it would make a loss from doing so (unless all other firms were to expand employment simultaneously) since the firm's workers would spend only a small fraction of their income on the firm's products. Thus, the economy will remain at an underemployed level. If the firm could pay its workers in its own product, the problem would disappear; in other words, the problem would not exist in a barter economy. If a worker's marginal product is ten tons of steel per week, he or she would be employed at a wage of, say, seven tons of steel. He or she will not, however, be employed at all at any wage payable in money because of the sequence problem – the firm has to sell the steel to obtain the money. In this case all firms would increase employment, paying wages with their output of steel, bread, etc., and the workers would exchange these among themselves. In terms of notional demand, there is a full employment equilibrium, but this cannot be made effective in any way without government intervention to break the vicious cycle. Clower argues that unemployment is more likely in a monetary than a barter economy; indeed, it may be a consequence of a monetary economy. This, of course, is an argument for government intervention in a monetary economy, not for the abolition of money. Nevertheless, Clower's argument has been challenged by, for example, Bliss in Parkin and Nobay (1975). More generally, Clower has opened interesting new avenues of research, see below in Section 8.5. The most interesting response is still that of Goodhart (in Harcourt, 1977). He argues by syllogism:

1. Increased uncertainty and reduced information reduce the level of output and employment (a standard result – see, for example, Hey, 1979).
2. The existence of money increases the quantity of information and reduces uncertainty.
3. Consequently, there will be less unemployment in a monetary world than in a barter world.

8.4 Disequilibrium, temporary equilibrium and the role of money

There have been numerous extensions of Clower's and Leijonhufvud's work. One stream of thought has sought to build formal models incorporating constraints of the sort hypothesised by Clower and Leijonhufvud.[2] The fundamental feature of this analysis is that price does not adjust instantaneously to clear at least one market, usually the goods or labour market. Rigid or 'sticky' wages are a typical example of such a phenomena. New Keynesian analysis has shown that such features may be optimal, Frank (1987), Blanchard and Fischer (1989, Chapter 9) and Carlin and Soskice (1990). The resulting level of price and quantity is called a temporary equilibrium or, perhaps more consistently, analysed as a disequilibrium. The simplest form of such analysis is presented in Figure 8.1, which shows a conventional supply-and-demand diagram. If the price were P_2, demand would be Q_4 and supply Q_1. Assuming perfect information, Q_1 transactions will occur, and there will be excess demand of $(Q_4 - Q_1)$. Such markets are termed 'supply dominated'. Similarly, at a price of P_1, there will be excess supply of $(Q_3 - Q_2)$ and actual sales of Q_2. Such markets are demand dominated. Some form of rationing or quantity constraint will prevail such that some agents do not transact as much as they

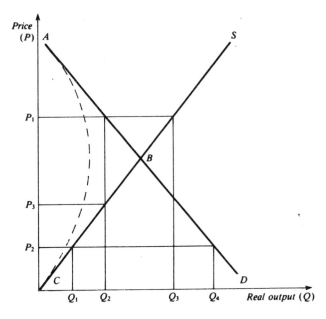

Figure 8.1 Disequilibrium

want to. In the labour market, in the case of excess supply, there is unemployment and certain workers ($Q_3 - Q_2$ in number) will be unable to sell their labour. It is interesting to note that Q_2 transactions take place at the price P_3 (with excess demand) as well as at P_1 (with excess supply). In fact, with perfect information, transactions take place along ABC, with the equilibrium B being a special case, when price clears the market. With imperfect information transactions occur along the dashed parabola, the distance between this and ABC measuring such phenomena as frictional unemployment. If various markets are analysed in this way the analyses can be combined to produce a model of '(temporary) general equilibrium' (from the title of Grandmont, 1977). Such models are subject to Walras' law, of course, so that the sum of excess demand in the markets (with excess demand) is equal to the sum of excess supply in the markets (with excess supply).

Malinvaud produced a simple classification of unemployment according to whether markets are supply or demand dominated. In particular, he wished to divide unemployment into 'Keynesian' and 'classical', where the distinguishing feature is whether a reduction in real wages will reduce unemployment. Keynesian unemployment requires a demand-dominated goods market, whereas when the goods market is supply dominated (or in equilibrium) unemployment is classical and can be eliminated by a reduction in real wages. Much of this area of economics is either recondite or outside the scope of this book, but some of its main features will be summarised briefly. To a large extent its significance for the questions under review here is that it has been written – in a Keynesian spirit – to refute a (possibly 'straw man') opposition mechanism that holds that unemployment is the fault of trade unions. Certainly nearly all the proponents of this school of Keynesians seek to challenge the notion that economies are self-righting. Many economists – whether self-styled Keynesians, like Blinder, or soi-disant monetarists, like Brunner – would agree that this is the crucial issue in macroeconomic theory (see Klamer, 1984). Whether the neoclassical paradigm is really as simplistic as its neo–Keynesian critics argue is doubtful, but this characterisation does justify such dicta as 'unions price their members out of a job'. This neoclassical model suggests that trade unions cause unemployment as a natural consequence of the exercise of monopoly power, lowering their output (that is, the number of jobs). Moreover, the unions keep real wages at an excess level which prevents market forces from eliminating unemployment. In contrast, the mathematical new Keynesians seek to show that it is possible that:

1. A reduction in real wages may not reduce unemployment.
2. Stickiness in real wages is neither (in economic theory) purely an *ad hoc* assumption nor (in practice) the consequence of union selfishness. Instead it could occur in competitive markets because of imperfections such as lack of information, inadequate signalling and problems of defining contracts or simply transaction costs.

Shackle and the other 'fundamentalist' Keynesians similarly seek to overthrow a mechanism which argues that economies are self-righting. They, however, lay stress on the nature of uncertainty, of Keynes' 'dark forces of time and ignorance', and reject any formal modelling of the problems it causes for economic policy. It is difficult to summarise Shackle *et al*'s views, if only because of the immaculate, elegant and precise prose in which they are expressed – in these respects his writings are as admirable as their inspiration, Chapter 12 of Keynes (1936). A vulgarisation of this position is that all behaviour depends upon expectations – inflationary expectations and those which influence investment being of paramount importance. Such expectations are not formed in the mechanistic fashion used by orthodox economists. Instead, they are likely to be influenced by such intangibles as the 'state of confidence'. Consequently, expectations are likely to be subject to change and unstable. Hence, at least, business cycles are likely. Moreover, persistent unemployment may be engendered by the consequences of a downturn.

The other two philosophies considered in this section are much closer to the main theme of this book in that they focus upon the role of money and the nature of optimal monetary policy. Post-Keynesian monetary theory, as advanced by Minsky for example (1982), Davidson (1978), Dow and Earl (1982) and Arestis (1988, pp.41–71), contains a number of strands. Some have been analysed elsewhere in this book; for example, a view that money may be endogenous and/or virtually impossible to control. An emphasis on Leijonhufvud's analysis that the existence of money is likely to produce a defective signalling is very marked, for example, 'Keynes has demonstrated that unemployment has its causes in the way in which monetary transactions are conducted' (Dow and Earl, 1982, p.251). Bufferism à la Bain is also an ingredient of this post-Keynesian dish, as is a dash of Shacklean expectations. What is unique to this school is the emphasis on the impact of the institutional structure and of speculation. The structure of financial institutions is not ignored by other economists; for example, Goodhart (1975) regards it as a reason why monetarist prescriptions may be appropriate for some but not all countries and why different methods of monetary control may also be appropriate in different countries. However, no other school treats it as being of central importance to *macroeconomic* analysis. The emphasis on the possible disruptive effects of speculation is even more distinctive. Speculation, it is argued, is likely both to create cycles in activity and to threaten the stability of the financial system, and so threaten a slump. Hence, monetary policy should concentrate on structural objectives and, in particular, upon the discouragement of speculation rather than on stabilisation policy. The other feature emphasised by post Keynesians is that money is credit determined but this is not distinctive to them, see pp.224ff.

8.5   Summary and conclusions

Clower and Leijonhufvud have changed the nature of how many macroeconomists analyse problems. This has led to a reappraisal of the microeconomic analytic foundations of the subject and of the role of money. Of particular relevance is the proposition that the existence of money is responsible for defects in the operation of economies, defects which may lead to the continuation of mass unemployment. Government intervention at a macroeconomic level may be justified (and only be justifiable) in terms of market-failure analysis of a sort normally only presented in micro-economic texts. Moreover, 'sticky' wages and prices could be the inevitable consequences of rational market behaviour and perhaps be beneficial rather than the undesirable result of irrational trade union behaviour.

Notes

1. The exegetical literature is enormous. Chick (1983), Gilbert (1982) and Coddington (1983) provide excellent surveys. Other important works for those interested in what Keynes really meant – besides Keynes (1971), especially Vols.XIII and XIV, and Keynes (1936) – include Johnson and Johnson (1978), Patinkin and Leith (1977), Minsky (1975), Davidson (1978), Shackle (1968, 1974), Wattel (1985) and Wood (1983).
2. Of particular importance or value in this area are: Barro and Grossman (1976), Benassy (1982), Grandmont (1983), Dixit (1976, 1977) and Malinvaud (1977). Two valuable textbook treatments are Cuddington *et al* (1984) which is exceptionally comprehensive and Sinclair (1987) which presents complex models in an exceptionally lucid manner and considers their practical relevance.

9

Debt Management and Government Finance

9.1 Theory and practice of debt management

All government activities must be financed, whether they take the form of expenditure on goods and services or the (net) acquisition of assets, or of lending to the private and overseas sectors. That part of the total outlay generated by these activities which is not financed by taxation must be borrowed and is called the PSBR, which has figured prominently in the preceding analysis. Government borrowing does have not only a short-run effect but also a long-run one, because the stock of loans is permanently increased and the government must pay interest on this. The purpose of this chapter is to examine the implications of interest payments and of an existing stock of debt, called the National Debt in the UK and the Public Debt (or, occasionally Federal Debt) in the USA. Any such debt must be managed; that is, its structure and form must be determined. An individual buying a house is engaging in debt management when he or she chooses the period and source of his or her mortgage. When circumstances change the borrower may change the source or type of housing finance, as many borrowers did in the UK in 1983 when a change in the tax regulations made endowment mortgages more attractive. The individual in doing this is presumably maximising his or her utility. The theory of debt management seeks to examine the elements of the relevant utility function for both governments and individuals and so consider how they would react to various shocks and stimuli.

The classical theory of debt management assumes that debt management has two objectives. The first is to minimise the level of interest payments; the level of the debt is, of course, predetermined. This would mean that a house buyer, having found that he or she needs to borrow £25,000, would choose the cheapest available mortgage. In practice, of course, the decisions about which house and which mortgage are interrelated but, as always, analytically it is better to decompose the decision-making process. The other objective is to maximise the maturity of the loan (that is, to postpone repayment for as long as possible). Thus, our hypothetical mortgagee would prefer a twenty-five-year mortgage to a fifteen-year one according to this criteria, other things being equal. The ranking of loans by this criteria is not always clear-cut. The potential borrower in the example might well hesitate between a mortgage which has to be repaid over twenty years in equal instalments and one on which no repayments are required for seven years but the mortgage has then to be repaid in its entirety. The reason for this preference for deferring repayment, other things being equal, is an assumption that liquidity always confers benefits and will therefore be chosen if it is available costlessly. If an individual can borrow and lend at the same rate, it is desirable to hold both assets and liabilities. If the individual could borrow for either one or two years and can repay the debt after one year, he or she will in these circumstances choose to borrow for two years and hold an asset for the second year. In the second year the individual has both a debt, on which he or she pays interest, and a loan, on which he or she receives interest. These payments cancel out and the individual is more liquid (because his assets are higher) at no cost. In many circumstances such liquidity is unlikely to be costless, so the objectives may conflict. This problem is considered in the next paragraph.

The classical theory of debt management argues that debt managers seek to attain two objectives: minimisation of interest payments and maximisation of repayment period. These may conflict. For example, the mortgagee considered above might find that he or she had to choose between a twenty-year mortgage with an interest rate of 10 per cent and a twenty-five-year one with a rate of 11 per cent. One criteria of choice suggested by some business-finance authors is to minimise the service cost of the debt (that is, the sum of interest payments and repayments of principal): on a loan of £100 at 15 per cent to be repaid over five years, the service charge in the first year is £35 – £15 interest plus £20 repayments. The service cost is clearly an important element in debt management and is obviously a function of the interest rate and maturity of the debt. Nevertheless, it seems unlikely that it would be the only criterion in choosing one's debt structure. For example, it implies that a three-year loan at 50 per cent interest (service cost, 83 per cent) is preferable to a one-year loan at 5 per cent (service cost, 105 per cent). One would have to be both desperate and pessimistic about the possibility of refinance to opt for the first alternative. More generally, it is assumed that the two objectives will be traded-off, so the conventional apparatus of microeconomics is used and the choice analysed using indifference curves and the other tools of choice theory.

The classical theory of debt management is obviously relevant to private individuals, companies and municipal authorities. It was relevant in the past to national governments but has been of little importance in the UK since 1947, when Dalton ceased to be Chancellor, and is of only minor importance in the USA although Mr Lawson often talked in these terms in 1986–7. Instead, debt management is used as a tool of economic policy.

It is clear that criteria other than the classical ones are relevant to government debt-management, since otherwise all government activities could be financed by the issue of currency. As the interest rate is zero and the effective maturity infinite, this is the perfect instrument of borrowing according to classical criteria. Even if no legal limit is imposed on the printing of currency, it is clear that governments would have to take note of the dangers of inflation or unemployment that the policy might cause. Such seems to have been the position in the UK since the First World War. Until then, Gladstonian principles have prevailed – classical debt management subject to a limit on currency creation. Between the wars classical and macroeconomic criteria were both important, but since 1947 macroeconomic criteria have prevailed.

The simplest of macroeconomic criteria is to use debt management to bring about the level and structure of interest rates that the authorities desire – either for its own sake, or as a tool to influence the money supply, the exchange rate or some other proximate target of policy. For example, if interest rates are perceived to be too low, the authorities can force them up by offering a higher rate of return on their own securities. More usually, the objective of debt management is to regulate the money supply. As was seen on page 17, any change in the size of private lending to the public sector will change the size of the money supply. If more debt is sold to the non-bank private sector, the money supply falls, and either currency or bank lending to the public sector is reduced. A repurchase of debt from the non-bank private sector (that is, a fall in private lending to the public sector) will increase the money supply. These transactions are referred to as open-market operations in the UK. In the USA the term is also used to describe sales or purchase of certain types of security (usually Treasury Bills) to or from banks. This is designed to affect the size of their holdings of reserve assets and so indirectly influence bank lending and the money supply. The most general objective of debt management would be to influence private sector portfolios so that their structure is optimal for the achievement of the authorities' macroeconomic objectives; control of the money supply is a special case of this, concerned with only a single asset. A Tobinite would be interested in the whole range of financial assets and might be much more concerned with changing the maturity of existing bond holdings than with sales or repurchases that affect total size. If private sector portfolios are shortened, the attempt to restore equilibrium would involve an increase in the demand for real assets.

9.2　The budget constraint

Since Blinder and Solow's (1973) seminal article the budget constraint has been one of the major themes of monetary literature. Blinder and Solow argued that other analyses ignored the role of interest payments on public sector debt. They argued that if these were explicitly taken account of, various striking results could be obtained. In particular, the conventional ranking of money- and bond-financed government spending would be reversed, at least in the long run. Godley has argued that the 'long run' may be very short (Godley and Coutts, 1984). Blinder and Solow's model is effectively one in which currency is the only form of money. Certainly it is critical for their model that government expenditure financed by money creation does not increase public sector interest payments. In practice this does not always hold, as the usual form of money creation involves the counterpart creation of bank claims on the government which do pay interest. This and the other limitations of the model are considered in the next section. If the assumption is accepted, the Blinder–Solow result is straightforward, as shown in Figure 9.1. The conventional comparison of bond- and money-financed expenditure (see pp.144ff) held that bond-financed expenditure would shift only the IS curve (from IS_1 to IS_2) so that income would rise only from Y_1 to Y_2. Money-financed expenditure, on the other hand, would shift both the IS and LM curves, so that

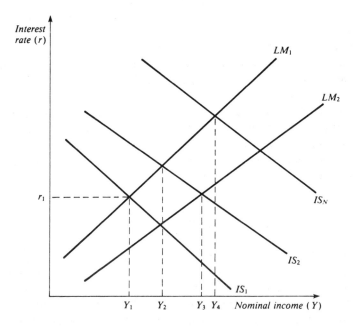

Figure 9.1 Money- and bond-financed expenditure: the budget constraint

income rises from Y_1 to Y_3. Blinder–Solow accept this as a short-term result. However, the increase in the quantity of bonds means that in the following period government expenditure rises again, in the form of transfer payments (that is, the additional payment of interest). Personal disposable income therefore rises, and the IS curve shifts outwards again. The increase in government outlays must be financed, so, holding the money supply constant, there must be a further increase in the bond stock. Thus, in the third period interest payments are still higher, and so the IS curve shifts again, and so on. Ultimately, Blinder and Solow argue, the IS curve will shift to IS_N, so that income is at Y_4. IS thus intersects LM_1 at a higher level of income than IS_2 intersects LM_2. Therefore, bond-financed government expenditure is ultimately more expansionary than money financed.[1]

A paradoxical extension of this model concerns the circumstances under which an increase in the money supply might be contractionary in its effect upon income. This occurs when the increase is brought about by a fall in private lending to the public sector. The LM curve shifts rightwards from LM_1 to LM_2, so income rises to Y_2 (Fig.9.2). However, the lower total of bonds means that interest payments are lower in the second period, so the IS curve shifts leftwards, and so on (that is, the exact converse of the previous result). Ultimately, this means that the IS curve shifts to IS_N in the Nth period and income is less, at Y_3, than initially, at Y_1.

These budget-constraint results clearly depend upon how far the IS shifts. Hence, it is important to consider why it is argued that the IS curve must shift far enough to produce the seemingly paradoxical results. The crux of the argument is that in long-run equilibrium, the budget must be balanced, strictly that the public sector's financial deficit be equal to zero. (The *PSFD* is equal to the *PSBR* less any public sector loans to the private sector.) This proposition starts by pointing out that, by definition, the IS and LM curves have ceased to shift in long-run equilibrium. If there is a budget deficit, it must be financed. If it is financed by money creation, the LM curve shifts in consequence. If it is not financed by money creation, the IS curve will shift because of the effects of the interest payments on the bonds sold to finance the deficit. Thus, in long-run equilibrium the budget must balance.

This condition can be incorporated by a modification to Figure

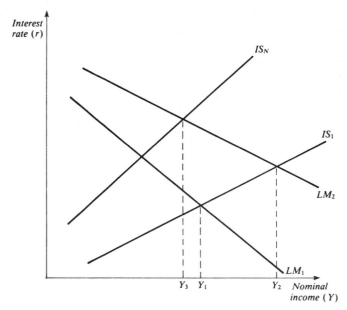

Figure 9.2 Paradoxical result of increasing the money supply

9.1 which is shown as Figure 9.3. The lower part of the diagram shows, for each level of Y, the level of government expenditure and taxation (all other components of the *PSBR* are assumed to be zero). Taxation (strictly, net of government transfer payments) is a positive function of income and so must slope upwards from left to right, although not necessarily linearly, as drawn. Government spending is taken to be independent of income. In the original equilibrium, at Y_1, government spending is G_1 and at this level is equal to taxation. The increase in government spending, by ΔG, can be financed by money creation or by the sale of bonds to the non-bank private sector. In the case of money creation, both IS and LM curves shift (as before). The shift is such that at the new equilibrium level of income, Y_3, both taxation and government spending must be equal, at G_1 plus ΔG. With bond-financed spending in the short run the shift in the IS curve to IS_2 is such that income rises to Y_2, at which level there is a budget deficit. This deficit occurs because the increase in

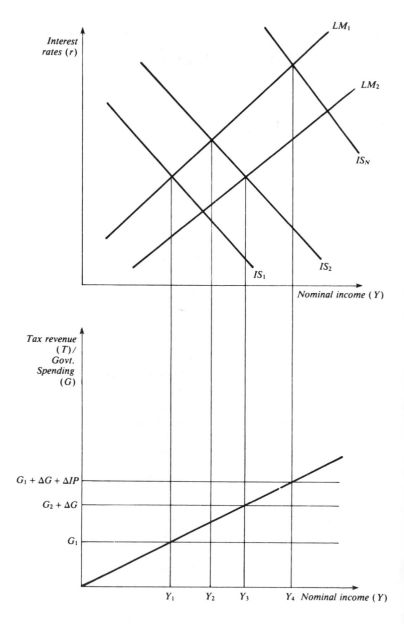

Figure 9.3 The budget constraint in equilibrium: a balanced budget

government spending is greater than the increase in taxation; since at Y_3 these are equal, at any lower level of income, the increase in taxation is less than the increase in expenditure. The deficit is further boosted by interest payments on the bonds. This is financed by further bond sales, and a further shift of the IS curve and rise in interest payments occur, as described above. This continues until the IS curve has shifted to IS_N. At this point the budget must be in balance, by definition, and so tax revenues must be such as to finance not merely G_1 and ΔG but also the (rise in) interest payments.

Thus tax revenues must be greater than at Y_3, when tax revenues are equal only to G_1 plus ΔG. If tax revenues are greater, then income must have been greater to generate them. (Of course, tax rates could have been raised, but in that case the comparison with money-financed expenditure would no longer be valid.) Thus IS_N must intersect LM_1 at a level of income greater than Y_3. This is the proof of the Blinder–Solow proposition. In a manner reminiscent of the elementary Keynesian model, it demonstrates the logical implication of equilibrium. The significance of this result is considered in the next section.

9.3   Significance of the budget constraint

The budget-constraint results were as prominent in academic literature in the 1970s as inside and outside money were in the 1960s, but it is still much harder to assess their overall significance, if only because of the greater elapse of time in the latter case. On the one hand, it is incontrovertible that interest payments were largely ignored in the literature prior to 1973. They have been of growing importance since then, especially in the USA, in the real world as well as in theoretical models. Moreover, the budget-constraint models have been among the foremost in producing explicitly dynamic macroeconomic models. There is considerable value in this and in emphasising that short-run results may not apply in the long run, nor vice versa. However, it may turn out that the original budget-constraint result is a mere theoretical curiosity; that is, money-financed expenditure is in practice more expansionary than bond-financed spending, and vice versa. Some arguments to this effect are:

1. That interest payments are equally affected by bond- and money-financed deficits because most money-financed expenditure is matched by increased bank holdings of government securities. In this case, one would need three analyses: for bond-financed, bank-money-financed and currency-financed expenditure respectively. Bank-money creation to finance government expenditure would lead to a shift of both the IS and LM curves in the short-run, as would currency finance (but not bond finance). However, for the bank money line the IS curve would creep outwards, as in the bond-finance case, but not in the currency case. In consequence, bank-money finance would be more expansionary in the long run than currency finance. It would also be more expansionary in the short run than bond finance, but both would be equally expansionary in the long run. However, as the authorities have very little control over the quantity of currency, the comparison may be of little practical value. Indeed, currency may be not only demand determined but also income determined; in which case the budget-constraint result collapses to a proposition that in the long run the expansionary effect of all government expenditure is identical, a result strangely reminiscent of 'American' new right results.

2. The comparison of bond- and money-financed deficits ignores Friedman's stock-flow argument (see p.147).

3. The results in Section 9.2 also ignore the wealth and other effects of the existing National Debt (see Section 9.4).

4. It may take many years, possibly even several centuries, for the long-run equilibrium to be reached (although Godley denies this). The short-run result may therefore be more relevant. Indeed, it may be that such an equilibrium would never be reached, nor even approached. The alternative is that the IS–LM model is not stable in the technical sense. This may not matter in a model designed only to analyse the effect of a *short-term* macroeconomic policy. Relaxation of some of the other factors held constant, such as fixed real capital stock, may be necessary for stability.

5. The whole concept of a long-run equilibrium of the sort analysed above may not be very useful. If results are only applicable in circumstances where budgets are balanced, their

importance is restricted. It may be better to concentrate on more short-run but more applicable results.

6. The models ignore any constraint on the size of the PSBR. In the UK, for example, PSBR targets are the norm. The budget process introduced into the USA in 1974 is, in principle, similar in its effect. Gramm–Rudman has rendered this a binding constraint at least in principle. The 1990 budget negotiations (between President Bush and Congress) confirmed that there is an effective if slightly fuzzy limit on the deficit. In these circumstances increases in interest payments lead to a reduction in other forms of expenditure rather than to higher deficits. The budget-constraint result would then be a model of the impact of short-run bond-financed expenditure on government transfers and real expenditure in the long run.

7. Blinder and Solow's model is very sparse in its financial sector. A richer specification of this, so that it includes assets other than money and government bonds, seems to change the results markedly (Cohen and McMenamin, 1978).

Whilst the specific 'budget-constraint' results may not be very important, the models are of great importance in extending and making consistent the basic IS–LM model. For example, they engender a dynamic version of the otherwise explicitly static IS–LM framework. Moreover, like Friedman's stock-flow point, budget-constraint models emphasise the peculiar status and possible inconsistency of a flow model in which stocks influence behaviour and are changing; for example, whenever saving is positive, personal sector wealth is increasing. Hicks himself made similar points on a number of occasions, for example Hicks (1983).

9.4 Existing National Debt and wealth effects

The comparison of the effect of bond- and money-financed government expenditure which comprised the basic budget-constraint result in Section 9.2 assumed that there was no pre-existing National Debt. It is obviously necessary to relax this assumption. Moreover, the consequent effects need to be taken into account in any analysis, even a short-run one in which the budget-constraint mechanism is ignored as an unimportant matter. The effects depend upon the form which the pre-existing National Debt takes. Two examples are illustrated here, one where the National Debt takes the form of consols and one where it takes the form of capital-certain assets, such as National Savings Bank accounts. Obviously, the actual National Debt is a combination of these and intermediate assets, but any realistic analysis can be obtained by a combination of the two models presented here.

In the case of the debt issued in infinitely dated form, such as consols, War Loans and other *de facto* irredeemable stocks in the UK, the interest payments are fixed but the capital value varies. If in one year (t) the government wishes to borrow £100 in this form, it issues a security which commits it to pay £r_t per year for ever, where r_t is the interest rate prevailing in year t. As discussed above (pp.70–1), this amount is fixed but its market value varies inversely with interest rates. In this situation the analysis is of an existing National Debt which commits the government to pay a specified sum per annum and so is a private sector portfolio which includes this as an asset. Any change in interest rates necessarily alters the market value of this asset and so the private sector's net wealth (the Keynes windfall effect; see p.153).

On the other hand, if the existing National Debt is in the form of capital-certain assets, then by definition, the market value of the debt never changes. In this case, if the government borrows £100 in period t, it commits itself to pay £r_i in each subsequent period i, where r_i is the market rate in period i. If the government borrows £100 at 5 per cent in the form of consols, it will pay £5 per year for ever. If it borrows it in a capital-certain form such as a National Savings Bank Deposit, it is committed to pay the current market rate. Hence, if interest rates double to 10 per cent in the consol case, the government continues to pay £5 per year and the market value of the debt falls to £50. If the debt is in capital-certain form, the government has to increase its interest payments to £10, but there is no change in the market value of the debt. In summary, with infinite debt the market value of the National Debt changes but not the government's outflow. In the capital-certain case the converse is true. With finite but non-capital-certain debt, like most gilt-edged securities, both change.

The first comparison is between money-financed and bond-financed public expenditure. Bond-financed public expenditure raises interest rates, so in this case there is a negative Keynes windfall effect, because the IS curve shifts leftwards (alternatively, the IS curves in Figures 9.1 and 9.3 have to pivot around r_1). Money-financed expenditure leads to a fall in interest rates, or, at worst, no alteration to them, so there is a positive Keynes windfall effect. Interest rates are always lower with money-financed than with bond-financed public expenditure. Hence, wealth is always higher, and so consumer expenditure is therefore higher at each level of income. In elementary Keynesian terms, the level of net injections therefore increases by more if there is money-financed than if there is bond-financed public expenditure, because the negative Keynes windfall effect has to be deducted from the bond-financed government spending and the positive Keynes windfall effect added to the money-financed government expenditure to obtain the relevant net injection. Hence, even if Blinder–Solow are right to argue that in the long run the income multiplier is higher for bond-financed public expenditure, this may be offset by the different sizes of injection.

If, on the other hand, the expenditure were financed by the issue of capital-certain assets, and the existing National Debt were in this form, none of these wealth effects would be operative. Instead, however, the government pays out much more in interest payments with the debt-financed expenditure, because it has to pay the increased market rate on the existing debt. This increases the consumers' expenditure at each level of output (because disposable income is higher) and so the IS curve in Figures 9.1 and 9.3 should shift further outwards for bond-financed expenditure than IS_2.

On the other hand, money-financed expenditure normally lowers the market interest rate and so reduces government interest payments. This in turn shifts the IS curve inwards in Figures 9.1 and 9.3 because consumers' expenditure falls. Thus, the relevant IS curve for bond-financed spending is to the right of IS_2 and for money-financed expenditure to the left of IS_1. This reinforces the Blinder–Solow result by generating a larger increase in income caused by bond-financed expenditure and a smaller one generated by money-financed expenditure. (Alternatively, one may incorporate these interest payments into the IS curve as suggested on p.154. In this case the IS curve pivots.) It may be in this case that even in the short run, bond-financed expenditure has a bigger effect on income than money-financed expenditure, but this is very much a perverse extreme case. The point that I would like to emphasise is that it is necessary for economists to take note of structural factors, such as the form of the national debt, in analysing macroeconomic policy. Financial sector influences matter and their size and form depends on the structure of the financial sector.

9.5 Monetarist arithmetic and mean lag theorems

There have been two powerful uses of the budget constraint: Sargent and Wallace's 'unpleasant monetarist arithmetic', reproduced as Chapter 5 of Sargent (1986), and the Godley mean lag theorem (Godley and Cripps, 1983). Sargent and Wallace use a variant of the budget-constraint model in which government securities are capital certain, paying the market rate of interest in each period. The analysis in the preceding section showed the importance of this difference from the Blinder–Solow approach. Sargent and Wallace considered a standard monetarist proposition: a budget deficit cannot cause inflation unless it is allowed to increase the money supply, that is a budget deficit matched by sales of securities to the non-bank private sector is not inflationary. Sargent and Wallace point out that this deficit will become ever larger, because of the cumulative effect of interest payments. Ultimately the deficit becomes so large that it is not possible to finance it by selling securities to the non-bank private sector so it has to be monetized. Hence security financing of a deficit has merely postponed inflation. Moreover because the deficit is then larger (because of interest payments) the effect is more inflation than if the original deficit had been monetized. The result rests on a number of critical assumptions, notably that the real interest rate exceeds the rate of growth of output. Sargent and Wallace argue that this shows the need to coordinate monetary and fiscal policy and that it is rash to assume in the USA that the Federal Reserve system can always counter the stupidity (as the authors see it) of Congress and the President. Similar views might have been expressed concerning Karl Pöhl and European politicians until the former's resignation. However, the crucial assumption does not seem necessarily true and the model has been subject to stringent criticism, for example, Buiter in Griffiths and Wood (1984).

Godley and Cripps use a conventional budget-constraint model. They then utilise one of its basic features, the ability to generate consistent stock and flow equilibria. In particular the general optimal wealth:income ratios for the various economic agents. They use these to calculate the mean lag theorem – that is, the period necessary for half the budget constraint to work through. This depends on a few simple parameters which can be estimated or generated (like Sargent and Wallace, Godley–Cripps rely heavily on simulations and sensitivity analysis). These suggest that most of the budget-constraint effect has worked through within less than two years.

9.6 Summary and conclusions

In managing the public sector's debt the monetary authorities usually subordinate other considerations to the objectives of monetary policy. However, neither the existence of such a debt nor the need to pay interest on it can be ignored in macroeconomic analysis. Blinder and Solow showed that the normal rankings of money- and bond-financed expenditure could be reversed once note was taken of interest payments. Their model is very much a special case but illustrates the potential importance of interest payments. Work by Sargent and Wallace and Godley and Cripps illustrates its policy relevance.

Notes

1. Throughout this chapter the short- and long-run effects of money-financed expenditure are taken to be identical. This is for expositional ease only. An initial surplus shifts the LM curve outwards and a deficit inwards until long-run equilibrium is reached.

10

Term structure of Interest Rates

10.1   Term structure and monetary policy

It is common for economists to talk about 'the rate of interest', whereas in fact there are many different rates of interest. Interest rates can be categorised in many ways; for example, according to the risk of the loan, according to the borrower – whether the interest rate is on a public, private or bank liability. Interest rates can be calculated on a real or nominal basis, depending on whether or not allowance is made for the impact of inflation on the return from a security. The formula for the real interest rate is

$$r = \frac{1 + i}{1 + \Delta P} - 1$$

where r is the real interest rate, i the nominal one and ΔP the change in prices. It is frequently presented as $r = i - \Delta P$ which is only an approximation. Different loans have different degrees of risk, analysable by various methods – see, for example, Weston and Brigham (1987, Chapters 6 and 16). All of these distinctions are very important in monetary economics, but the most important is the distinction between interest rates for loans of different periods. This is called the term structure of interest rates and is usually illustrated by a *yield curve*, such as Figure

10.1, which has the duration of the loan (maturity) along the horizontal axis and the rate of interest on the vertical axis. In Figure 10.1, for example, if it were desired to borrow for t_1 years the interest rate would be r_1. If the loan were wanted for t_2 years, the borrower would have to pay r_2. A yield curve is drawn for a particular category of loan so that nothing but maturity changes as we move along it. Thus, at one time there will be several yield curves – one for government stocks, one for first-class (aaa) companies, and so on.

The term structure of interest rates (that is, theories which seek to explain the slope of the yield curve) is important for three reasons. The first is that it is a potentially important transmission mechanism for monetary and financial policy. The monetary authorities normally operate in short-term financial markets, so they tend to influence directly only short-term interest rates. Most forms of economic activity are influenced by longer-term rates, or at least so the conventional wisdom states. Hence, for a moderate Keynesian the impact of monetary policy on expenditure is likely to be dependent upon whether and by how much a

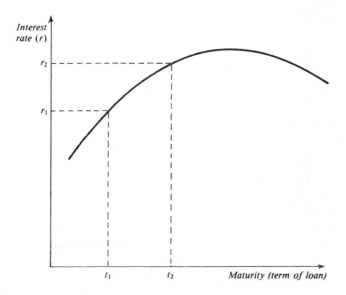

Figure 10.1 The yield curve

change in short-term interest rates affects longer-term ones, so the impact of monetary policy depends upon the nature of the term structure relationship. All other things being equal, the maturity of a loan is an inverse measure of its liquidity, so a theory of the term structure is an explanation of how the neo-Keynesian version of Tobin's model operates.

Moreover, the term structure of interest rates is a very important determinant of the money supply. In the UK, at least, the structure of interest rates is just as important a determinant of the stock of money as the absolute level of interest rates (Gowland, 1982, 1991a). (The relationship between bank and public sector interest rates is important as well as the term structure.) Finally, the relationship is important to the pure theorist since if there is a determinate relationship between the interest rates (and prices) of bonds of different maturities, then it is possible to substitute *the* bond rate (and bond stock) for the potentially infinite range of types of bond of different maturities. Thus, the correct degree of aggregation in models of the monetary sector is dependent upon the term structure.

The term structure is of vital concern to those who execute and formulate monetary policy. The authorities are constantly seeking to manipulate the relationship to achieve some goal or other. Two notable examples are 'operation twist' in the USA in the 1960s and the 'Duke of York' strategy used in the UK after 1974. 'Operation twist' was an attempt to reduce long-term interest rates (to stimulate investment) while increasing short-term ones (to stimulate capital inflows to support the exchange rate). Much of the revival of interest in the term structure in the 1960s arose from this episode. The 'Duke of York' strategy is an ingenious method of persuading investors to buy government bonds, and so reduce the money supply (for a detailed explanation of its mechanics, see Gowland, 1982, p.148). As the name implies, the authorities seek first to increase and then reduce interest rates to render their debt more attractive. A crucial feature of this involves an increase in long-term interest rates relative to short-term ones. Most government debt is long term, whereas most of the alternatives are short term, so that if long-term assets are more attractive, funds are switched to government bonds.

10.2 Expectations theory

The earliest and most basic of the theories of the term structure of interest rates is the expectations theory, which is usually associated with Hicks (1946), and Lutz (1940). For simplicity of exposition the relationship between the one-year interest rate and the two-year interest rate will be analysed, but all the results can be generalised in a straightforward manner. The one-year interest rate in 1991 will be written as $R_1(1991)$, the two-year rate as $R_2(1991)$, and so on. It also simplifies the expectations theory to start by assuming a world of perfect certainty; this highlights certain key features of the model which also apply in more realistic situations.

In a world of perfect certainty, a two-year bond is a perfect substitute for two one-year bonds. This follows from the investment opportunities open to investors. An investor can hold a two-year bond (1991–3) or he or she can hold a one-year bond from 1991 until it matures in 1992 and reinvest the proceeds in a second one-year bond from 1992 to 1993. This investor knows what the one-year rate will be in a year's time because it is a world of perfect certainty. Hence, he or she will regard these alternatives as perfect substitutes. Thus, this investor will never hold two-year bonds unless the return from them is at least equal to that from the two one-year bonds. He or she will receive R_1 (1991) + R_1 (1992) on the two one-year bonds and R_2 (1991) twice on the two-year bond. So, two-year bonds will only be held if:

$$2R_2 \ (1991) \geq R_1 \ (1991) + R_1 \ (1992) \tag{1}$$

or, more conveniently, if:

$$R_2 \ (1991) \geq \frac{R_1 \ (1991)}{2} + \frac{R_2 \ (1992)}{2} \tag{2}$$

Strictly, this formula is only an approximation since if the income in the first year is greater from the one-year bond, this can also be invested in a one-year bond for the second year (or vice versa). For example, a 12 per cent bond 1991–2 and an 8 per cent bond 1992–3 offer a fractionally higher return (by 0.16 per cent) than a 10 per cent two-year bond 1991–3, because the extra 2 per cent received in 1992 can be invested at 8 per cent from 1992 to 1993 and is therefore worth more than the extra 2 per cent due to be received in 1993 on the two-year bond.[1] The exact formula is that the two-year rate is the geometric average of the two one-year rates, rather than an arithmetic one. However, the arithmetic average is usually used in textbooks for simplicity. Unless condition (2) holds investors will always choose to hold one-year bonds and never two-year bonds so (2) is a necessary condition for the existence of two-year bonds in this model.

Similarly, an investor has a choice between a one-year bond, on which he or she will receive R_1, and holding a two-year bond for one year and selling it. In 1992 the two-year bond (1991–3) has only one year left to maturity, so it has become a one-year bond. Thus, it will be sold at a price on which its yield is R_1 (1992). Thus, the yield from this investment is $2R_2$ (1991) − R_1 (1992), that is, what would be received if the two-year bond were held for two years less the return that the second purchaser will get in 1992–3. Thus, the condition for the existence of a one-year bond in 1992 is:

$$R_1 \ (1991) \geq 2R_2 \ (1991) - R_1 \ (1992) \tag{3}$$

If this is not fulfilled, all one-year investors will choose to hold two-year bonds and sell them after one year. Condition (3) can be rearranged as follows:

$$R_1 \ (1991) + R_1 \ (1992) \geq 2R_2 \ (1992) \tag{4}$$

that is:

$$\frac{R_1 \ (1991)}{2} + \frac{R_2 \ (1992)}{2} \geq R_2 \ (1992) \tag{5}$$

As both the inequalities (2) and (5) must hold, then the inequality must be replaced by an equality sign (for the non-mathematically minded, if A must be at least as big as B, and B at least as big as A, then necessarily A and B are the same size). Thus, the basic equation of the Hicksian model is derived, that the two-year interest rate is an average of the one-year rate in 1991 and in 1992:

$$R_2 \ (1991) = \frac{R_1 \ (1991)}{2} + \frac{R_1 \ (1992)}{2} \tag{6}$$

This type of relationship is central to Hicks' theory. The one- and two-year interest rates are interdependent because one type of bond will be substituted for the other according to the level of *future* short-term interest rates and arbitrage between two- and one-year bonds will take place unless the returns from the investment policies outlined are identical; that is, unless (6) holds. When the present and future short rates are equal, the present long-term rate must equal the present short-term rate. For example, if the one-year rate in 1991 is 10 per cent and the one-year rate in 1992 will be 10 per cent, the two-year rate in 1991 must be 10 per cent because the average of 10 and 10 is 10. When R_1 (1991) is equal to R_1 (1992) the resultant yield curve is known as the normal slope. In a world of perfect certainty this is horizontal (Fig. 10.2a).

When future short-term interest rates exceed present ones, the (present) long rate must exceed the present short-term one. For example, if R_1 (1992) is 15 per cent and R_1 (1991) is 7 per cent, R_2 is 11 per cent, which is of course greater than 7 per cent. Thus, when future short-term interest rates exceed present ones, the yield curve is upward sloping, as in Figure 10.2(b). This relationship applies in reverse. When long rates exceed short-term interest rates, then necessarily the future short-term interest rate exceeds the present one. Hence, forecasts of changes in interest rates can be derived from the yield curve: an upward-sloping curve implies that rates will rise. Conversely, if the present short rate is greater than the future short rate, it will also exceed the present long rate. Moreover, if the short rate exceeds the long rate, interest rates must fall. To take two examples: if the one-year rate is 8 per cent and the two-year rate is 10 per cent, the one-year rate in one year's time must be 12 per cent if (6) is to be satisfied. Similarly, if one-year rates are 10 per cent and two-year rates 9 per cent, the one-year rate will have fallen to 8 per cent in a year's time. The yield curve necessarily incorporates a prediction of future movements in interest rates. This idea is crucial to the expectations model even when it is amended to allow for uncertainty; it is, of course, rather empty to derive predictions in a world of certainty.

The expectations theory has two key elements even in a world of uncertainty:

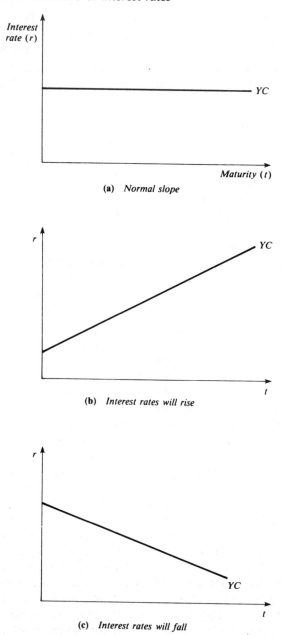

Figure 10.2 The term structure in a world of certainty

1. The relationship between one- and two-year rates depends on future one-year rates, which determine substitution between the two bonds.
2. It is possible to derive forecasts of interest rate changes from observation of one- and two-year rates or from the yield curve generally.

The basic amendment to the theory in a world of uncertainty is to substitute the expected future short rate for the known value of it in equation (6). Hence the name of the theory. If this is done, the basic equation becomes:

$$R_2 = \frac{R_1\ (1991)}{2} + \frac{E(R_1\ (1992))}{2} \tag{7}$$

This relationship is called the *pure expectations* theory, associated with Lutz.

The pure expectations theory assumes risk neutrality, and it may be more plausible to assume risk aversion. In this case the basic equation is modified to incorporate a risk premium (l) and becomes

$$R_2\ (1991) = \frac{R_1\ (1991)}{2} + \frac{E(R_2\ (1992))}{2} + l \tag{8}$$

l can be either negative or positive because there are two types of risk involved in holding bonds. One is capital risk, often known as liquidity preference. The capital value of a series of one-year bonds will fluctuate less than longer-term bonds (see p.120) and is known with certainty for each date of maturity. If interest rates are higher than expected in one year's time, in 1992 the value of the two-year bond will be less than the £100 received by the holder of the one-year bond due to mature then. Thus, if the investor holding a two-year bond has to sell it after a year because of some unforeseen contingency, he or she will be worse off than if he or she had invested in a one-year bond (with the intention of reinvesting if the contingency did not arise). By definition, for a risk-averse investor this risk more than offsets the chance of gain if rates are lower than expected in one year's time when the contingency occurs. A capital risk-averse investor will accordingly prefer to hold short-term bonds. If all investors are capital risk averse, l will be positive and there will be a liquidity premium because long rates will exceed short ones when no change is expected in (short-term) interest rates. Hicks expected that capital risk aversion would be the norm.

However, there is another sort of risk aversion: income risk aversion. The holder of a two-year bond knows what his or her income will be in each year of the life of the bond. The holder of two successive one-year bonds does not. His or her income in the second year will depend upon the level of (one-year) interest rates in a year's time. Therefore, if the objective is to guarantee (money) income, a long-term bond is preferable to a succession of short-term ones. An institution with known liabilities for a long period – such as a pension fund – should be in this position and has every reason to be income risk averse. The income risk averter will thus prefer longer-dated bonds. If all investors were income risk averse, l would be negative and short rates would exceed long ones when no change in interest rates was expected. If investors were risk loving, these risk premiums would be reversed, so that an income risk-loving investor preferred short-term bonds and a capital risk lover (a gambler) long-term ones.

When risk aversion is present, the normal slope of the yield curve is no longer horizontal. When capital risk aversion predominates and l is positive, it is upward sloping, since R_2 (1991) exceeds R_1 (1991) when R_1 (1991) is equal to R_1 (1992) (Fig. 10.3a). Normal slopes can be derived from more complex assumptions. For example, Bank of England researchers (Good-hart, 1975) have on occasion hypothesised that income risk averters dominate in long-dated bonds and capital risk averters in short-term ones in such a way that the yield curve initially slopes upwards and then turns down, with the two halves joined between four and eight years to maturity (sometimes called the 'walking stick' hypothesis, from the consequent shape of the normal yield curve; Fig. 10.3c).

It is still possible to derive forecasts of interest rate changes from any pair of (present) interest rates of different maturity, but the procedure is more complex than when rates are known with certainty or if the pure expectations hypothesis is valid. It is no longer the case that rates are expected to rise if long rates exceed short rates but they are expected to rise if long rates exceed short ones by more than the normal amount. This is most clearly seen using the yield curve. If the slope of the actual yield curve

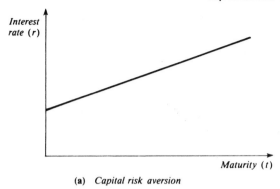

(a) *Capital risk aversion*

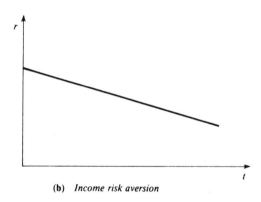

(b) *Income risk aversion*

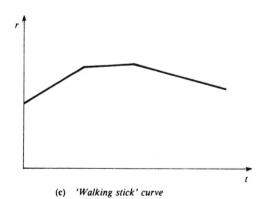

(c) *'Walking stick' curve*

Figure 10.3 Normal slopes in a world of uncertainty

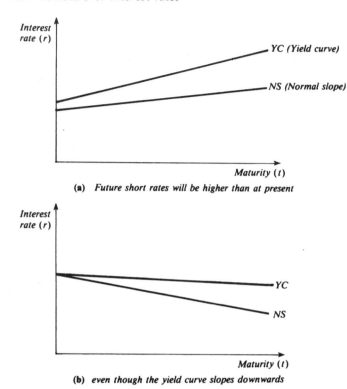

(a) *Future short rates will be higher than at present*

(b) *even though the yield curve slopes downwards*

Figure 10.4 Expectations of a rise in interest rates

exceeds the normal slope, interest rates are expected to rise (Fig. 10.4a). This can also occur if the yield curve is downward sloping but by less than the normal amount (Fig. 10.4b). Similarly, if the observed yield curve slopes downwards by more than the normal slope, or, by extension, upwards by less than the normal slope, interest rates are expected to fall (Fig. 10.5). Finally, it is important to be aware that while the theory has been presented in terms of utility-maximising lenders, it could have been presented in terms of utility-maximising borrowers. For example, the certainty analysis could have started with a borrower who could borrow for two successive periods of one year or for two years and sought to minimise his or her interest payment. Deviations from (5) could also be exploited by borrowing for two

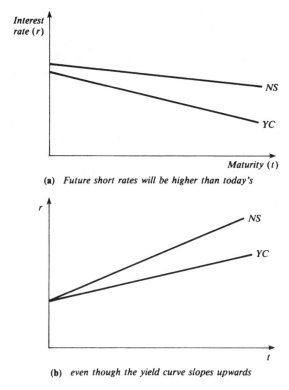

(a) *Future short rates will be higher than today's*

(b) *even though the yield curve slopes upwards*

Figure 10.5 Interest rates expected to fall

years and using the funds to hold two successive one-year bonds (or vice versa). There is not, however, perfect symmetry. Notably 'credit availability' has no equivalent for a lender.

It is important to consider the above point in some detail and its implications. If a lender wishes to invest for a period of ten years, he or she might well be tempted to invest in two successive five-year bonds if the expected return is greater. Suppose that this expectation turns out to be wrong, then the investor merely receives a smaller income. Even if no attractive investment is available for the second five-year period, then the investor can hold a bank deposit. Hence, it is not unreasonable to assume that investors regard long and short bonds as substitutes for each other. However, they may not be perfect substitutes (as in the expectations theory). The preferred habitat model (section 11.4) deals with the case of imperfect substitutes. In these models the investor trades off a higher expected return from one strategy with less risk from another. The risk facing a borrower is fundamentally different. Suppose that a married couple, Mr and Mrs Smith, wish to borrow for a period of 20 years to buy a house. A 20-year mortgage is obviously attractive. Suppose that their belief is that it will be cheaper to borrow for 10 years and then to re-borrow for a second period of 10 years. It is now necessary to examine the consequences if their belief is wrong. Suppose that they cannot find a second lender, after 10 years. In this case, they face the risk of being homeless. It is unlikely that a small reduction in the expected cost of the loan will compensate for this risk. This is the credit availability point developed above. Obviously this risk is greater for some types of borrowers than others. However, this merely underlines the proposition that borrowers are different and that it is necessary to look at the specific character of borrowers. The argument is that these, the supply-side factors, will influence the term structure. The simplest model in which this is true is the market segmentation theory.

10.3 Market segmentation

A polar extreme to the expectations theory is the market-segmentation theory associated with Culbertson (1957, 1972), Ben Friedman and Cuthbertson. Whereas the expectations theory is a theory of substitution between bonds of different maturities, the market segmentation assumes that substitution of this sort never occurs. Some investors, such as banks, prefer short-term assets for structural reasons, possibly even legal reasons. Prior to 1987 UK building societies could not hold bonds with more than five years to mature. Other investors prefer long-term ones; insurance companies and pension funds are often cited. Similar institutional constraints also divide borrowers into those who wish or are forced to borrow for short periods and those who borrow long. Thus there are distinct short- and long-term markets. There is no relationship between these markets in long- and short-term assets; the two are segmented, hence the name. Supply-and-demand factors will determine the equilibrium rate in each market independently, and the yield curve can no more be 'explained' than any other sequence of unrelated events, such as a particular pattern of numbers which emerges at the roulette table.

10.4 Preferred habitat

The expectations and market-segmentation theories were incorporated as polar extremes into the preferred habitat theory developed by Modigliani (Modigliani and Sutch, 1966), which is therefore a much more general theory than either of its predecessors. The market-segmentation theory assumes no substitution between long- and short-term bonds. Expectations theory assumes perfect substitution since, even in a world of uncertainty, arbitrage will occur to maintain the fixed differential (l) between the actual value of the long-term rate and that derived from the pure expectations theory. A potentially infinite volume of arbitrage funds is available to maintain this fixed differential; that is, to exploit the opportunity for profit available whenever equation (7) is not fulfilled.

Modigliani argued that substitution would occur but that the elasticity need not be infinite nor in consequence need the risk premium be constant. His theory incorporated the institutional and structural factors rightly stressed by the market-segmentation theory but denied that these meant that no substitution would take place. Both those who borrowed and those who lent had strong preferences for assets or liabilities of a specific date. Nevertheless, they could be tempted away from this maturity, their 'preferred habitat', by an interest rate incentive. A bank might wish to hold a one-year bond but could be persuaded to hold a two-year one instead if the margin offered by the two-year bond were substantial enough. The bank would compare the two-year rate with that implied by the one-year rate and its expectation of the one-year rate in a year's time. According to the expectations theory, it would buy the bond if the margin exceeded a critical level l; according to the market-segmentation theory, it would never buy it. Modigliani argued that whether it would purchase it or not depends upon the margin, the degree of certainty about its expectations and other relevant considerations. Moreover, the decision need not be an all-or-nothing one; the bank might shift part of its portfolio if the margin were 0.25 per cent, more if it were 0.5 per cent, and so on, but would never be prepared to move completely into longer bonds. Preferred-habitat models are very similar in spirit to the neo-Keynesian version of Tobin's model (see pp.121ff) and the imperfect substitutability of preferred habitat would justify the neo-Keynesian transmission mechanism postulated by Tobin (so long as either long-dated financial assets are substitutes for real ones or spending on real goods is interest sensitive). Because preferred habitat incorporates arbitrage, even though on a limited scale, the forecasting procedure developed from the expectations theory still holds. If the yield curve slopes upwards more steeply than the normal slope, rates are expected to rise, and so on. There are problems with preferred habitat. It assumes that supply factors need no separate analysis, see Goodhart (1989a, p.250). Borrowers and lenders are treated as identical agents without any special treatment of credit availability. Nevertheless, it is the incorporation of implicit forecasts of movements in interest rates which has cast doubt upon the theory. When tested as a theory, the model performed very well. (See Goodhart, 1989a, pp.251–3 for a comprehensive survey of the literature.) However, the implicit predictors of future interest rates could be tested and performed uniformly badly. (Hamburger and Platt were the first of a number of economists to do this; this literature is summarised by Goodhart, 1989a.) Moreover, the theory had to be reconciled with the rational and efficient markets hypothesis and with its empirical counterpart, the random walk (Goodhart and Gowland, 1977, 1978), which were also upheld by the data. Most of the evidence seems to sustain the rational critique of the preferred habitat (Pippenger and Phillips, 1977; Carleton and Cooper, 1976), so it is necessary to examine this critique.

This is an extension of the efficient-market analysis developed earlier in this book in the context of the speculative demand for money (see p.64). It was shown that if the bond market were in equilibrium, it would necessarily be the case that the expected changes in bond prices would equal zero. Similarly, if the preferred-habitat (or expectations) model were valid, then market agents could use its predictions to make money. For example, if interest rates were predicted to fall, market agents would want to sell bonds. Thus there would be an excess supply of bonds at present prices, so bond prices could not be at their present price. Indeed, they would be lower such that no further fall in their price was expected. Thus, the impeccable logic of Modigliani has been challenged by the devastating and equally coherent idea of rational markets. So far, no solution has emerged but the likeliest solution seems to be that both views are right. A limited range of the infinite number of preferred-habitat models generate only predictions that do not engender profit-making chances. For example, in some cases any potential profits (by selling bonds) are offset by a fall in income (by holding lower-yielding short-term bonds instead of higher-yielding long-term ones). In other cases, the potential profit is less than the transaction costs necessary to obtain it. Perhaps term-structure modelling will ultimately rely upon this restricted version of the preferred-habitat model. Goodhart's pessimistic conclusion seems valid:

> This research leaves the expectations theory with relatively little role in the determination of long-term rates. We seem to know less than we had believed we knew in the early 1970s. (Goodhart, 1989a, p.257)

Other research is more positive in its implications, notably the attempts to build a richer, more realistic model of the financial sector and incorporate it into macroeconomic models (Blanchard and Fischer, 1989, pp.532–6).

10.5 Summary and conclusions

Term-structure models seek to explain the relationships between short- and long-term interest rates. The expectations model argues that these are determined by the expected future level of interest rates. This approach incorporates the assumption that borrowing is simply negative lending. It is not because of problems of credit availability. Market segmentation suggests that they are determined by institutional forces. Both theories are special cases of preferred habitat. This model seems, however, to suggest that the bond market is not an efficient one. Whilst the models are formally consistent – preferred habitat assumes risk aversion, efficient-markets theory assumes risks neutrality – this dilemma is so far unresolved.

Notes

1. Even in the case of a two-year bond it is, of course, the one-year rate in year two which is earned on any interest reinvested (a point missed by one reader of the typescript).

11

Banking Sector and Supply of Money

11.1 Supply of money

Both monetarist theory and the policy prescriptions derived from it rest upon two presumptions about the money supply:

1. It is controllable by the authorities.
2. It is not determined by income.

These hypotheses are theories about the nature of the supply of money (see p.137). Indeed Friedman (1969) in defining the distinctive features of monetarism, chose to state these propositions as a theory of the supply of money; namely that there is at least one factor which influences the supply curve for money but does not influence the demand curve. The argument about this issue can be presented in many ways. For example, a beguilingly simple Keynesian view in the 1950s was that the money supply was totally demand determined; others have revived it in the debate anent Thatcherism (for example, Kaldor, 1982). This argument was that income (and possible interest rates) were determined by a number of variables, such as government spending, but crucially, money was not one of these variables. Income and interest rates determine the demand for money. The authorities then adjusted the money supply so that it was equal to the amount demanded. This account may or may not have been true. More important, it left unclear whether or not the authorities were forced to adjust the supply of money or merely chose to do so. Arguing that they are forced to adjust it is a hard-core Keynesian view (especially in post-Keynesian thought), whereas claiming that they merely choose to is consistent with most forms of monetarism. Indeed, it is a crucial point that monetarists do not need to argue that the money supply has been controlled by the authorities, merely that it could (and should) be. Friedman has criticised the US monetary authorities for over thirty years for failing to control the money supply.[1] Indeed, his criticisms have often taken the form of arguments that they have mistakenly adjusted the money supply to income and so increased the long-term rate of both unemployment and inflation. Thus, Friedman and other monetarists accept that the money supply may have been indirectly determined by income through the (mistaken) reactions of policy makers to observed changes in inflation and unemployment. Their thesis is that the supply of money could be, and should have been, controlled by the authorities. Hence, as always, in economics the debate about the nature of the supply of money can only be considered within an appropriate formal framework. In general, debates about the supply of money are best considered within the flow-of-funds framework; that is, using the money-creation equation:

Δ Money supply = *PSBR*

+ Δ Bank loans to the non-bank private sector (*BLP*)

− Δ Non-bank private sector loans to the public sector (*PLG*)

+ Overseas impact on the money supply

The framework is neutral. The debate is about what determines the four supply-side counterparts and what the interrelationship amongst them is. A hard-line Keynesian could easily find a reason why each is solely determined by income. *PLG*, for example, must depend at least in part upon the level of saving and so of income, so it is not totally ludicrous to argue that it depends only upon income. Post-Keynesian analysis in particular lays stress on the view that *BLP* (credit) determines *M* only. Credit in turn depends upon income. These views seem special cases of the orthodox position. The orthodox analysis is that the money supply is determined by the interaction of official action and private sector behaviour. The authorities set the level of government expenditure and tax rates. These, together with income, determine the *PSBR*. The authorities also fix interest rates. The non-bank private sector then determines the level of its borrowing from banks and its lending to the public sector given these interest rates. In effect, the authorities are faced with demand curves for credit and government bonds determined by the non-bank private sector. These curves, in turn, may in part depend upon income. The authorities can then determine the quantities of *BLP* and *PLG* so long as they do not care about the level of interest rates. It seems to me that the difference between the post-Keynesian Arestis (1988) and the orthodox Goodhart (1984, 1989a) is that Goodhart assumes interest rates are potentially exogenous. Post-Keynesians also assume a greater, even infinite elasticity – Moore's (1988) horizontalism. Similar considerations apply to the overseas impact on the money supply, where the private sector makes decisions given the exchange rate and interest rates; various theories offer different views about the determinants of the exchange rate (Gowland, 1984), but do not affect the validity of this description. The model implies that the supply of money is partially but not totally dependent upon income, and thus the authorities can control it by suitable manipulation of interest rates, government spending, tax rates and the like (see pp.253ff).

There are two criticisms that can and have been made of this model. One is that it would be desirable to render the authorities endogenous rather than to treat official policy actions as exogenous. This is usually done by use of reaction functions, which seek to make government policy a predictable reaction to external stimuli such as inflation or unemployment.[2] This approach has defects. One is that a reaction function can be relevant only to a particular place and time – a Republican administration in the USA (let alone a Republican-appointed chairman of the Federal Reserve) is unlikely to respond to a change in the inflation rate in the same way as a socialist President of France. Moreover, it is not clear what the gain from a reaction function is. Monetary theory seeks to elucidate the consequences of alternative policies and to suggest which are the better targets and instruments. For this purpose it is better to treat official reactions as exogenous. The other criticism of the model is that it says nothing about banks. They are either ignored or treated as passive. Instead, it is suggested, the supply function should include an explicit model of banking. This seems a reasonable argument, so alternative models of banking are considered in the rest of this chapter. Finally, some macro-economic models which incorporate an endogenous supply of money are presented.

11.2 Banking models: an introduction

It is conventional in textbooks to illustrate the nature of banking models and their objectives by reference to stylised descriptions of early banks. From one point of view this is absurd since there is very little in common between the Midland Bank and a seventeenth-century goldsmith. On the other hand, it does demonstrate the generality of the models and can be used to emphasise the chief characteristics of the two rival schools of analysis: the multiplier and the 'new view'.

Modern banking emerged from the Italian financiers of the late twelfth century, of whom the Bardi are the best known. They came from the Lombard and Tuscan cities of northern Italy, especially Siena and Florence, and have given their name to Lombard Street, near the Bank of England and where the Institute of Bankers is located, and the Rue des Lombards in Paris, the centre of French finance until the time of Napoleon. These entrepreneurs operated an extensive money-transmission mechanism, designed to serve the Pope (who received taxes in all countries, but wished to spend them in Rome), various kings (fighting wars abroad) and the merchants who traded at the great fairs of Champagne, where merchants from northern and southern Europe met to trade goods. The Italian firms operated by receiving cash (usually gold and silver) in one centre and giving a receipt that could be encashed at another one of their branches; formal branches seem to have been established about 1290. Hence, a London merchant could hand over gold in London to the Bardi, obtain a receipt, travel to Champagne and buy silk from an Italian merchant. The London merchant would pay with the receipt which the Italian could cash in Siena. Thus, neither merchant had to transport cash. Moreover, the Bardi also dealt with the very complex foreign exchange problems that emerged. Some of these transactions would offset each other, but the Bardi would have to ship enough gold to meet any net claims. If, for example, English merchants had bought more than they sold in Champagne, it would be necessary to ship bullion from London to Italy. The Bardi, of course, made a profit by charging a commission for their services. The Italian financiers also started to lend funds, originally by extending credit to customers who bought goods from them; the Bardi and others were also traders. At some point they found it convenient to make loans by issuing the certificates that entitled the holder to receive bullion from one of their branches. For example, if the King of England wished to send an ambassador to the Pope in Rome, he could finance the trip by a loan from the Bardi. He would do this by obtaining a certificate entitling his emissary to draw gold in Italy. The Italian financiers quickly realised that they could issue more certificates than they had bullion; indeed it is unlikely that their Paris agent had much idea how much cash was held in Siena, or vice versa. Hence, modern banking emerged. By issuing certificates to a borrower, the Italian bankers were creating money. They chose to lend and in doing so created liabilities on themselves which were money. In the eighteenth century English banks performed the same operation by printing notes so that they could lend them. Modern banks do the same, but the creation is concealed behind entries in ledgers and on computer discs.

Banking economists have sought to answer two questions about this process. The first is why it emerged (and continued). The second is what determines the amount of credit a bank extends (that is, the quantity of money it creates). The first can be answered easily. The Bardi and their confrères made loans because it was profitable (or in many cases because powerful monarchs coerced them). This is still true for banks, although residual finance (see p.15) is a smoother method of borrowing than some of Philip the Fair's methods.[3] The second is a much more complex and crucial question. Indeed, the question can be posed as the converse of the first problem – why is money not created? It might seem that if banks can create money, the natural result would be creation on an infinite scale. The models of banking seek to analyse the constraints over money creation and so explain the quantity created. Basically, there are two answers: the multiplier and the 'new view'. Both of these can, however, be viewed as special cases of the portfolio model of banking.

The Italian banks, according to the multiplier approach, were constrained by the need to redeem the certificates they had issued. The bank had to exchange certificates for gold (more or less) on demand. Thus, a reserve had to be held to meet these claims. Prudence and experience revealed what was the best ratio; that is, what proportion of deposits it was sufficient to hold as reserves to meet likely claims. This might be, for example, 40 per cent. Critically, for multiplier analysis, the ratio was constant. In this case the main determinant of loans extended was gold inflows and outflows. When the reserves were depleted by the encashment of certificates, the bank would cease to make loans until more cash was deposited. If extra deposits were received, the bank could and would choose to extend more loans, issue more certificates (in fact equal to over twice the inflow) without the ratio falling below the critical level. The 'new view' would regard this as an overmechanistic and simplistic model. Banks would have to hold reserves but not as a fixed proportion of deposits. The quantity of loans would depend upon the number of customers wanting to borrow, what security they offered, and so on. Banks, in short, were profit-maximising firms. They should therefore be analysed using the normal marginal tools of microeconomic analysis.

11.3 Multiplier approach

Any model of banking must perform two closely related functions. It has to explain the limits to the creation of money by banks and the nature of the supply schedule of bank loans, that is, of credit. The 'old view' of money does this by emphasising that a bank must hold reserve assets to meet any repayments. The proponents of this model usually start by imagining a bank receiving a deposit in cash, say £1,000. It must decide how much it needs to hold in case the depositor wishes to draw part of his or her money out. It is an essential feature of the multiplier model that this is a predictable amount and, more or less, common to all banks. To illustrate the example it will be assumed that this is 20 per cent. Thus, the bank holds £200 of its deposit as a reserve. It can lend a borrower £800 and either directly loan him or her the cash or have it ready to pay out when he or she spends a loan created in the form of a bank deposit. Either way a claim of £800 on the bank is created and is satisfied by the cash. The money supply is now £1,800, the £1,000 deposit together with the £800 cash instead of £1,000 cash before the deposit was made. However, the story continues by assuming that the £800 is redeposited in either the original or another bank. This is certainly possible, for example if the borrower spends the money on a hi-fi system the shopkeeper is very likely to pay these takings into his or her bank account. The £800 cash receipt by the bank leads to the same reaction as before: it loans 80 per cent (£640) and retains 20 per cent (£160). Hence bank deposits are £1,800, reserves £360 and loans £1,440 – the balance sheet constraint is not violated. As £640 cash is also held by the private sector the money supply at this point is £2,440. This process continues, the third-round loan being 80 per cent of £640 (that is, £512) and so on. Ultimately, the banking sector as a whole holds the entire £1,000 as a reserve against deposits of £5,000, having made £4,000 of loans (the sum to infinity of the geometric series £800 + £640 + £512 + £409.60 + ...). This series of transactions is set out in Table 11.1.

Table 11.1 The credit multiplier

		BANK LIABILITIES		ASSETS		Reserve
		Deposits (£s)	Δ Loans (£s)	Loans (£s)	Reserves (£s)	ratio (%)
	initial deposit	1,000	0	0	1,000	100
Round	(1)	*Bank lends excess reserves (£800); after redeposit:*				
		1,800	800	800	1,000	44
"	(2)	*Bank lends excess reserves (£640); after redeposit:*				
		2,440	640	1,440	1,000	41
"	(3)	2,952	512	1,952	1,000	34
"	(4)	3,362	410	2,362	1,000	30
"	(5)	3,690	328	2,690	1,000	27
"	(6)	3,952	262	2,952	1,000	25
"	(7)	4,162	210	3,162	1,000	24
"	(8)	4,330	168	3,330	1,000	23
Final position		5,000	0	4,000	1,000	20

In this world, the quantity of both bank loans and deposits is directly determined by the quantity of reserve assets, in this case cash. *Crucially, causality runs from reserves to loans.* The size of the change in deposits is equal to the injection of cash times the reciprocal of the reserve ratio (in this case 5, the reciprocal of 0.2, 20 per cent or symbolically $1/z$, where z is the ratio). The change in bank loans is equal to the change in deposits less the change in reserve assets; that is, $(1/z)$ times the injection of cash. These relationships lead to the model being called the multiplier model. The ratio of credit to reserve injection is usually called the credit multiplier. This quantity is invariant with respect to the interest charged on bank loans, so it is a perfectly inelastic supply curve. Banks' desired loans depend upon their holdings of reserves. In this case the demand for credit function will determine the equilibrium interest rate (r_E), as in Figure 11.1. The quantity of credit is determined by the availability of reserve assets. In summary:

1. The restriction on bank creation of money comes from the need to hold reserves. It is worth re-emphasising that bank

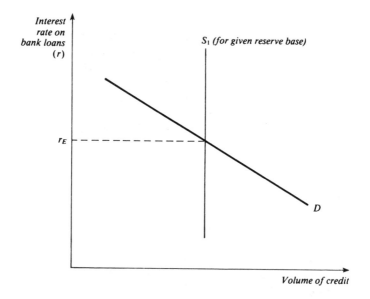

Figure 11.1 The simple ratio model

loans create money; this model seeks to explain the constraint on money creation by arguing that banks will lend only when they have sufficient reserves.

2. The supply of credit is inelastic.
3. Causality runs from reserves to loans.

These features remain when one of the simple features of the model is relaxed. This is the possibility of a cash leak; that is, the private sector does not redeposit all of the amount loaned out but instead chooses to hold some of it as cash. It is usual in the multiplier model to assume that the private sector holds a fixed ratio of cash to deposits. In this case the size of the credit multiplier depends upon the two ratios – cash–deposits ratio and bank–reserve ratio. Hence, this model is usually called the *ratios model*. The consequent modifications to the previous story are simple. For simplicity it will be assumed that the private sector chooses to hold 50 per cent of its money holdings as cash (or in general the fraction e), and 50 per cent as bank deposits, or in general $(1 - e)$. In this case a cash injection of £1,000 into the system as a whole will mean an injection of only £500 into the banks, since £500 will be held by the private sector. Of this the bank will retain £100 as a reserve and loan out £400 (Table 11.2). The private sector does not want to hold £400 of extra bank deposits, instead it wants to hold £200 of deposits and £200 of cash. For example, if the borrower buys a hi-fi system for £400,

Table 11.2   Cash leak

	PRIVATE SECTOR				BANK ASSETS				
Cash (£s)	Bank deposits (£s)	Cash ratio (%)	Debts to Bank	Net worth (£s)	Bank liabilities (Deposits) (£s)	Loans (£s)	Reserves (£s)	Reserve ratio (%)	Money (£s)
1,000		100		1,000					1,000
Private sector holds too much cash									
500	500	50		1,000	500		500	100	1,000
Bank reserves too high									
100	500	64	400	1,000		400	100	20	1,400
Private sector holds too much cash									
700	700	50	400	1,000	700	400	300	43	1,400
860	700	55	560	1,000	700	560	140	20	1,560
780	780	50	560	1,000	780	560	220	28	1,560
833	833	50	666	1,000	833	666	167	20	1,666

the shopkeeper will only pay £200 into the bank and retain £200 to pay staff salaries. Hence, at this stage the private sector holds £700 of bank deposits. The bank holds £300 of cash and £400 of loans as assets against liabilities of £700. Thus, balance sheets balance and the private sector is in equilibrium, but the banks hold excess reserves; their reserves are 3/7 instead of 1/5. As they hold excess reserves, they will lend more; in fact 80 per cent of the second-round injection of £200 they have received – £160. In the simplistic model each round of lending could be calculated by multiplying the previous round by $(1 - z)$; that is, one minus the reserve ratio. Now it is necessary to allow for cash leaks by multiplying it by $(1 - e)$ as well. Thus, the new round is the previous round times $(1 - z)(1 - e)$; in this example $(1 - 0.2)(1 - 0.5) = 0.4$. This can be verified in the example where the new round of lending £160 is 0.4 of the previous one (£400). £160 leads to a subsequent round of loans of £64 (the full details are set out in Table 11.2). The final outcome is that the private sector holds £883 of cash and £883 of deposits. The banks hold £167 of cash and have made loans of £666. Thus, balance sheets balance and both sectors are in equilibrium (that is, they have maintained the ratios). This is the standard model of the multiplier system in which the supply of credit is determined by reserve assets because the constraint on bank credit creation is the need to hold reserves. It has been widely used, especially by monetarist authors, such as Cagan (1965) and Friedman and Schwartz (1963). It is useful to set the ratios model out algebraically using the general values of e for the cash–deposits ratio and z for the reserve ratio. In the general form of the model, cash is not necessarily the reserve asset. In this case:

$$M \equiv D + C_p \tag{1}$$

where M is money, D deposits and C_p private sector holdings of currency. The equation

$$C_p = eM \tag{2}$$

represents the private sector's choice to hold a fixed cash–deposit ratio:

$$R = ZD$$

so:

$$D = \frac{R}{Z} \tag{3}$$

Banks always hold reserves equal to the reserve ratio (Z) times their deposits. If (2) and (3) are substituted into (1), then:

$$M = eM + \frac{R}{Z}$$

so:

$$M - eM = \frac{R}{Z}$$

$$M(1 - e) = \frac{R}{Z}$$

so:

$$M = \frac{R}{Z(1 - e)} \tag{4}$$

This is the basic equation of the ratios model.

An interesting and much-utilised special case can be derived if cash is the only reserve asset. In this case R is equal to bank holdings of cash, which necessarily equal total cash into the system (C) less private holdings of cash (C_p). Hence, ($C - C_p$) can be substituted for R:

$$M = \frac{(C - C_p)}{Z(1 - e)}$$

However as $C_p = eM$:

$$M = \frac{C - eM}{Z(1 - e)}$$

$$M(Z)(1 - e) = C - eM$$

so:

$$ZM - eZM + eM = C$$

so:

$$M = \frac{C}{Z + e - eZ} \tag{5}$$

This can be checked by recalculating the above example where $C = £1,000$, $Z = 0.2$ and $e = 0.5$. The answer is £1,666 as before.

Cash injections into the system usually follow from government spending. This leads to the distinction between first- and second-round effects of the *PSBR*. Government spending of £1,000 leads to a first-round money creation of £1,000, as set out in (3) above, so long as it is not financed by private lending to the public sector. If this £1,000 is a cash injection into the system, there will be further second-round effects as the increase in cash induces banks to lend more.

The old view is still the one most frequently presented in textbooks, but there are a number of major objections to it. The first is that in the UK at least, banks do not observe fixed ratios nor have they ever done so. In some countries the model can be defended by reference to legally imposed ratios (for example, in Germany, the USA and Australia), but not in the UK. The UK authorities have never attempted to operate a textbook reserve-ratio/reserve-base system of this kind, although there have been superficially similar ratios.[4] Some authors (for example, Coghlan, 1980, 1983) nevertheless believe that a useful, if complex, ratios equation can be developed.

A model can be constructed in which the reserve ratio depends upon the rate of interest. This sort of model is quite realistic for the USA and useful for the UK because it captures an element of portfolio management in the UK. In this model the ratios equation no longer determines the actual supply curve but the maximum that supply can be – S_{MAX} (Fig.11.2). As illustrated, S_{ACT} – the actual supply curve – is upward sloping and asymptotic to S_{MAX}. The rationale is simple. The distance between S_{MAX} and S_{ACT} is equal to the loans that could be but are not made, that is, to excess reserves multiplied by the credit multiplier, $(1 - e)(1 - z)$. This quantity declines as r rises because excess reserves fall. The higher the reserves held the lower the probability that a bank will be unable to repay a deposit on demand. On the other hand, the higher the reserve ratio, the greater the loss by holding (usually non-interest-bearing) reserves, such as cash, instead of interest-bearing assets, such as loans. Hence, a bank will trade the two off and determine

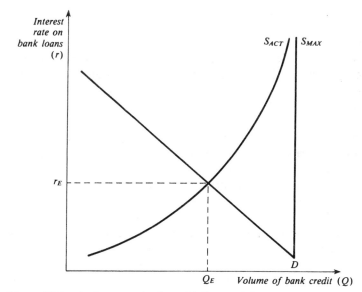

Figure 11.2 An interest-elastic multiplier model

an optimal ratio and lend accordingly. The key point is that as interest rates rise, so the cost of holding reserves rises, so fewer will be held (that is, more will be loaned per unit of reserves). This is reinforced by a further reason for holding reserves, an ability to meet a request for a loan if a customer unexpectedly asks for one. Again, this is useful for a bank but a bank will find it more costly as interest rates rise and so will want less of the facility. In a system where the reserve ratio is legally imposed, the argument is restated in terms of excess reserves (that is, in excess of those required). A bank will hold excess reserves to reduce the danger of falling below the minimum and to accommodate customers but will hold less as interest rates rise. In this model the supply curve is a normal one, so supply and demand interact to determine price and quantity in the credit market – at Q_E and r_E (Fig.11.2).

Another objection to the model is that private sector demand for currency is not a fixed proportion of money holdings but may depend upon the level of interest rates (for example, those paid on bank deposits) or of money holdings or income. It is possible to incorporate this into the model but at a cost of horrendous complexity.[5]

The most sophisticated critique of the multiplier model is that it is misleading because it misstates the direction of causality between loans, reserves and deposits. The model presupposes that available reserves determine loans and so deposits. Instead, it may be that banks calculate desired loans and/or deposits and then obtain the necessary reserves. In this case the only influence of reserves on banks will be through their cost. In other words, the reserve-base/multiplier models assume that banks' holdings of reserve assets are exogenous, whereas they may be endogenous. Models can be constructed to incorporate this but not only the essential simplicity of the basic model but also its predictive usefulness disappear. It is better to incorporate a cost of reserves into the alternative approach, the 'new view'.

This problem lies at the heart of Goodhart's (1975) devastating and mordantly witty critique of the ratios model. He points out that ratio models of the most absurd kind can be created which formally are as valid as the reserve ratio. For example, the level of UK national income (Y) necessarily equals the numbers of sardines eaten in York (S) multiplied by the sardine ratio, so long as this is defined as Y/S:

$$Y = S \times \frac{Y}{S} \tag{6}$$

Historically Y/S is at least as constant as the banks' reserve ratio, so it follows by multiplier analysis that sardine consumption in York determines national income and that inflation and unemployment can be affected by influencing the eating habits of York residents. Formally, this proposition is as valid as the analogous conclusions derived from the ratios model of banking; namely, that reserves determine credit. Of course the difference is that a semi-plausible theory of behaviour (the credit multiplier) justifies analysis using the ratios model. Nevertheless, as Goodhart (1975, p.133) puts it:

> However, in order to use such an approach to explain variations in the larger total as contrasted with describing such movements – which definitional multipliers, however ridiculous, can always do – some further conditions are necessary . . . . [Moreover] If it is necessary to specify the structure of the system in order to understand why the

multiplier works as it does, it is difficult to see what advantage is to be gained by using it as an analytical tool in the first place.

11.4   Profit maximisation: the new view

The second approach to the modelling of banking starts with the concept that the important constraint upon a bank is to persuade enough depositors to hold claims on it so that its liabilities equal its desired assets. In a simple form this has often been practised by UK banks (liability management). These are usually run by those who give priority to lending and then consider where to find the necessary deposits. In the short run this will almost inevitably be the case as the maturity of deposits is so much less than that of loans. Hence, day-to-day management of a bank is very much a question of finding deposits to match assets. Marginal deposits are often obtained on the overnight interbank market.

More generally, however, a very simple model of banking can be constructed from this basic idea so long as an objective function for the bank is added. The simplest and most obvious is profit maximisation. A bank therefore has to calculate its marginal cost and marginal revenue schedules for different levels of output, that is, for different levels of loans. If a bank makes a loan it incurs two sorts of costs. The first are administrative costs, shown as *MAC* in Figure 11.3. These include the cost of processing a loan, of attracting customers, perhaps by advertising, and so on. In addition a bank must induce or obtain a total of deposits equal to its loans (less any own capital). It therefore has to calculate the cost of attracting deposits – interest payments, advertising, free gifts, free or subsidised services such as cheque clearing. All of these are shown in Figure 11.3 as *MIC* and the sum of *MAC* and *MIC* as *MC*. The bank can in principle calculate the demand for its loans. It has, however, to allow for default risk – customers may not pay back. If it is maximising expected profit it calculates revenue by deducting the risk of default from interest payments to calculate the marginal revenue from a loan. This is a reasonable approach for lending to the personal sector since with a large number of loans an actuarial approach is possible. If not, a risk preference has to be assumed,

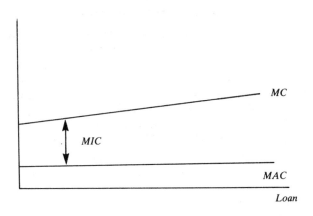

Figure 11.3 The new view: bank cost function

see below. The resulting curves are just like those of any other firm and so profit maximisation occurs where they intersect – Figure 11.4 – so long of course as the firm switches from profit to loss at this point. The returns from loans are usually interest payments and so are some of the costs of deposits. However, the rate of interest receivable on loans is not the same as that paid on loans. An increase of the same size in both may not influence the quantity of deposits supplied, whereas a change in the differential between them will influence the quantity supplied. This is an example of the supply of money depending upon relative, as well as absolute, interest rates (for example, Gowland, 1982). The whole model is summarized in Figure 11.5.

If desired, it is easy to incorporate a reserve-asset mechanism into this model, Figure 11.6. If there is a reserve ratio of 20 per cent, then to lend £100, £125 of deposits must be raised so that £25 can be held as reserves and £100 lent out. In this case the cost

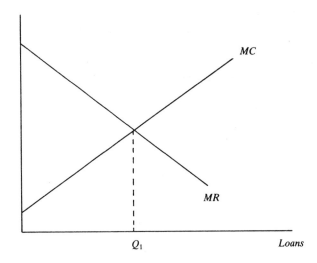

Figure 11.4 Optimal quantity of loans

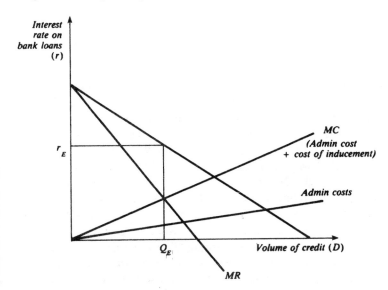

Figure 11.5 The new view

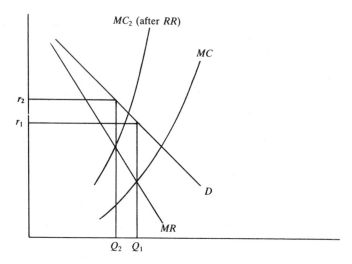

Note: Q_1r_1 – no reserve ratio; Q_2r_2 – after reserve ratio

Figure 11.6 The new view with a reserve ratio

of £100 of loans includes the interest paid on £125 of deposits rather than on £100, as would be the case if no reserve ratio existed. In consequence the *MC* curve moves upwards to reflect the higher inducement costs. A reserve ratio works like a tax and its impact, if any, is through increasing interest rates. In the new view loans create reserves and are in elastic supply to the banks.

If banks are competitive, then it is possible to derive the supply curve for loans (credit), and this will normally be upward sloping. In this case one has arrived at the same analytical model as in the multiplier model but without the need either to treat banks as special or to use such distinctive and dubious apparatus. As Tobin (1963, p.122) puts it, 'thus the new view is a very simple and very flexible approach to the analysis of banks'. For example, it is easy to incorporate different utility functions for the banks, such as sales maximisation or risk aversion. Marginalist tools, always so powerful in economics, render monetary analysis very simple. Indeed the whole of modern banking theory is based upon this approach. It seems reasonable to assume banks are risk averse especially with large loans – although their behaviour in practice often suggests that this plausible assumption is ill-founded. The Third World debt crisis has made this topical and made economists focus upon it – especially Hefferan (see the survey by Ciarrapico, 1991). In general, portfolio models of banking incorporate many assets with different risk-return frontiers. A bank then maximises its utility subject to any constraints, such as minimum legal reserve ratios.

Moreover, the 'new view' has other advantages: the importance of private sector behaviour is emphasised by the need to examine the private sector's demand for loans, which determines the banks' marginal revenue schedule, and the private sector's demand for deposits, which determines the banks' marginal cost curves. It is worth emphasising that Friedman, Brunner and other soi-disant monetarists would regard the 'new view' as being appropriate in analysing an individual bank or even banking as an industry. However, for macroeconomic purposes they believe that the multiplier model is more appropriate to explain money creation by the banking system as a whole. Individual banks can always obtain reserve assets at a price. However, if the total of reserves is fixed, this price will be such as to make the quantity of loans equal to the prediction of the ratios model. 'New view or old view' is an empirical question depending on the supply elasticity of reserves.

11.5 Asset and liability management and the portfolio approach

Practising bankers tend to analyse banking by reference to asset and liability management. In the case of asset management, a bank takes its deposits (liabilities) as predetermined and adjusts its assets to maximise its objective function. It is easy to see that asset management is a necessary condition for a reserve-base system. In this model, banks adjust the size of their assets, loans and reserves according to exogenous shifts in deposits (and reserve inflows). With liability management a bank determines its assets and then obtains the necessary deposits. This necessarily implies the 'new view', although this is not true in reverse because the 'new view' is consistent with either asset or liability management. The consensus of opinion is that liability management is practised in the UK. In fact one assumes that liability management describes a bank in the short run as it seeks to attain the equilibrium level of output predicted by the new view. A bank's loan portfolio is given in the short run, by decentralised decision making and prior commitments. Deposits are raised to match this total. If the outcome is not profit maximising the bank adjusts interest rates until this is achieved. If a bank seeks to manage both assets and liabilities, it is practising portfolio management, which is the most general approach to banking. In fact, both multiplier and profit maximisation can be regarded as special cases of the portfolio approach. The bank has a portfolio of assets. These include cash, any other reserve assets, as well as loans, analysed earlier. However, in most portfolio models the menu of assets is much richer as loans are categorised by type of borrower (for example, public sector, industrial companies, personal sector), degree of risk, liquidity, and so on. The banks' liabilities are constrained to be equal to assets, but again there is usually a richer menu of choice for the bank as different types of deposit may be taken. The bank maximises its utility function by appropriate choice of the size and composition of its assets and liabilities. Profit is likely to appear in the utility function but so may risk aversion, liquidity, the size of assets and, indeed, many other variables.

The reserve-base model is a special case of this model, where the desire to maintain a minimum quantity of reserves is the only relevant consideration, because reserves are exogenous (that is, in inelastic supply and so a binding constraint upon banks). If a bank's objectives are restricted, then the 'new view' emerges. For example, if profit maximisation is the sole objective of banks, this simplifies the asset choice facing a bank such that the basic 'new-view' model is appropriate. Some portfolio model is bound to be correct because it is so general, but to be useful it has to be simplified. The simplification is usually a profit-maximising model of some sort, hence proponents of the 'new view' would argue that their approach is correct and the portfolio approach is merely a slight elaboration of their basic model. It is interesting to note that a plausible special case of the portfolio model generates a multiplier model with a *negative* coefficient; that is, extra reserve assets (or an increase in bank lending to the public sector) lead to a fall in bank lending to the private sector. Jaffee (1975) argues that such a model is highly plausible in the USA. His elegant presentation rests upon an assumption of credit rationing (p.245). The results can also be generated by plausible assumptions about bank objectives; for example:

1. Banks (in managerial–coalition theory, of the firm style) have a target level of assets. Accordingly, extra public sector assets imply fewer private sector ones.
2. Banks' utility functions include size (positive) and risk (negative); that is, their controllers desire to be as large as possible but to take as few risks as possible. Public sector assets are less risky than private sector ones. Extra government spending causing an increase in bank holdings of public sector debt means that (by reducing private sector lending by a proportion of this) banks can be both larger and take fewer risks. Including leisure or profits or both in the utility function complicates this analysis but does not change the result.

Banks' desire to lend to the private sector may very well change when bank lending to the public sector rises or falls. This is a particular form of crowding-out or crowding-in.

11.6 Creditism and credit rationing

Keynesian economists have always placed considerable emphasis on the role of credit as opposed to money, even though there is only one *en passant* reference to credit in the *General Theory* (1936, p.158). Credit is what an individual owes, the extent of his or her indebtedness, whereas money is what an individual owns, his or her stock of perfectly liquid assets. Milton Friedman and monetarists generally argue that the behaviour of economic agents is largely influenced by their stock of assets and by the liquidity of this stock. In the simplest form of monetarism, 'money burns a hole in your pocket'. Keynesians have always denied that money was very important in its own right although it might be indirectly important through its effect on interest rates, exchange rates or credit. Keynesians stressed in the 1950s particularly the role of availability, known in Federal Reserve circles as the *availability* doctrine. The argument was originally *ad hoc*. Casual empiricism suggested that especially in the days before effective financial liberalisation (1950s in the USA, 1980s in the UK) individual and small-company spending plans were frequently frustrated by an inability to borrow. Keynesians at this period therefore often argued that credit restraint could halt economic expansion but not promote it (Hansen, 1953; Radcliffe, 1959). This assumed that credit availability was the only possible money transmission mechanism and that its role was restricted to 'the bank manager says No'. Johnson in a whole series of articles trenchantly attacked this, for example those reprinted in Johnson (1972). In response the Keynesian position was reformulated by Radcliffe (1959). In addition to the classical definition of liquidity in terms of the cost, speed and certainty of converting assets to purchasing power a fourth dimension was added: *collateral value*. Assets were liquid if one could borrow against their security. Keynesian analysis developed further with Clower (1965) and Leijonhufvud (1968). They justified the Keynesian consumption function as a liquidity constraint. In a neoclassical world economic agents use borrowing and saving to ensure a smooth path of consumption in the face of uneven income – as in the famous Ando–Modigliani (1963) life cycle or the Friedman (1957) permanent income model. This follows from the principle of diminishing marginal utility. To consume $x + 1$ in period 1 and $x - 1$ in period 2 or vice versa is less attractive than to consume x in each since the extra utility gained from the xth unit is greater than that from the $(x + 1)$th forgone to obtain it. Hence, individuals will not respond to shocks and the consequent variations in income by adjusting income. Instead they will borrow or dissave if their income falls. Hence the marginal propensity to consume will be approximately equal to zero. Hence there will be no magnification of shocks to the economy: the multiplier process will not exist. Clower and Leijonhufvud argued that the multiplier was an illiquidity phenomenon –

individuals could not borrow as much as they wanted. Hence consumption plans were constrained by income. Hence effective demand (as predicted by a Keynesian consumption function) would differ from notional demand (as predicted by neoclassical analysis). Soi-disant monetarists like Brunner and Meltzer (1989) for example retrospectively followed suit by giving debt a role in their analysis. However, credit remained a theoretical curiosity to which little attention was paid until the 1980s when it became Hicks-topical. Then (Ben) Friedman (1983) argued that statistically credit aggregates were better predictions of income than monetary ones. He and Blinder (1989) developed models in which there was a role for credit (bank assets or loans to the private sector). These models were part of a general realisation that many of the arguments for monetary targets were really arguments for *any* target expressed in terms of a financial aggregate – DCE, government bonds, credit, etc. In a world of perfect certainty all would be equivalent in that any one would imply values for the rest. In a world of uncertainty the form of the uncertainty would determine which is preferable, see Chapter 12. Of course, such arguments are bound to be inconclusive and, as Laidler (1982) points out, miss the point of monetarism. If there were enough information to make it possible to determine whether a credit or money target were better, then there would be enough to select a still better policy, either discretionary or 'open loop', based on some combination of the two.

However, what really gave impetus to the revival of creditism was the discovery that credit rationing was not only prevalent but in many ways an optimal response to the market failure generated by imperfect and asymmetric information. Neither borrowers nor lenders have perfect information but it is likely that the borrower will have more information than the lender about what he or she intends to do with a loan and the prospects of any investment project. This is reinforced by the possibility of bankruptcy. If a borrower defaults he or she goes bankrupt. It is then immaterial to him or her whether his or her assets are sufficient to repay 50 or 60 per cent of his or her debts. On the other hand, the bank is concerned for obvious reasons. At the other end of the distribution, the reverse is true. The bank normally receives either a fixed return, agreed interest plus principal, or the borrower defaults and the bank has to *sauve qui pent.* However well the project prospers it will receive none of the excess. Hence the borrower has an incentive to take more risks than the bank would like and so to pretend that the project is less risky than it really is. To illustrate, assume that the interest rate on bank loans is 10 per cent. Consider a variety of projects all with an expected return of 10 per cent, and so all equally socially desirable. The borrower is taken to be a limited liability company investing only in this project and entirely financed by the bank loan. The first project offers 10 per cent with perfect certainty. The borrower will find this unattractive – its net return is zero. On the other hand, it would be very attractive to the bank – it would always receive its agreed interest. The next project offers a 50 per cent chance of a return of 5 per cent and a 50 per cent chance of a return of 15 per cent. If it pays 15 per cent, the borrower receives an amount equal to a net 5 per cent (15 − 10) of the amount invested on an investment of zero. The bank receives the agreed 10 per cent. If it pays 5 per cent, the borrower defaults (earns 0 per cent) and the bank recovers its investment plus 5 per cent: all the available funds. The borrower therefore has an expected net return of 2.5 per cent. The bank's expected return is 7.5 per cent. Hence the bank would prefer the less risky alternative, the borrower the riskier. Hence a borrower has an incentive to pretend that projects of the second type are projects of the first type or more generally to conceal the risk element.

This example illustrates a key proposition of the credit-rationing school – the higher the interest rate, the riskier will be the loans demanded. Assume there are a large number of entrepreneurs some of whom can invest in the safe project above and some in the risky. For simplicity assume that the bank cannot distinguish them. If the interest rate is 9 per cent both types will demand loans. The safe project offers a return to the borrower equal to 1 per cent (10 − 9) of the project's cost. The risky project offers the borrower either 6 (15 − 9) or default. The bank receives a 9 per cent return from the first group and either 9 or 5 (in the case of default) from the second, that is 7 per cent. If there were equal numbers of each project it would receive an overall return of 8 per cent. If the bank raised the interest rate to 11 per cent, borrowers would not wish to borrow to finance the safe project: 10 is less than 11. However, the second type of project is still attractive – offering either 4 (15 – 11) or default. Thus the bank would find all its loans were to risky customers and it would receive a return of 8 per cent, 11 when the project paid 15, 5 when it did not and the borrower defaulted.

In general therefore a high interest rate has an adverse selection effect which may outweigh any risk premium effect even to a risk-neutral bank. In other words, charging a higher interest rate to a riskier borrower may have a lower expected return than a low rate to a safer one. It is interesting to muse on the effects of combining deposit insurance analysis (Gowland, 1991a) with the analysis here. Banks are searching for risky loans when faced with borrowers who are pretending their loans are less risky than they are. The thrifts crisis in the USA was a consequence of this (Gowland, 1991a). Many thrifts (US equivalent of building societies) were insolvent at a total cost to the US Federal budget of $500 billion. Hence the thrifts may have sought a risky portfolio but obtained a still more risky one.

Banks can protect themselves from the problem in part by demanding collateral or by insisting that the borrower provide equity funds to provide a cushion for the bank and to ensure the borrower pays in the event of bankruptcy. Information about projects may be obtainable at a price (Williamson, 1986); for example, accountants can be asked to verify the data provided by a would-be borrower. Finally the bank may demand that its return be related to the overall return on the project: an equity kicker. All of these are real-world phenomena and are termed equilibrium rationing by Jaffee. The crucial point is that all involve a limit on the amount a borrower is available to borrow, determined by his or her collateral or by available equity funds. This limit will not be relaxed by a willingness to pay more. In other words there is a rationale for the availability doctrine.

The analysis can be extended to derive the familiar result that a bank would rather lend to a large company than a small to finance the same project – since its other activities provide collateral. Moral hazard may also apply. Once a loan has been obtained the borrower has an incentive to change his or her behaviour so as to take more risks.

In general credit rationing provides a micro-foundation for the availability doctrine and the Keynesian consumption function. To conclude, modern monetary theory analyses banks as if they were ordinary firms. The result is a rich portfolio of Hicks-topical analysis of current policy problems with many counter-intuitive results.

11.7 IS–LM models incorporating an endogenous money supply

In most eyes one of the most restrictive features of the basic IS–LM model is the assumption that the money supply is exogenously determined by the authorities. Fully articulated models of the financial system have been developed, but their complexity has led to a search for an IS–LM model incorporating a simple but realistic process of money supply determination. The benefits are clear, given the ubiquity of the IS–LM model. In particular, attention has been paid to models in which the monetary authorities' instrument is taken to be some financial variable which influences the money supply. The money supply is determined by market responses to this variable. The basic structure of the models is unaffected. The IS curve and its derivation are unchanged. The equilibrium condition for the financial sector is still that the money supply and demand be equal. However, the locus of equilibrium for the financial sector is no longer strictly an LM curve (which assumes a fixed money supply) and so is called an MM curve. In the model analysed here the authorities are assumed to determine the reserve base of the banking system. This model assumes some sort of multiplier model of banking, so the money supply is interest elastic (see p.235) and is appropriate for analysis of the USA.

In the model, in which the authorities determine the reserve base, the basic result is that the MM curve is more elastic than the equivalent LM curve, and so more 'Keynesian' results are generated. The process underlying this result is simple. When interest rates rise, there is not only a fall in the demand for money but also an increase in the supply of money. The resulting disequilibrium in the money market is therefore greater than with a fixed money supply. Hence, the rise in income necessary to eliminate the excess supply would be larger. This means that the MM curve is more elastic than the LM curve (Fig.11.7). Figure 11.7 compares LM_1 (when the money supply is fixed at M_A) with

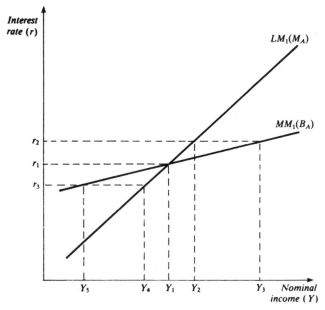

Figure 11.7 An interest-elastic money supply

MM_1 (when the reserve base is fixed at B_A). When interest rates are r_1, B_A leads to a money supply equal to M_A, so the two curves are coincident; (r_1, Y_1) is an equilibrium in both cases. When interest rates rise to r_2, there is a bigger excess supply when the reserve base is fixed. Thus, a larger increase in income would be necessary to eliminate the disequilibrium. Hence, when the money supply is fixed, (r_2, Y_2) is an equilibrium and so is on the LM curve, whereas when the reserve base is fixed, (r_2, Y_3) is an equilibrium and so is on the MM curve. By a similar argument, when interest rates fall, a larger fall in income would be necessary to restore equilibrium if the reserve base were fixed than if the money supply were fixed. Hence, whereas (r_3, Y_4) is on the LM curve, the equivalent point on the MM curve is (r_3, Y_5). By extending this inductive process, it can be seen that MM_1 is more elastic than LM_1.

In fact, the slope of MM depends not on the interest responsiveness of the demand for money (as the LM curve) but on the sum of this and the interest responsiveness of the supply of money. This can be seen if the MM curve is derived algebraically:

$$M_s = M_D \tag{7}$$

Equilibrium for the money market is when the money supply (M_s) is equal to the demand for it:

$$M_D = a + bY - cr \tag{8}$$

This is a conventional demand for money function in which the demand for money is positively related to income (Y) and negatively related to the rate of interest (r):

$$M_s = d + eB + fr \tag{9}$$

This represents the money supply process (see p.234; also Fig.11.2) in which the reserve base determines the maximum supply through determining the maximum size of credit (S_{MAX}) and actual credit (and so money) supply (S_{ACT}), asymptotic to this, rising with interest rates. S_{MAX} and S_{ACT} shift when the reserve is altered. The functional form in equation (9) assumes the shift in S_{ACT} is parallel:

$$B = \bar{B}_A \tag{10}$$

The reserve base is exogenously determined by the authorities at B_A. The equation for MM_1 is when:

$$M_s = M_D$$

that is:

$$d + eB_A + fr = a + bY - cr$$

that is:

$$Y = \frac{d - a + eB_A + cr + fr}{b}$$

Thus the slope of MM is $c + f/b$; that is, it depends upon the sum of the interest responsiveness of the demand for money (c) and of the supply of money (f). A more realistic variant of this model makes the actual reserve base held by the banks also depend upon the level of interest rates. It is then assumed that the authorities determine the total of reserve assets. However, the private sector holds some of these, so the quantity held by the banks is endogenous. As the private sector's demand is negatively related to the rate of interest, the size of the reserve base is also interest elastic. Alternatively an excess reserve function may be added. In this case the slope of the MM curve depends on the sum of the interest responsiveness of:

1. Demand for money
2. Supply of money
3. Effective quantity of reserve assets (private sector behaviour and/or excess reserves).

In this case the MM curve is still more elastic and so even more 'Keynesian' results can be derived.

Yet another variant allows income as well as interest rates to be a determinant of the demand for currency and/or the private sector's optimal deposit–currency ratio. If the personal sector's holdings of currency relative to deposits fall as income rises, then the reserve assets available to the banks rise and the MM curve is still more elastic, and vice versa. However, on balance this version does seem more plausible.

A major defect of the standard presentation of this sort of model is that it rests upon certain hidden assumptions about the working and structure of financial markets. For example, as described above, the model assumes that the credit market is supply dominated. This follows because when interest rates rise it is assumed not only that banks wish to lend more but that they succeed in doing so. This implies that the private sector is willing to borrow more when interest rates rise, which of course means that there must have been excess demand at the prevailing price and that the market outcome is always determined by the supply curve.

This assumption (of supply determination) implies that banks do not raise their loan rates sufficiently to clear the market. This is credit rationing but should be explicitly modelled.

11.8 Summary and conclusions

The flow-of-funds approach is the best framework in which to analyse the money supply process. Within this, however, it is necessary to model banking explicitly. The multiplier and 'new-view' approaches can both be used for this purpose. The 'new view' is the more flexible as well as the simplest. Both, like liability and asset management, are special cases of the portmanteau portfolio model approach. Such models can be incorporated into IS–LM models.

Notes

1. Friedman's criticisms have usually appeared in *Newsweek*. Some have been reprinted in, for example, Friedman (1968b).
2. For a discussion of the reaction function literature, see Coghlan (1980, p.68). More modern work in this area can be found in Chapters 6 and 7 of Barro (1989), which puts it in a different context.
3. See Favier (1963), Strayer (1980) and Pegues (1962).
4. See, for example, Gowland (1982, p.7), Gowland (1990, Chapter 3) and Goodhart (1975, 1984).
5. See, for example, Griffiths (1970).

12

Monetary Policy

12.1 Introduction

This chapter is devoted to two topics. The first is an analysis of
how the money supply can be controlled and the problems that
arise in seeking to do so (section 12.2). This is clearly a crucial
issue, since any monetarist policy prescription is based upon the
belief that the money supply should be controlled and so,
logically, that it can be. The rest of the chapter presents some
arguments concerning monetary targets. Since any argument for
a monetary target presupposes some relationship between money
and income, the whole of this book is an analysis of this issue.
Nevertheless, there are some more specific issues that have to be
analysed.

12.2 Techniques of monetary control

The monetary authorities in the UK sought to control a broad
definition of money in 1975–85; that is, a definition which
includes (nearly) all the bank deposits held by the non-bank
private sector as well as all the notes and coins held by them. In
1984–5 Mr Lawson abandoned this policy with apparently

disastrous effects (Gowland, 1990, Chapter 2; for details of the various definitions see the Appendix to Chapter 1).

The quantity of money in existence can be controlled in the same way as the quantity of any other good; that is, by rationing it or by making it more expensive. Money is, however, slightly more complicated than other goods, because a central bank such as the Bank of England can either seek to control the size of deposits and currency directly, or, alternatively, it can seek to influence the means whereby money is created and so indirectly determine the money supply. The direct methods are sometimes called demand-side and the indirect methods supply-side means of control.

The most obvious demand-side method is to seek to persuade individuals to hold fewer bank deposits by making them less attractive relative to other assets. This involves raising the rate of interest on those assets which are alternatives to holding money and reducing the rate of interest, if any, paid on bank deposits. In practice this method cannot be used because it is impossible to change the structure of interest rates in this way. If the Bank of England raises interest rates, banks immediately increase the interest they pay on deposits, while many of the bodies offering alternative homes for funds, such as unit trusts, do not. This would mean that bank deposits probably become more attractive not less attractive. This is a particular example of one of the most important problems facing all monetary authorities. As argued elsewhere, for example p.238, the supply of money depends upon relative interest rates, that is the structure of rates, as well as their absolute level. The Bank of England has few problems in changing the level of rates, but it is exceptionally difficult to change the structure of interest rates. The US authorities, especially when Democratic administrations have been in power, have tried to solve the problem by 'regulation Q', which put a ceiling on the interest rate paid by banks. This *modus operandi* is hard to clarify as either a price or a quantity device. It seems, in practice, to combine the worst of both groups of control. In any case it has been rendered ineffective by the growth of black markets – especially managed money funds.

Because the Bank of England could not rely on the price mechanism it tried to ration (interest-bearing) bank deposits between 1974 and 1980. This was a scheme called the *'IBELs* ceiling' or, inelegantly, 'the corset' (an *IBEL*, Interest-Bearing Eligible Liability, is a technical legal term for an interest-bearing bank deposit). Each bank was told what was the maximum of interest-bearing deposits that it could accept; the total varied from bank to bank and depended on the quantity of such deposits that the banks had when the scheme was introduced. If a bank exceeded the ceiling, it had to pay a stiff financial penalty, by lodging a substantial deposit interest-free with the Bank of England; this was called a supplementary special deposit.

Any system of rationing of any good has a number of disadvantages, of which the two most important are (a) that it can be evaded and that in consequence (b) the authorities do not know the true size of the market. Any form of rationing is apt to lead to a black market, and rationing in financial markets is no exception. A black market is used in its basic microeconomic sense and implies nothing pejorative, let alone illegal. The black market took the form of *off-balance-sheet lending* then called *disintermediation*; that is, in form (but not in reality) a bank ceased to be involved in the transaction. This is merely an example of the general microeconomic proposition: rationing leads to black markets. A bank can perform the normal banking function by introducing a borrower to a lender and guaranteeing the loan rather than accepting and on-lending a deposit. In this case, the transaction does not appear in the bank's balance sheet even though the investor holds an indirect claim on the banking system: off-balance-sheet lending. If a bank lends by discounting and accepting a bill of exchange, and sells this to a potential depositor, this is what has happened, hence 'bill leak'. Thus, the form of the control is satisfied but the authorities' intention is evaded. All the key features of intermediation are unchanged: A's funds go to B because A trusts the bank and because of the bank's specialist skills. This was sometimes also called the 'letter of acceptance' leak, from the name of a particular type of bill. After the abolition of exchange control in the UK in late 1979 evasion involved 'booking' deposits abroad, that is, one form of *offshore banking*. In the simplest case, instead of A holding a bank deposit with, say, Midland's York branch which grants B a loan, A holds the deposit with Midland's Paris branch and B's loan is similarly granted by this overseas branch. Unless exchange control were reintroduced, such evasion is a danger with any direct control on either bank liabilities or assets, that is, credit. The quantity of evasion was very large, especially between 1979 and 1980. Unfortunately, the authorities can never know the total of black market transactions, so they did not know the size of the effective money supply; that is, the measured money supply plus the black market deposits. This is obviously a serious handicap to monetary policy.

The supply-side means of controlling the money supply can best be analysed by using the flow-of-funds equation:

Money supply = Public Sector Borrowing Requirement (*PSBR*)
+ Bank lending to the non-bank private sector
− Non-bank private sector lending to the public sector
+ Overseas effect

This is also the money-creation equation, since a change in one of the right-hand-side variables is the only means by which the money supply can be created or destroyed (see pp.14ff). UK governments from 1974 to 1985 adjusted the *PSBR* so as to change the money supply. So as to reduce the money supply, or at least its rate of growth, the UK government had, between 1974 and 1985

1. Reduced expenditure on goods and services and on transfers; for example, by the Conservative government in January 1984, the Labour government in June 1976 and the Conservative government in July 1983.
2. Increased taxation; for example, in the 1981 budget petrol tax was increased by 20p per gallon so as 'to reduce inflation'(!) through its effects on the money supply (higher tax rate leads to higher yield depending on elasticity; higher tax yield leads to lower *PSBR* and hence lower money supply).
3. Sold assets, initiated by the Labour government's sale of BP shares in 1977 and followed by Conservative sales of council houses, more BP shares on three further occasions, Cable and Wireless, Amersham, Britoil, British Steel, British Gas, Telecom and many others from 1979 onwards.
4. Raised nationalised industry prices. This acts in the same way as a tax to reduce the *PSBR*; again this was initiated by the

Labour government and carried further by Mrs Thatcher's government who, for example, have doubled gas prices (then publicly owned) 'as an essential part of our anti-inflation strategy', to quote a Cabinet Minister.

5. Reduced public sector lending to the private sector. This was practised on a large scale by the 1974–9 Labour government, who, for example, virtually stopped local authorities from lending to certain categories of house purchasers. Indeed, they persuaded building societies to take over this function.

Bank lending to the non-bank private sector is also a primary cause of money creation, as the old adage put it 'every loan creates a deposit' (see pp.16–17). Until 1971 the authorities in the UK sought to control bank lending and so the money supply by rationing bank loans through credit ceilings. These were abandoned because the authorities believed they were evaded by disintermediation and by the growth of parallel markets; that is, by the growth of bodies that were banks in all but name (who carried on banking business unhindered by the ceilings). From 1971 to 1973 and since 1979, the Bank of England has relied on the price mechanism to control bank lending. By inducing the banks to increase the interest they charge on loans, the authorities hope to persuade the private sector to borrow less and to reduce monetary growth, or vice versa. In principle there is a third method of influencing bank lending: the reserve asset mechanism. However, this has never been used in the UK, whereas it has in the USA and a number of other countries (OECD, 1979). This method argues that the *supply* of bank lending depends upon the size of the reserve base (usually central bank deposits) and the reserve ratio, by a process usually known as the credit multiplier (see pp.228–37 above), such that, for example with a reserve ratio of 20 per cent, a change of one in the reserve base causes a change of five in the money supply. The UK authorities have always argued that such a scheme is both impracticable and undesirable in the UK (Gowland, 1990, Chapter 3 and 1991a).

Non-bank private sector lending to the public sector reduces the money supply in exactly the same way as taxation or asset sales by the government. If a private individual writes a cheque to the government for £100, the money supply falls by £100 for exactly the same reason, whether this person is paying income tax or buying savings certificates, even though the one is a lower *PSBR* and the other a higher level of private lending to the public sector. Private lending to the public sector can, as ever, be influenced by price mechanisms or by quantity controls. The latter, 'forced loans', have rarely been used in the UK, although post-war credits in the Second World War and import deposits in 1968 are exceptions. An import deposit compels the purchaser of imports to lodge a percentage of their price interest-free with the authorities for a period, usually either six months or a year. Forced loans are used more extensively in Germany and Belgium. The UK government relied upon a variety of devices to induce the non-bank private sector to purchase public sector debt, both in the form of gilt-edged securities and national savings. National savings were rendered more attractive both by increasing the rate of interest offered on them and by introducing new types of security, such as income bonds and index-linked securities. Gilt-edged securities were sold on a number of occasions by the 'Duke of York' technique, so-called because interest rates are first of all increased and then reduced, like the Grand Old Duke's military manoeuvre: the rationale was that bonds are most attractive when their price is low but rising. Other devices have included indexation and a variety of innovative marketing devices such as tender issues, convertible stock, part-paid stock and variable-rate bonds. The most dramatic change in debt management policy in the UK occurred in October 1985. Until then, discretionary debt management policy had been a major and very successful instrument of monetary control. Mr Lawson abjured such policy and instead used bond sales to ensure public sector contribution to monetary growth was zero. This was ferociously criticised by monetarists who thought it bore considerable responsibility for the problems that arose from excess monetary growth.

The overseas effect works in a variety of ways to influence the money supply (see pp.18–20) and may again be influenced by either quantity devices or price inducements. The Conservative government since 1979 has on occasion used both to provoke a capital outflow intended to reduce the money supply, the abolition of exchange control in November 1979 and a higher exchange rate being the respective devices.

Thus, there are at least twelve methods of monetary control, of which ten have been used in the UK. They may conveniently be grouped into two groups: those which rely on quantity controls and those which rely on the price mechanism (usually on interest rates). When analysing the influence of interest rates it is important to note that different interest rates influence the money supply in different ways. Indeed, it may be that the structure of interest rates matters as much as the level of interest rates. For example, the demand for savings certificates probably depends upon the rate of interest offered on them relative to that offered by building societies, rather than on the absolute rate. Prior to 1971, during the period of the 'old approach', the authorities relied upon quantity controls. These were abandoned because of the problem of 'black markets', which produced evasion and distorted statistics, so that the authorities believed that a coherent monetary policy was no longer possible. Moreover, rationing is usually both inefficient and unfair. In consequence, the 'new approach' to 'competition and credit control' was introduced in 1971; this was designed so as to use only the price mechanism. The new scheme was abandoned in December 1973 after the money supply had grown by over 60 per cent in twenty-seven months. The scheme had failed because the authorities found the implications of their own scheme unacceptable. In particular, the 'new approach' implied that interest rates needed to vary much more and to reach much higher nominal levels than the then Prime Minister, Edward Heath, was prepared to tolerate. He believed that low stable interest rates were both electorally popular and economically desirable in order to promote growth. From 1974 to 1979, the Labour government relied upon both quantity controls, the *IBELs* ceiling and the price mechanism, on government debt sales, as well as manipulation of the *PSBR*. The Conservatives dropped the *IBELs* ceiling because evasion had rendered it useless. They added a whole plethora of new devices to control the money supply, but their record of monetary control was still not very good, especially between 1979 and 1981, when monetary growth was over 20 per cent per annum. In the middle 1980s monetary policy was successful. The later 1980s showed the still greater cost of not trying to control the money supply.

12.3 Nature of monetary targets

A belief in the desirability of monetary targets is the *sine qua non* of monetarism. Indeed, such a belief is probably the best definition of monetarism. Certainly it is the most useful in practice, because the most important effect of the monetarist resurgence was the widespread introduction of monetary targets, especially between 1975 and 1980 (Foot, 1981).[1] Such targets were almost invariably in part the response to monetarist pressure, although not the result of an overnight conversion to its tenets by central bankers. A monetary target is best defined as 'the acceptance, as an overriding objective, by the policy-making authorities of a country of the need to achieve a specific rate of growth of some monetary aggregate or aggregates'. There are two key features of such a target. One is that the target variable must be an observable quantity rather than either a price (such as an interest rate or exchange rate) or a synthetic artefact such as fiscal leverage[2] or the high employment budget deficit. Keynesians usually prefer a target which is a price or some synthetic target (Ben Friedman's créditisme being the main exception). The other crucial feature of a target is that the authorities are willing to sacrifice other variables to achieve their monetary goal. In practice the other variables will include at least one of the following: the interest rate, the exchange rate and the public sector borrowing requirement (*PSBR*), or some other measure of the budget deficit widely defined. It is easiest to illustrate this within the flow-of-funds framework:

$$\Delta M = PSBR + \Delta BLP - \Delta PLG + O$$

where M is the money supply (broadly defined), BLP is the stock of bank loans to the non-bank private sector, PLG is the stock of non-bank private sector loans to the public sector, and O is the overseas impact on the money supply. Achievement of a monetary target necessarily involves the sum of the four right-hand-side variables equalling the desired rate of monetary growth, even though these variables may not be independent of each other. Moreover, many of the techniques of monetary control involve the direct or indirect manipulation of these variables (Gowland, 1982, Chapter 2). In particular, the techniques used in the UK have concentrated on the manipulation of these variables (see pp.254–9).

A government might seek to manipulate one or more of the right-hand-side variables by quantity controls, but these are neither costless nor very effective, at least in the USA and the UK; in fact they have been more effective in France. Hence, a government must either subordinate its spending and tax policies (the *PSBR*) to monetary purposes or rely on the price effects of interest rates and exchange rates to influence money growth. Both interest rates and the exchange rate influence the overseas impact: higher interest rates increase private lending to the public sector and reduce bank lending, so in both ways they reduce monetary growth. However, different interest rates influence different aggregates, so the structure of interest rates matters as much as their level. Hence, a government which pursues a monetary target must accept that at least one of exchange rates, the level and structure of interest rates, and the *PSBR* must be subordinate to monetary policy. Even if monetary targets could be achieved by quantity controls or by a reserve-base system, the attempt to control money would still have implications for interest rates (Gowland, 1982, Chapter 3). These implications, however unpleasant, must be accepted if the commitment to a monetary target is to have any meaning. In the UK in recent years the issue has been presented as a choice between control of the money supply and of the exchange rate. Advocates of exchange rate management in the UK usually argue for membership of the exchange rate mechanism (ERM) of the EMS. This debate has continued since the UK joined the ERM in 1990. Now the debate focuses on the correctness of this decision, the desirability of narrowing exchange rate fluctuations within the ERM and the desirability of monetary union.

The necessity for sacrificing other objectives if a monetary target is to be meaningful is best seen in the case where an unexpected development – a shock of some sort – hits the economy. Any shock will show up in one or more of the right-hand-side variables. The favourite example of textbooks is an exogenous shift in the savings function so that less is saved at each level of income. In this case lending would be above the expected level and in consequence the monetary target would be exceeded. The authorities would have to take action to ensure that their target was met. They might reduce the *PSBR* or raise interest rates to curb bank lending and/or increase debt sales to the public or allow/cause an exchange rate rise to induce a (capital) outflow. All of these would reduce monetary growth, but whichever the authorities choose to do, they would have sacrificed something to achieve their goal.

It is, perhaps, semantic to define monetarism, but it *is* important to define a meaningful monetary target. A willingness to forgo other intermediate objectives in pursuit of the monetary goal is essential if a monetary target is to be meaningful. A further element of the commitment involved in a meaningful monetary target is that it forswears any discretionary action for the duration of the target. As in the above example, the authorities can respond to a shock only to offset the impact of monetary growth. They cannot choose to make a different response (e.g. that which a fine-tuner might feel to be more appropriate). Indeed, this preference for a rule compared to discretion is often held to be a crucial feature of monetarism (Mayer, 1978). However, different monetarist positions imply different amounts of discretion. Friedman (1983) wishes to deny any discretion and prefers a rule which fixes the rate of monetary growth for ever. 'Pragmatic monetarists', such as Paul Volcker and his successor, Alan Greenspan, in the USA (and in the UK Sir Geoffrey Howe), retain considerable discretion by reserving the right to vary the target from year to year. They seem to favour at least as much discretion as those Keynesians, such as Dow (1964), who argue that lack of knowledge restricts the ambit of fine-tuning. Similar problems apply to any instrument of economic policy. The argument between rooms and discretion is independent of agreements about which is the relevant variable. In practice, very few members of the UK policy community now argue for discretion.

Other aspects of a monetary target are regrettably less clear. One vexed question is the period over which a target should be observed. If a target of 13 per cent growth is set for a period of one year, this implies 1 per cent for each month, 0.22 per cent for each week, 0.02 per cent for each day and 0.001 per cent for each hour. Does it matter if any or all of these implicit targets are missed so long as the annual target is met? Economic theory offers no answer; the monetarist case is based much more on comparative statics than on explicit real-time dynamics – in this respect it is like all macroeconomics. It might seem absurd to try to meet hourly targets but reasonable to observe quarterly ones and a moot point about monthly ones – such certainly seemed to be City orthodoxy in the UK in the early 1980s. However, there is no convincing reason for this belief; it probably owes as much to the availability of data as anything else.[3] In the USA, weekly data are available, unlike the UK, and there orthodoxy in financial circles is that monthly targets are *de rigeur* and weekly ones desirable but not essential.

Some points seem relevant to this problem.

1. Seasonal variations affect monetary growth and produce uneven patterns of monetary growth on a monthly basis. It seems very reasonable to use seasonally adjusted data, but seasonal adjustment is not very exact in practice (in the UK at least) so it is both inevitable and reasonable to accept some variation in monetary growth.[4]

2. The argument that some variability in monetary growth is acceptable if it ensures greater stability in interest rates is widely accepted. However reasonable this is, it is a derogation from a monetary target, since formally the argument for allowing the money supply to grow faster on Thursday than on Friday so as to maintain stable interest rates is the same as the argument for allowing faster monetary growth in 1992 than 1991 for the same reason. One might be able to justify the former but not the latter by a cost–benefit analysis of transactions costs involved in changing interest rates against the benefits of monetary stability. Almost certainly such a calculation would find annual targets much more justified than daily ones – but no one has done this, at least so far. Another justification of the periodicity of targets might lie in the duration of wage contracts, although the relationship might not be straightforward, especially given overlapping wage contracts.

3. With respect to the practical argument that a 'stitch in time saves nine', if the money supply grows by twice the implicit target rate in one month, it is not clear at the time whether this is a random fluctuation which will be offset by a later negative stochastic event or the start of sustained deviation.

Even if action would not be justified in the former case, the authorities should still change their policy instruments, because if it is the start of a sustained period of excess growth, the cost of curbing it too late is much greater than that of, say, a temporary rise in bank base rates. It seems clear that acting too late is a major fault of policy making in the UK – for example, between 1972 and 1973, in 1978 and 1979, in 1983, in 1984–5 and in 1988–9 (Gowland, 1982, 1991a) – and anything which adds to the decision lag is to be deplored. The costs of delay when action is needed (so far) seem to outweigh the costs of an unnecessary response to a short-term deviation. This conclusion would follow if policy makers have a quadratic loss function. It would also apply if there are costs of adjusting policy variables. However, as argued above, the whole issue needs to be subject to a rigorous cost-benefit analysis.

The next unsettled question is whether a monetary target should be the same for ever. For over thirty years Friedman has argued vigorously for a fixed target (Friedman, 1953). Consequently, this position is widely regarded as being coterminous with monetarism. Friedman (1969) has suggested various methods of fixing the amount by which money should grow but has made it clear that the advantages of any fixed rule outweigh any minor differences in the merits of 0, 2 or 5 per cent. On the other hand, other monetarists do not agree. The leading exceptions are Laidler (1975a) and Parkin and Nobay (1975), who have argued for gradualism; that is, for each year's monetary target being less than the previous year's. This is a particularly important proposition, because it was accepted by the Conservative government in the UK in 1979 and was embodied in the *Medium-Term Financial Strategy* which was the basic document of their monetarist approach at least in principle, however much ignored in practice, (Browning, 1986).

Laidler's and Parkin's arguments were based on aggregate supply considerations. In the eyes of monetarists, the money supply determines aggregate demand, so it is at least conceivable that shifts in aggregate supply might change the optimal level of aggregate demand. Laidler's and Parkin's arguments were based on Friedman's expectations model (1968a) (analysed in Gowland,

1990). Briefly, in this model aggregate supply curves depend upon the level of inflationary expectations and these in turn on past inflation. A small rise in unemployment will suffice to reduce inflation below its expected level and shift the aggregate supply curve to the right. Moreover, there will be a further shift of aggregate supply in each period so that the declining rate of monetary growth produces a declining rate of inflation and a constant but not very high level of unemployment. Once price stability has been attained, Friedman's rule should be applied. Compared to the 'clean kill policy' of an immediate reduction in money growth to this level, unemployment does not rise to so high a level but is above the natural level for longer. This seems preferable to the gradualists for obvious reasons, although the choice must depend upon how large the difference is and for how long it is sustained and, of course, on how quickly following a clean kill unemployment falls below the level produced by gradualism.

Here, all that is relevant is that the argument is logically valid. Although the policy may not be easy to apply in practice, Stein's (1982) simulations for the USA suggest that a clean kill is the better policy since the difference in unemployment is small. UK experience between 1979 and 1981 has revealed the operational problems of implementing gradualism. In principle, virtually any shift in the aggregate supply function would justify a variation in the monetary target. In practice, most monetarists would regard such an argument as special pleading and would believe that many of the virtues of monetarism would be lost – in particular, any hope of influencing expectations.

The best case for such flexible policy is in response to a sudden and unpredictable shock, such as the 1973 OPEC oil price increase. If the monetary authorities leave their target unchanged in response to this, the effect in a monetarist model is that unemployment would rise while the effect on inflation is unpredictable (Gowland, 1983b and p.178 above). Instead, the monetary authorities could increase the money supply so that a rise in unemployment would be averted, although prices would rise. If such a rise in prices were a once-and-for-all increase with no effect on subsequent inflation, such a policy would make sense for the most hardline of Friedmanites. However, if inflationary expectations respond to the rise in prices, the inflationary cost would be large. Moreover, the knowledge that the monetary discipline was weakened would change behaviour and affect expectations such that it might be that all of extra monetary growth would go into prices and none into output.

Theoretically, shifts in the demand for money functions also justify variations in the monetary growth rate. For example, Keynes' bugbear of a collapse in confidence – that is, an increase in pessimism – would mean that more money was demanded at each level of income and interest rates than when the prevailing psychology was 'normal'. In the world of the elementary IS–LM model this causes a shift to the left of the LM curve, and there is every reason to increase monetary growth to avoid an unwanted fall in (the growth rate of) nominal income. Thus, Volcker, chairman of the US Federal Reserve, was not necessarily unmonetarist when he argued in October 1982 that a shift in the demand for money was the reason for the temporary abandonment of the US money supply target – his reasons being a change in the attractiveness of money because of the unwinding of All Savers Certificates and changes in *IRA*s (Individual Retirement Accounts). Nevertheless, virtually all commentators rightly regarded it as the abandonment of his tight money policy. Arguments about shifts in the demand for money are regarded with extreme suspicion by monetarists because they are too convenient for the central banker and too hard to predict (see Hamburger, 1973, for a critique of an earlier alleged shift). Moreover, any such abandonment may weaken credibility – perhaps the key issue. Similar considerations applied in the UK between 1985 and 1989 when Mr Lawson cited financial innovation as a reason for abandonment of monetary targets. The argument did not make very much sense (Gowland, 1990, p.13). In principle, such arguments can be correct, but in practice, they are usually an excuse for abandoning monetary discipline.

Similar scepticism is general amongst monetarists about any argument for varying monetary targets; theoretically the case may be impeccable, but practically the authorities are unlikely to have enough knowledge. Thus, except for gradualism, monetarists reject nearly all arguments for variable monetary targets. The least extreme of monetarists would combine a demand for a carefully specified argument with strong scepticism. The only exception to this is when there has been a past error – say it is agreed that optimal monetary growth is 5 per cent, but in year n monetary growth is 7 per cent. Some monetarists would argue for a target of 3 per cent in year $(n + 1)$ to offset the error, others that bygones are bygones and so the target should remain at 5 per cent. Other arguments are possible, such as 'wedging the error in'; that is, offsetting it over time by a series of targets such as 4, 4.5, 4.75, etc. in successive years so that the actual target gradually reverts to 5 per cent. In fact there are no very convincing arguments for any position. It is important to distinguish this argument of substance from the UK debate about whether to *express* targets as a percentage of the previous target or of the previous actual level. If the level at the start of the year n is £100 billion and the target growth rate is 5 per cent, the target level is £105 billion at the year end. If, instead, growth is 7 per cent, the actual level is £107 billion. Should a new target be expressed as a percentage of 105 or 107? This is independent of the decision about whether to offset the error. If the error is to be offset, the new target level is £110.25 billion, which is either 3 per cent growth if the base is 107 or 5 per cent if it is 105. If the error is not to be offset, the target can be expressed as either 7 or 5 per cent growth from 105 and 107 respectively. The UK authorities have varied the base from actual to previous target level, or vice versa, several times so as to influence expectations by making the policy seem more consistent or tougher than it was. Only if the authorities are committed to announcing a given figure are the decisions related – an unlikely contingency. Undoubtedly the structure and form of monetary targets has to be such as to maintain and if possible maximise the credibility of monetary policy. Credibility is necessary for a successful policy because the impact of policy depends in large part upon how the private sector changes its behaviour in response to targets. If the private sector believes a policy is temporary or unlikely to be adhered to then the policy is unlikely to work. Keynes (1936, p.203) first emphasised this:

> Thus a monetary policy which strikes public opinion as being experimental in character or easily liable to change may fail in its objective . . . . The same policy may easily prove successful if it appeals to public opinion as being reasonable and practicable and in the public interest, rooted in strong conviction, and promoted by an authority unlikely to be superseded.

Credibility is analysed below.

These operational problems are secondary to the main proposition: a monetarist policy involves adherence to a monetary target even if costs must be borne to meet it. If an exchange rate policy is adopted, it is necessary to bear costs to ensure that it is met. It may be that the best target is the one that is most credible in the eyes of economic decision makers.

12.4 The case for monetary targets

There are three arguments that have been put in favour of monetary targets, in addition to the proposition that monetary factors are the main determinants of nominal income. The first is an argument that a money supply target acts as an automatic stabiliser; that is, it will reduce the deviation of output from its trend level. This can be accepted by many Keynesians since it is agreed that the action necessary to meet a monetary target will frequently reduce the impact of shocks on output. The difference, of course, is that Friedman and Brunner have argued that this reduction of the impact of shocks is the most that is attainable, whereas Tobin and other self-styled Keynesians believe that more is possible. However, less emphasis is now given to this aspect of 'Keynesian' beliefs since the implicit fine-tuning discretionary policy is very hard to implement successfully.

The stabilising nature of monetary targets is most easily demonstrated by reference to the flow-of-funds equation:

$$\Delta M = PSBR + \Delta BLP - \Delta PLG + O$$

The shock analysed is a fall in exports caused, for example, by a world recession. This will reduce the overseas impact (O) below what it would otherwise be. In this case it is necessary to influence one of the other items so that it is larger (or less negative) than it otherwise would be and thus offset the monetary effects of the fall in exports. Any action that would do this would be expansionary in any model – whether lower interest rates, higher public spending or a relaxation of credit ceilings. Consequently, the reduction in output and employment caused by a fall in exports would be offset. The monetarist argument is that by setting the economy on an automatic pilot in this way, better results will ensue than if the authorities use their judgement about how to respond to the shock.

Foot (1981, p.17) developed an interesting extension of this based on what was then almost a Bank house theory (also to be found in, for example, Price, 1972). This argument presupposes that monetary and interest rate data are available sooner or are of higher quality than data on price and output. In this case if the demand for money function is known, one can solve it to derive estimates of the income variables (if the demand for money is $10 + 0.9Y - 0.6r$, the money supply 94 and interest rates 10 per cent, income must be 100). This argument, of course, assumes in addition that the money market is in equilibrium or that money is demand determined. Nevertheless, if one accepts the assumptions, a smooth path of monetary growth ensures a smooth path of income. Shocks will lead to interest rate adjustments – a downturn in activity will reduce monetary growth and, whether viewed from a demand or supply perspective, necessitates action such as a lowering of interest rates.

Hence, it is universally accepted that observance of a monetary target will be stabilising. However, whereas Brunner and Friedman argue that this is the maximum attainable degree of stability, Keynesian writers would either rely on discretionary action or on automatic stabilisers of a fiscal kind, investigated by those paladins of the Keynesian establishment in the 1960s, Hansen (1969) and Heller *et al* (1968).

A much more controversial argument for a monetary target is that it may influence expectations. This argument can range from a purely economic argument to one incorporating a large element of politics. Minford (in Griffiths and Wood, 1981), for example, argued that the function of monetary targets was to show that the government meant 'business about inflation'. (He went on to add: 'It is this that the UK authorities should build up. They still have a long way to go.') This issue, credibility, is considered below.

The simplest argument concerning monetary targets is beguilingly attractive. The private sector needs information about the public sector's behaviour if it is to plan its activities optimally. Information about government monetary policy is the most useful information that private sector agents could have, so a government should commit itself to a specific path of monetary growth.

This proposition is very similar to the arguments put forward for indicative planning in the 1960s – for example, at the time of George Brown's ill-starred national plan of 1965. The counter-arguments of opponents of monetary targets are that more useful information could be given (for example, a commitment to price stability or full employment) or that the benefits of more information are less than the costs imposed by monetary targets.

Much more attention has been given in the UK, at least, to the more sophisticated argument of the role of the money supply in the formation of inflationary expectations. Since Friedman's seminal article (1968a), it has become almost universal in macroeconomic models of all varieties, Keynesian and monetarist, to attribute key significance to inflationary expectations (see, for example, Gowland, 1990, Chapter 4). Friedman's own analysis concentrated on the role of past inflation in the formation of expectations. Various economists have analysed the role of extraneous events in the formation of expectations. Laidler and Parkin (1975) argued that the 1967 devaluation in the UK marked a watershed in post-war economic history by its effect on inflationary expectations. Virtually every defender of incomes policy in the 1970s relied upon the argument that incomes policy could break the link between expected and past inflation and so reduce the unemployment cost of reducing inflation. (Inflation in Friedman's model is equal to demand inflation plus expected inflation. Incomes policy might lower expected inflation. Similar arguments have been made in favour of monetary targets, the ERM and various other devices which it is hoped will break the link between inflation and inflationary expectations.) Within this tradition of political economy, it is reasonable to argue that government policy is a crucial determinant of inflationary expectations. Monetary policy is, at the least, an important element of economic policy, so it must influence inflationary expectations and so a monetary target may have a beneficial effect upon inflationary expectations. If inflationary expectations can be lowered, then it is possible to reduce inflation without a cost in terms of unemployment. Similarly, the costs of a short-term rise in inflation is much less if this does not feed through into inflationary expectations. These simple propositions are uncontroversial (see for example Gowland, 1991a). It has been argued successively that incomes policies, monetary targets and now membership of the ERM can achieve this. The problems arise not with the formal logic of the argument but with what, if anything, will have an impact upon private sector decision making. There has been a long academic argument about the impact of anticipated policy (see Barro, 1989 and Buiter and Miller 1982 for the two sides of this debate). It is not necessary to go into this debate here, since the problem is not what happens if Government policy is anticipated and influences inflationary expectations, but whether it will do so.

The argument that a monetary target influences inflationary expectations can also be derived more fashionably using the concept of rational expectations (Begg, 1982, Frydman and Phelps, 1983 and Sheffrin, 1983, provide detailed critiques; see also Evans, 1980). This issue has been analysed exhaustively, perhaps excessively, the best known being Buiter and Miller (1982) – which is very critical of the Thatcherite position. Rational private sector agents seek to maximise their utility. To do this they have to form expectations of future inflation, since these are crucial to all manner of decisions – such as those in labour-contract negotiations, the level of savings, real and financial investment. Such expectations will be formed in the best available manner and should be statistically unbiased, since consistent underprediction or overprediction can be eliminated by adding or subtracting a constant from one's basic forecast so long as the event is continuous rather than discrete. The expectation, however formed, must imply some view of how the economy operates. Thus far the model is incontrovertible, although it is necessary to note that as it is costly to forecast (if only in time) individuals may find that the most efficient forecast is fairly crude and may involve a rule of thumb. Friedman's assumption that expected inflation will be equal to last year's could be justified in this way if agents believe that the benefits of a more accurate forecast are not worth the effort.

The rational expectations school usually assumes that forecasting is costless, so it follows that individuals will seek to use the best possible model to predict inflation; as any forecast implies some view about how the economy will operate, the best forecast incorporates the best view. This is usually taken by supporters of rational expectations to be the model they are using, so that inflationary expectations become equal to the mathematical expectation derived from the model, which is usually dependent on expected monetary growth (model-consistent rational expectations). A much more moderate assertion would in fact suffice. One influence upon inflation is past, present and future monetary growth, so agents will incorporate expectations about monetary growth into their information set so as to forecast inflation as well as possible. Government monetary targets then become relevant to the formation of inflationary expectations. The implications of model-consistent rational expectations – the so-called irrelevance hypothesis – are considered at the end of this section. However, it is in fact virtually incontrovertible that expectations about government policy will influence behaviour and that official announcements and varied policy may influence these expectations. Most of the main arguments about monetary targets depend only upon this weak proposition.

The crucial problems, however, stem from the fact that the private sector may not believe that the target will be met (or not attribute a 100 per cent probability to it). Minford in several places seemed to argue for monetary targets in a way very similar to the standard case for incomes policy. If the government *announced* a monetary target of x per cent, private sector agents, crucially trade unions, would lower their inflationary expectations so that they were in line with the target. Consequently, the aggregate supply curve would shift outwards such that inflation could be eliminated with little or no unemployment cost. Such a response assumes not merely that expectations of monetary growth are the main determinant of inflationary expectations (itself dubious) but that the official target is the best predictor of monetary growth. This has not proved to be the case in the UK (Gowland, 1991a). Similar arguments have been made in favour of the exchange rate mechanism of the EMS. The argument is again that the behaviour of trade unions will be influenced by the macroeconomic framework in which they bargain. Time will show whether this is in fact the case.

However, a defence of the role of the value of 'missed targets' has been made by Fforde (a prime architect of monetary policy throughout the 1970s) and Minford (in his comment on Foot, 1981, cited above). Fforde (1983) distinguished the political economy of monetary targets from their 'practical macroeconomic' or 'operational significance'. Accepting that the latter role was minimal, he defended them on the former ground. These include the value of a flow-of-funds approach to macro-economic policy as a means of achieving a coherent and consistent policy (of course, this does not necessarily involve a monetary target). However, he emphasises the 'vitally important' role of targets 'to signal a decisive break with the past . . . to enable the authorities to stand back from output and employ-ment' (that is, abandon a commitment to full employment). Minford put this case succinctly; the objective was 'to show the government meant business' about inflation.

The case for this starts with the Keynesian argument that full employment existed in the 1950s and 1960s not because of the direct effect of official policy but because of the indirect effect of the commitment to it, or rather the belief in it (Graham, 1980; Gowland, 1990). There was full employment in the 1950s because the private sector believed that the government would maintain full employment. In consequence of this belief the private sector altered its behaviour such that there was full employment.

In particular, businessmen invested more. Full employment implied that demand and expenditure (that is, future sales) would remain high. Thus it would be profitable to invest to satisfy this demand. Moreover, a belief in full employment boosted such intangible forces as business confidence, and so caused a further rise in investment.

One category of investment does not depend in any way on expectations of future sales. This is housebuilding which is of especial importance because some studies suggest that it was a significant cause of the high levels of employment experienced in the late 1950s (Matthews, 1968). In Keynesian terms, it was the injection which kept the economy at a high level of demand. However, the housebuilding boom depended in large part on the enormous personal sector demand for housing which was matched by a willingness to accept long-term mortgage commit-ments to finance house purchase. Keynesian economists plausibly argue that the belief in full employment was at least a necessary condition for people being prepared to do this. If someone takes out a mortgage they are committing themselves to making repayments over a period of at least 20 years. No one would do this if he or she feared that they were likely to lose their job in the near future; nor for that matter would any building society (who had a monopoly of mortgage lending in the 1950s) lend to him or her. Moreover, house purchasers have to consider the prospects of resale which depend on both the state of the economy in general and other people's willingness to take out mortgages in particular. Hence, the belief in full employment was again one of the causes of extra demand.

Finally, in the 1950s employers started to hoard labour, that is, they did not dispense with spare labour because they believed that they would not be able to find labour in the future when they did require it. Hence in the 1950s the government's commitment to full employment was self-fulfilling.

In the 1960s, less favourable consequences of the belief in full employment became clear – the so-called English disease. In particular, because trade union leaders believed in full employment, they ceased to believe that the threat of unemployment need constrain wage demands. Hence they asked for large-scale wage increases. Employers acceded to these demands, in part because their belief in full employment meant they thought they would be able to pass the wage increases on as price increases and consequent high demand. Hence the belief in full employment led to cost increases, and so to upward movements of aggregate supply curves.

Moreover, a belief in full employment generates the inefficient use of resources in the longer term in other ways. In elementary arguments for capitalism, it is argued that if firms seek to maximise profits the result will be a minimisation of costs and an economically efficient allocation of resources (at least under certain circumstances, see Gowland, 1983a, Chapter 8). However, it is acknowledged that in reality those running firms may be interested in other goals – sales, prestige, leisure, perks and so on – besides profits. The presence of many of these will lead to excessive costs and so to economic inefficiency (this sort of economic inefficiency is often called X-inefficiency, see Leibenstein (1976)). Advocates of market capitalism rely upon competitive pressures to restrict such activity by forcing managers to aim to minimise costs and maximise profits. A belief in full employment weakens the strength of such pressures and so generates inefficiency. Less formally, the effects of a belief in full employment on management are to induce complacency. The belief in buoyant demand (which generated extra investment) meant that firms believed that they could sell their products at home irrespective of price, quality, design or reliability. The growing success of imports in the UK revealed and reveals the hollowness of this belief. Indeed the belief, by generating complacency, is counter-productive. Adeney (1989) describes this process in graphic detail in the motor industry.

On the arguments presented above, a belief in full employment generated changes in behaviour which reduced efficiency and so shifted the aggregate supply curve upwards and leftwards. The consequences are obvious in terms of output and price. Moreover, by this argument, many of the UK's longer-term problems can be attributed to those malign effects of full employment policies. In summary, inefficiency was generated by the effect of the belief in full employment on the behaviour of both trade union leaders and businessmen. In consequence the AS curve shifted inwards.

Almost all commentators would agree with this diagnosis of the problems of the UK economy in the 1970s. What is less obvious is the solution. Marxists would argue that it showed capitalism to be inconsistent or at least only possible with a 'reserve army of the unemployed'. Social democrats would cite the necessity of planning and an incomes policy. Mrs Thatcher took the view that it was necessary to end the commitment to full employment (Fforde, 1983). In the 1980s it may be that once more businessmen reacted before trade union leaders and thereby produced a worst-of-all-worlds short-run scenario that was the mirror image of the 1950s. (See Gowland, 1990, pp.30–3 and 58–60 for a fuller discussion of this hypothesis.) In summary it seemed that *perceived* abandonment of the commitment was necessary if inflation was to be reduced.

The most obvious course of action would have been for the government to announce that it aimed to ensure price stability *irrespective of the cost in terms of unemployment*. Fforde argues that this would not have been politically possible in the UK. Indeed, a very large part of his argument rests upon this point, that a government would not say 'we have abandoned full employment' but could say 'we are monetarist'. This is possible but many Tory Wets concentrated on the illogicality of a commitment to a financial aggregate. (Wets were the Tory opponents of Mrs Thatcher.) Commitment to price stability at any cost might have been easier. Moreover, both Mrs Thatcher and Sir Geoffrey Howe made statements very similar to this. In 1988–9 the same issue arose again after Mr Lawson's bungling caused inflation to rise when Mrs Thatcher and Mr Major made statements to this effect. Similarly, 'there is no alternative' and 'the lady's not for turning' influenced (and were meant to influence) opinion to believe that the government would press on to the (bitter or sweet) end. Nevertheless, the essential point is that the Fforde–Minford case depends upon the impact on private sector expectations. Otherwise the government would merely pursue its policy. The argument is much more sophisticated than the argument that money supply targets are *directly* taken into account in formulating, say, wage claims. Nevertheless, it still depends upon the effect on expectations. It is in this respect that the case is weakest. It would seem that only the *fact* of large-scale unemployment changed expectations in the UK. The role of an announced target would be to reduce the (unemployment) cost of an anti-inflationary policy. Indeed, following the Fforde–Minford argument, the failure to hit monetary targets may have increased the unemployment cost of eliminating inflation by reducing government credibility. (Mrs Thatcher's credibility was restored by her behaviour during the Falklands crisis, and thereafter the problems caused by missing targets were much reduced.) Similar arguments arose about the impact of the ERM on inflationary expectations.

It may have been desirable to eliminate perceptions of full employment; indeed, it almost certainly was. The relevant question is 'was it worth it?', to which responses legitimately differ. Nevertheless, monetary targets do not seem to have contributed to this goal. Experience in the period has strengthened the case for targets that are not merely set but observed, in that (to quote Buiter's (1981) statement of the elements of the case for targets that he cannot refute) 'they eliminate uncertainty about current and future policy-instrument values' and avoid 'authorities [who] either pursue the wrong objectives or pursue the right objectives in inept ways'. As Minford put it in *The Daily Telegraph* (22 November 1990):

> To communicate monetary intentions, they first have to be coherent, then clearly expressed. They are neither. Monetary poker is the antithesis of monetary policy designed to set a stable framework for private decisions.

The third argument for monetary targets, hinted at by Buiter, is that they are necessary to constrain or discipline governments. Buchanan has been a frequent proponent of this view (for example, in Buchanan and Brennan, 1981) but it is even more closely associated with Friedman (1962). Buchanan's views can also be found in Buchanan *et al* (1986). This view can be put in a rather illiberal, undemocratic fashion: governments, left to themselves, will pursue policies that cause inflation, perhaps to buy votes, so it is necessary to find devices which will constrain them. This method of presentation is, however, unfair to its proponents who, to use Buchanan's terminology, want to see the introduction of an 'economic constitution'. Governments have enormous potential political power but accept constraints upon it, either through a written constitution as in the USA or tacitly as in the UK. Such constraints involve both an acceptance of 'rules of the game' (the opposition is not kept out of power by force) and of rights such as freedom of the press, as well as procedural safeguards such as trial by jury. Buchanan and Friedman would argue that it is equally necessary to constrain the economic power of government by analogous devices. In this form the argument is not unreasonable, although one may argue that the majority's right to use economic power is sufficiently circumscribed by a political constitution. Nevertheless, it is worthy of note that this last argument is new to monetarism in the twentieth century – traditionally monetarists believed in discretion not fixed rules; for example, in their contests in the nineteenth century with supporters of the gold standard.

Many of these arguments can be analysed in the time-consistency framework developed by Kydland and Prescott (1977); see the survey by Chari *et al* in Barro (1989, pp.265–305). The concept of a time-inconsistent policy is straightforward – one that will not be credible because it includes future actions that will be irrational at the time of implementation. A simple example involves examinations. It is frequently argued that the main purpose of exams is to make students revise for them and this will be assumed. Hence a rational educational authority will announce a ferocious test to induce students to revise. On the day of the exam, the test will be cancelled. There is no need to hold it and incur all the costs on students and examiners since its purpose has been achieved. Students have worked hard in a disciplined framework and developed their potential. This practice frequently occurs in infant and primary or lower schools with variants like postponing the test. However, it runs into a danger – that students will work out the logic of the system and not revise. This renders the policy of announcing examinations time inconsistent. Students can calculate that on the day of the test, the exam will be cancelled. Hence they do not work. Of course, if an examiner does set a test disaster occurs (and it is argued below that this is what Mrs Thatcher did). What is necessary is a legal or external requirement that exams be taken. Once the option of cancelling exams disappears students work etc. Guisso and Teruzzese (1990) extend this analysis to both promises and threats – time consistency and sub game perfection.

The application of this parable to economic policy is clear-cut. The obvious policy for a government is to pursue a high-demand policy in the short run but announce that they will deflate next period. The latter reduces inflationary expectations and so increases employment and lowers inflation in the present period. In the second period they again pursue a high-demand policy and announce that they will deflate. The threat of deflation, like the exam, is never put into practice. This certainly matches UK experience from the late 1950s to the late 1970s; governments were always announcing hard-line policies which they did not implement. Hence, of course, no one believed that they would deflate. When Mrs Thatcher did in 1979–81, the effect was like setting an exam to ill-prepared students – economic agents assumed soft policies, formulated expectations accordingly and got hard-line deflation.

Given the obvious incentive for governments to renege on anti-inflationary policies, how can credible anti-inflationary policies exist? A monetary target or some other form of precommitment is the obvious answer; Blanchard and Fischer (1989, pp.592–614), Rogoff in Barro (1989, pp.236–65). However, the monetary authorities might renege on a target. What then? Rogoff and others have analysed models in which punishments, loss of reputation, etc., are the consequence and developed elaborate models. An important argument is that one needs independent ultra-conservative central bankers – Volcker (USA), Pöhl (Germany). In New Zealand, this has been reinforced by relating Central Bank salaries to the price level – negatively so that if the monetary authorities permit large-scale inflation they suffer. Again there are a large number of ways of seeking to achieve the same objective: exchange rate targets (such as the ERM), monetary targets, and central bank independence, etc. It is a problem in political economy which would be the most effective.

However, this raises the underlying political issue – does a democratic electorate wish to see policies pursued which maximise long-run economic welfare, by eliminating inflation, at the cost of short-run unemployment? Goodhart (1989a, p.368) encapsulates this by the following quote from Cagan (1986, pp.31–3).

> In Barro's model . . . the preferred position of lower inflation and the same unemployment is not reached because the authorities cannot be trusted to foreswear unannounced stimulus to reduce unemployment . . . . But that credibility problem is not insuperable. . . . It is the public's insistence, shared and accepted by the authorities, not to subordinate low unemployment to other objectives . . .

> Let me substitute for the rational-expectation, market-clearing framework of his model the traditional notions of price inflexibility and long lags in the effect of monetary policy. . . . They were an accepted view before Keynes . . . .

> In this reformulated version of Barro's model, a stable equilibrium appears unlikely. When inflation develops, the authorities can be counted on to slow it down, but they are hesitant to press down too hard and are certainly unwilling to reverse an increase in prices by deflating them. Inflationary pressures from a previous overstimulus may not be eliminated before the next bout of unemployment . . . . There is a tendency, therefore, towards escalation of inflation. If the rate of inflation gets high enough, the resolve to bring it down may stiffen, and the objective of low or lower inflation may predominate for a while, as since 1980. . . . Can this process be stopped by nondiscretionary methods of the kind Barro discusses? Yes, of course it can. Will it? I doubt it. I see no evidence that the public is willing to accept nondiscretionary policies and to give up the option to deal not only with severe unemployment but also financial crises. There is today a heightened awareness of the advantages of price stability, and perhaps a new desire to avoid the worst excesses of fine tuning. But no government today would surrender its freedom to deal as it sees fit with macroeconomic problems and would never say that it would.

This raises its head in the context of the ERM of the EMS, another automatic device designed to eliminate discretion. All of what had been a rather arcane academic debate became central to political controversy in the UK in 1989 fuelled by Mr Lawson's resignation, the debate about UK entry into the ERM of the EMS, and its entry in October 1990, and even the successful challenge to Mrs Thatcher's leadership of the Conservative party. This is not the place to discuss the reasons for Mrs Thatcher's downfall, but certainly arguments about the ERM precipitated the challenge to her leadership. Mrs Thatcher put the orthodox Keynesian argument that democratic governments need the freedom to do what their electorates require and want. Ironically her critics, for example the *Guardian*, put the traditional right-wing arguments:

(a) Governments do not have sufficient knowledge to exercise discretion or use autonomy: Friedman's view.

(b) Markets work so well that intervention is unnecessary (the new classical argument).

(c) Governments are likely to manipulate the economy so as to win general elections – the so-called political business cycle. Using the Friedman model of inflation, Chapter 8 above:

Year 1 government reflates

Year 2 output rises and unemployment falls: general election

Year 3 high inflation, government deflates.

(d) If economic agents have low inflationary expectations, economic policy is easy and likely to succeed: one can stay on the short-run AS or Phillips curve. If agents have high ones the reverse is true. Similarly, it is obviously advantageous for policy makers if short-term fluctuations in the inflation rate do not feed through into inflationary expectations. This arises when the commitment of policy makers to an anti-inflationary strategy is credible, that is when economic agents believe that they will introduce policies to offset any such shocks.

Discretion in the kinds of governments is likely to generate high inflationary expectations. Economic agents are likely to fear the political business cycle or a well-meaning but imprudent attempt to reduce unemployment. Hence an external check is necessary to give credibility (and so low inflationary expectations):

Inflationary expectations are much lower in countries where there is a widespread and deep seated belief that the authorities will not let up – credibility is easily lost and hard to regain. (Governor of the Bank of England, 16 November 1990)

Credibility might be given by:

(a)   a monetary target
(b)   a fixed exchange rate – that is, the ERM or EMU, which prevents governments running budget deficits or pursuing discretionary monetary policy
(c)   an independent central bank – either for its own sake or to ensure (a) or (b); most supporters of EMU assume an independent central bank and many Tory critics of Mrs Thatcher wanted to make the Bank of England independent, especially Mr Lawson.

To summarise, monetarists believe that governments should accept a commitment to a monetary target and should be prepared to make sacrifices to achieve the target. This is justified because of the impact of monetary targets on expectations and because their adoption constrains governments and tends to stabilise output. None of these is without foundation. The 'automatic stabiliser' proposition is incontestably valid; the dispute is whether discretion or an alternative rule could do better. Monetary targets do convey information and influence expectations but it is as easy to overstate as to ignore this case for their introduction.

Nevertheless, a missing link in this case is 'why money?' Similar arguments could be constructed for interest rate targets, for other quantity targets, for exchange rate targets or for more complex rules. This is seen most clearly in the discipline case. Buchanan acknowledges that a balanced budget rule (or a maximum tax to GDP ratio) or fixed exchange rates (for example, the gold standard) may be better constraints on governments. Hayek (1976) suggested that total government withdrawal from money markets was the best solution – so having competitive money. This argument about how best to constrain governments can only be conducted in the framework of a particular set of political institutions and history, since a large part of the case would have to rest upon the legitimacy of the various options. However, the relative merits of monetary and other targets can be considered in a narrower economic framework, and this analysis forms the rest of this chapter.

The new classical school have put forward a number of important propositions concerning the role of monetary policy. All rest on the assumption that economic agents act rationally within their environments. This assumption implies that agents assemble and use information in an efficient manner (Barro, 1989, p.1).

Austrian and post-Keynesian economists would challenge the first part of this (Hodgson, 1989) but few others would, whether Keynesian, monetarist or anything else. Certainly the implication that macroeconomics needs a rigorous micro-foundation is generally accepted. The second sense is not tautologous but it is the implications of this which leads to the startling results of new classical analysis. These divide new classicists as sharply from Milton Friedman as from any Keynesian; indeed more sharply than from some new Keynesians like Ben Friedman. This is, of course, the interpretation of rational expectations used by Barro and his school.

It is undeniable that some human actions depend upon expectations of the future, for example a decision whether to wear a fur coat or a bikini depends upon an expectation about the weather. Many economic decisions certainly depend upon expectations, notably the role of inflationary expectations in the determination of output (see Chapter 8). In the weak sense used by Barro these will be formed optimally. The debate hinges upon what is meant by optimal. Barro etc. argue that optimal means unbiased, that is, equally likely to be right or wrong in either direction, that is, has a random error. The argument is that one can always adjust a forecast to achieve this by adding or subtracting a constant, thus achieving what statisticians call an efficient forecast. If a holidaymaker wishes to know the weather and on each of the first three days it is cooler than the radio forecast says, he or she can improve his or her forecast by simply deducting three degrees from the radio forecast. The assumption that forecasts are unbiased leads to the conclusion that what happens depends not upon whether news is good or bad but whether it is better or worse than expected. This can often be observed on the Stock Exchange: when a company's results are announced a large rise in profits is often followed by a fall in the price of the company's shares because the market was expecting a still larger rise. The implication of unbiased expectations is that if a company's profits rise 100 per cent, the share price is just as likely to fall as rise since it is just as likely that the market expected a rise in excess of 100 per cent as one of less than 100 per cent. In general, in the new classical world the reaction to an event is unpredictable, since one is reacting to the surprise element (the difference between forecast and actual) and this is random. This crucial result depends upon four assumptions:

(a)   that it is costless to forecast. If forecasting is costly one may not feel it is worthwhile to form an efficient forecast, or rather subconsciously one does not think about the problem at all. One either accepts the going forecast or ignores the problem. Say I am deciding whether to buy shares in Vickers. One of their minor interests is Rolls-Royce cars. It is too costly for me to evaluate the latter systematically so I may accept the *Investor's Chronicle* view that sales of luxury cars will rise (even if this is a biased forecast) or just buy the shares anyway. In either case my implicit forecast of Rolls-Royce sales is not efficient in the statistical sense but is in the economic sense, in that it would not be worth investing further resources to improve my forecast.

(b) . that it be a repeated event (game). The adjustment process described above only makes sense if approximately the same event takes place more than once. Otherwise there is no data by which one can decide what constant adjustment is possible.

(c)   that the event be continuous, rather than discrete. A discrete event would be, for example, whether the UK joined the ERM, that is, there is a 'yes'/'no' element. A continuous event – for example, the level of the exchange rate – can take any value. For a discrete event, the response will be in the same direction as in the naive world. Imagine a share currently priced £1. It will be worth £2 if the Conservatives win the next election and 1p if they do not. In the naive world (without expectations) the share will rise £1 if they win and fall 99p otherwise. When expectations are formed, these will influence the price. If there is an 80 per cent chance the Conservatives will win the price might be

£1.60, if a 10 per cent chance perhaps 20p. However, the movement of the share will be in the same direction as in the naive case.

(d) risk neutrality. One may not act on one's expectation if one is risk averse. To simplify the exposition it is assumed that I have correctly forecast that a small oil company will discover oil and that its shares (now 5p) will then be worth 200p. I and others with the same forecast will buy shares. However, we are unlikely to run the price up to 200p. We may be wrong by there being either less oil or more oil. We are likely to be more influenced by the danger that there is less oil than we think than more. Hence the price may rest at 190p. The expected 10p of profit fails to compensate for the risk. Thus when the oil strike is announced the price rises as in the naive case but by 10p instead of 195p.

Given these assumptions, forecasts will be unbiased. However, it is necessary to examine what people seek to forecast. Keynes' beauty contest is appropriate. In the 1930s, newspapers ran contests in which readers were asked to rank pictures of young women in order of pulchritude (rather like goal of the month). However, the ranking was not done by an expert panel but by counting the entries. Thus the most beautiful woman was the one who appeared as first on most entries. Hence one had not to select the most beautiful but estimate what other people thought about beauty. As everyone was in this position, everyone was trying to guess what other people would guess estimate other people's estimate to be. This sort of game is relevant to many areas of economic life. Roman Frydman and Phelps (1983) include studies of when agents seek to predict the Walrasian equilibrium and when they seek to predict others' expectations, and of course when the latter converges to the former. If this critique can be ignored an unbiased expectation can be derived: model consistent.

The use of this can be seen with the aid of Figure 12.1. This shows Friedman's analysis of the effect of expansionary policy in terms of either *AS/AD* or Phillips curve analysis. The economy moves from 1 to 2 to 3. Expansionary policy has a short-term effect in raising output, although this disappears in the long run. However, in this world people expect inflation to equal the level of the previous year. Inflation is rising. Hence they always

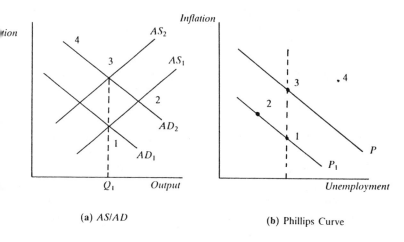

(a) *AS/AD*

(b) Phillips Curve

Figure 12.1 Rational expectations or Friedman analysis

underpredict so their forecast is inefficient. The new classical school say that the economy is just as likely to finish up at 4 as 2 in the short run and that 3 is the average of all the places the economy might finish up.

This analysis can be extended. Their particular point is that no anticipated economic policy can have any effect upon output: the *irrelevance hypothesis*.

Only shocks and unanticipated developments affect the economy. In consequence they are often said to believe in the 'Surprise! Surprise!' supply function.

This is accompanied by a belief that virtually all stabilisation policy will be predictable and so ineffective. Alternatively its effects are unpredictable as in the Friedman case.

In fact anticipated policy may be rendered ineffective, strengthened or left unaltered.

(i)   *An ineffective policy*

If the authorities varied income tax so as to influence disposable income in an attempt to produce a fluctuating pattern of consumers' expenditure in order to offset fluctuations in export demand, private action would render this ineffective. The private sector would realise quickly what the authorities were doing and would finance higher tax payments by reducing savings when the government raised tax rates (and therefore not reduce spending). The savings would be rebuilt when tax rates were lowered and, again, the authorities' attempt to vary spending would be frustrated. (Alternatively, the private sector would vary its borrowing, borrowing to pay higher taxes and repaying the loans when taxation was reduced, with the same effect on net saving as above.) The use of tax policy to produce a contra-cyclical variation in consumers' spending would be frustrated because the private sector could adjust its savings and borrowing to offset official actions and maintain a stable level of consumption. This is a good example of the sort of mechanism envisaged by rational new classicists.

(ii)   *No action may be possible*

If I know death duties will rise tomorrow I am unlikely to commit suicide.

(iii)   *Intervention could be reinforced or self-fulfilling*

If the authorities introduced a tax credit or other incentive to induce greater investment, a rational response would be: 'They are always changing these allowances. I had better take advantage as quickly as possible.' In this case, the contra-cyclical effect of a policy of varying investment incentives would be reinforced because it was believed to be temporary.

Rational expectations have had a greater influence on macroeconomic theory than any other development in the late 1970s. In the process, macroeconomic models have become far more complex. In return, there seem to be a number of gains:

1. A recognition that companies and individuals are not dummies easily manipulated by governments; this had often been stated but rarely incorporated in formal theory.
2. A recognition that the formation of expectations is crucial and cannot simply be added on to an existing model, as was done so often in the 1960s and 1970s.

3. A recognition that consistency is necessary in model construction and that certain forms of consistency were not present in existing models.

Within the new classical model there is scope for policy designed to increase the long-run natural level of output or minimise deviations round it. More generally, there will be scope for policy as Barro (1989, pp.1–18) recognises as much as his arch critic Buiter (1980a). The argument is that interventionist policy must be justified by some observed market failure and designed approximately.

12.5 Money and interest rate targets

The choice between money and interest rate targets has been analysed in a number of distinct frameworks. The traditional conclusion was that the choice of optimal intermediate target was dependent upon what assets were direct substitutes for money. If the direct substitutes were only a narrow class of liquid short-term financial assets, an interest rate target was preferable, but if money were a substitute for all assets, real as well as financial, a money target was preferred. Indeed, in 1970 there was little doubt that this was the dividing line between monetarist and anti-monetarist, as illustrated in Goodhart's enormously influential and authoritative article (1970). It is easiest to see the analytical foundation for this relationship between patterns of substitution by using the two simplifications of Tobin's (1969) general equilibrium model of monetary policy (see pp.122–7; also Chick, 1973, pp.91ff; Gowland, 1979, pp.104–7).

This approach, however, implicitly assumes uncertainty or imperfect knowledge. Otherwise policies using the different targets would be indistinguishable since one could calculate the relationship between bond rates and the money supply, and y per cent monetary growth and x per cent bonds yields would be equivalent targets. The reason that it is preferable to have a target which is a direct substitute for real assets arises because of lack of knowledge and/or certainty about the workings of the financial sector. This led Poole (1970) to argue that one should explicitly model uncertainty rather than use *ad hoc* arguments.

Poole used the ubiquitous IS–LM framework as the basis of his analysis. This made obvious sense in that the IS–LM model was and is the most common macroeconomic teaching vehicle in the Western world, yet this model reveals nothing about the case for monetary against interest rate targets, even though this is the crucial issue. The reason for this is shown in Figure 12.2. The authorities believe the optimal income level to be Y^* (following Poole, all arguments are in terms of levels, generalisation to changes is straightforward). A money supply of M^* would mean that the relevant LM curve is LM^*, which would achieve the target level of nominal income Y^* (Poole assumed fixed prices, so a target level of nominal income implied a level of real income, but this is unnecessarily restrictive). However, an interest rate target of r^* would also achieve the optimal level of nominal income. In fact, the two targets are indistinguishable: a money target of M^* leads to an interest rate of r^* just as an interest rate target of r^* would require open-market operations that would lead to a money supply of M^*. Similarly, if an alternative income level of Y_A were preferred, this could be achieved either by an

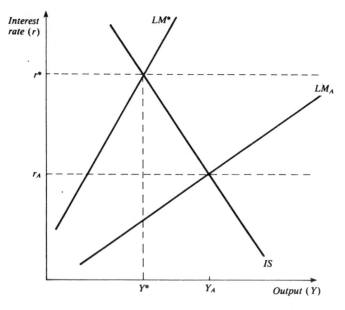

Figure 12.2 The equivalence of money and interest rate targets

increase in the money supply to M_A, to shift the LM curve to LM_A, or by a reduction in interest rates to r_A. One cannot distinguish moving along an IS curve (changing r) from shifting the LM curve (changing the money supply) since both occur simultaneously.

The two, however, become distinguishable once uncertainty or imperfect information is added so that one is no longer certain as to the position of the IS curve or the LM curve or both. This may arise because a curve is state contingent; that is, its position is dependent upon the size of another variable whose future value is now known at the time that the policy is set. This would be the case, for example, if in Figure 12.3 the IS curve were IS_1 when oil prices were \$30 per barrel and IS_2 when they were \$25. There are, however, a number of other reasons why the policy makers might be uncertain of the position of a curve, see p.292 below. Figure 12.3 illustrates the first form which uncertainty can take, that is where there are random shocks, or any of the other factors, present in the goods market but not in the money

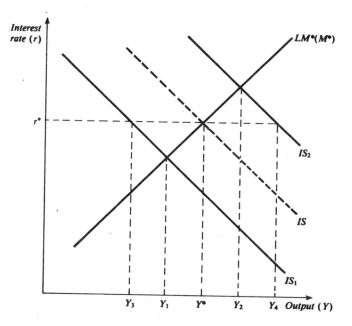

Figure 12.3 Goods-market instability

market. For simplicity, the case illustrated has only two possibilities, IS_1 and IS_2, with a 50 per cent probability of each occurring. This could mean either that each will be the case 50 per cent of the time or that only one will be the case but that it is impossible to ascertain which at the time that the policy is set. The IS curve in the certainty case (Fig. 12.2) is the dashed IS curve in Figure 12.3, i.e. the average of the two. This example can be generalised to any distribution of possible IS curves so long as intersections with LM^* produce a symmetric distribution of values of Y around Y^*. Here the targets can be compared. If the money supply is fixed at M^*, income will be Y_1 when the operative IS curve is IS_1, and Y_2 when IS_2 is operative. On the other hand, if r^* is adopted as the policy target, income will be either Y_3 or Y_4, as the operative IS curve is IS_1 or IS_2 respectively. It is easy to see that income deviates less from Y^* when the authorities have set a money supply target than with an interest rate target. This is generalisable: the variance of income is always less if a monetary target is adopted so long as uncertainty is about goods-market forces (that is, about the IS curve).

The other simple case occurs when uncertainty is about monetary factors (that is, the LM curve but not the IS curve). This can occur because of random shocks, an unstable LM curve, econometric ignorance or, to take a Keynes favourite, because there is a different demand for money equation according to the level of stock market prices, or any other unknowable factor. The case illustrated in Figure 12.4 is where M^* can lead to LM curve LM_1 in 50 per cent of cases and LM_2 in 50 per cent of cases, where these are symmetric around the certainty case LM^*. In this case the result is very clear-cut. Income is at the optimal level Y^* with an interest rate target r^* but not with a money supply target; in which çase it is either Y_5 or Y_6. In general, when there is uncertainty about monetary forces but not goods-market forces income is less variable with an interest rate target.

Finally, Poole (1970, p.713) generalised his results still further by saying that if there is more uncertainty about goods-market forces than money-market forces, a money target is to be preferred, and vice versa. Ford and Driscoll (1982) have demonstrated that this simple, elegant conclusion may not apply in all cases. In particular, uncertainty about the *slope* of the IS

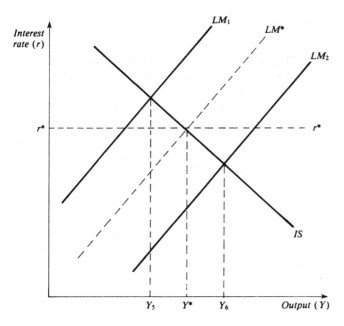

Figure 12.4 Money-market instability

curve can take a form such that Poole's result no longer holds. Nevertheless, Poole's result still seems to apply because it is much more likely than not that the nature of ignorance will be such that it can satisfy the conditions necessary for Poole's conclusion. Hence, Poole argued that monetary targets were to be preferred if the demand for money were relatively stable compared to the equations which underlie the IS curve. In this way he echoed the famous Friedman–Meiselman (1963) result in which the debate rested on the relative stability of money and Keynesian multipliers. (Econometrically, Poole's model would test interest-dependent versions of Friedman's multiplier functions.) The argument that a stable demand for money is a necessary condition for a monetary target to be desirable also follows from Poole's work.

It is interesting to note the various reasons why there may be uncertainty about the position of either the IS curve or the LM curve or both:

1. Econometric ignorance. The reason for the uncertainty about the IS or LM curve may be simply that econometric techniques are currently incapable of identifying the curves with sufficient precision. By the way, this point provides an interesting counter to Hahn's (in Surrey, 1976) critique of Friedman (1969). (Hahn argued that greater stability of the demand-for-money function – compared to the demand for goods – cannot settle any *theoretical* dispute about monetarism. Poole shows that the policy debate could nevertheless be so dependent.)
2. Either curve could be state contingent; that is, for example, IS_A would be the case if Labour won the next general election, IS_B if the Conservatives did.
3. The curves could depend on unpredictable variables, such as stock market prices (2 and 3 are similar but formally distinct).
4. The curves could shift within the policy period. For example, if policy variables were set for one year at a time and the IS curve had a systematic seasonal component, the monetary target case follows.
5. Behaviour in either market includes random elements.
6. The economic system is subject to shocks in the everyday sense; for example, generated by strikes, OPEC, etc.

Statistically many of these are similar or identical, but practically most policy makers would regard an LM curve that shifted in a known fashion in response to US interest rates as being very different to one that shifted whenever there was a war in the Middle East, even though formally both could be analysed as shocks.

Leroy and Waud (1977) argued that Poole's analysis was inappropriate. This argument is left to Section 12.7 below on contingent targets. Cagan and others have frequently pointed out that Poole's model is mistaken in treating the interest rate as an instrument whereas most central banks and governments seem to regard it as a final target, or at the least they believe that stabilisation of the level of interest rates is one of the prime goals of financial policy. Poole's analysis shows this defect with most economic models, which invariably treat interest rates as an instrument or intermediate target rather than a final target or goal variable. Cagan suggests that one should accept this as a stylised if irrational fact of life and incorporate into macro-economic models an additional objective, to minimise the variance of interest rates. This addition seems desirable but is not irrational. Stability of interest rates may in fact be an instrument of policy with an orthodox goal in terms of price and output stability – if, for example, investment is a function of the variance of interest rates as well as their level, as the CBI often argue. However, this effect is probably small and it is better to regard stability of interest rates as a goal for the following reasons:

(a) Central banks have structural goals as well as macro-economic ones (see Gowland, 1991a). One of these is maintaining the stability of the financial system *inter alia* by avoiding bank failures. Stable interest rates reduce the risk of bank failure. By a slight extension of this argument stability of interest rates is taken as representative of the goals of structural monetary policy just as low unemployment and inflation are of macroeconomic monetary policy. The two are frequently in conflict, so adding an objective in terms of stabilising interest rates captures this aspect of monetary policy.

(b) Changes in interest rates redistribute income and wealth. An increase in interest rates benefits the old and, para-doxically, the poor at the expense of the young and the rich (Gowland, 1983b). Such redistributions may be undesirable or desirable in their own right so there is a case for a particular level of interest rates as a final target, the level being the one which generates the optimal distribution of income and wealth. Moreover, it is easy to argue that frequent redistribution of income and wealth which are soon reversed are highly undesirable – if only on grounds of the diminishing marginal utility of consumption. Hence there is a case for stabilising interest rates to avoid such redistributions.

(c) Interest rates have a further 'political' element in that governments might feel that *any* redistribution is bad because losers complain whereas winners are ungrateful. Moreover, a rise in interest rates may be viewed as a symbol of failure, so it is better to have a relatively constant rather than a variable level in order to avoid this criticism. These points are in addition to distributional arguments such as that an electioneering government might reduce interest rates to gain the votes of mortgagees or raise them to attract old age pensioners.

The other arguments about interest rate and money targets have centred upon the defects of interest rates as an indicator of policy. Friedman (reprinted in 1969) argued that a high interest rate is not an indicator of a tight policy but of a past slack one. The link is that a fast rate of monetary growth in the past will have caused inflation and so positive inflationary expectations. Consequently, nominal interest rates would have risen. Hence, Friedman regards interest rates as an imperfect indicator of past policy not as an indicator of present policy.

A similar mechanism underlay the author's argument that monetary targets are preferable because of response lags by the authorities (Gowland, 1978). Consequently, inflationary expectations rise before the authorities increase interest rates, and steeply rising nominal rates may lag behind inflationary expectations such that real rates fall. In 1973 nominal rates were increased by 6 per cent in three months, yet it was not clear at the end of the period whether or not real rates had risen, as inflationary expectations had accelerated so much. The same happened in the second half of 1988. Any reliance on interest rates as either a tool or target of policy demands rapid reactions by policy makers if this problem is to be avoided.

Both this point and Friedman's can be regarded as special cases of a proposition that seems to have originated with Wicksell but has received much more attention in recent years as a central feature of rational expectations models. This is the belief that the price level is indeterminate with an interest rate target. In a Friedman or Stein–Laidler model this is only a long-run result; in the short term, inflationary expectations determine the price level – as Friedman demonstrated in his 'monetary framework' (Gordon, 1974). Both Griffiths and Wood (1981, p.7) and Minford stated that this is the crucial argument for monetary targets (Minford's comments appear in Griffiths and Wood, 1981). In essence the argument is very simple; the authorities are potentially committed to being prepared to increase the money supply *ad infinitum* to peg bond rates. Hence, money is unstable and so, therefore, are nominal income and prices. Certainly, in a world in which inflationary expectations exist, a very weak form of this argument is sufficient to destroy the case for nominal interest rate targets. If nominal rates are pegged, the real rate is determined by the private sector's inflationary expectations. If this real rate ever falls below the (unobservable) natural rate, inflationary expectations, inflation and monetary growth will accelerate for ever. If inflationary expectations ever receive a shock, the effect can be catastrophic.

A real interest rate target is more attractive but in the end runs into similar problems. Setting the real rate equal to its natural rate should produce stable inflation, and any rate above this should produce declining inflation. However, real interest rates are unobservable and the natural real rate of interest is unknowable. The former is partially weakened in the UK by the existence of index-linked government securities, so a real rate is observable. However, as the authorities operate in both indexed and non-indexed markets and all sorts of risk and institutional factors supervene, the observed rate is not the one relevant to the textbook model.

It is not at all clear what would happen, either theoretically or in the real world, if the authorities announced that indexed securities would always be available at a real yield of x per cent. Israeli, Brazilian and Finnish experience suggests that it does not make prices determinate.

In general some quantity target is necessary to anchor the system and make the price level determinate. However, it may be that institutional factors perform this task in practice. It is less clear what are the implications of uncertainty in a wider sense – when the structure is unknown (Goodhart, 1989a, p.349 ff.) or even unknowable (Arestis, 1988).

12.6 Exchange rate targets

In recent years there have been many advocates of exchange rate targets – international monetarists (for example, Beenstock, 1982) and neo–Keynesians (for example, Buiter and Miller, 1982) alike. Whilst many, especially in the USA, advocate a return to the gold standard, the usual form in Europe is membership of the ERM of the EMS or full monetary union. They propose a clear alternative to a money supply target, since exchange rate and monetary targets are incompatible. In principle, as a price target, an exchange rate target is open to the same objections as an interest rate target, especially the indeterminacy of the price level. This is especially true of a 'real' exchange rate target, usually defined using an index of 'competitiveness', so that the optimal exchange rate depends on the relative price level at home and abroad. In this case it is likely that some vicious cycle would emerge in which the exchange rate seems too high measured by some index. A depreciation is therefore apparently necessary. This leads to a rise in domestic prices (probably equivalent to the depreciation). This, in turn, leads to arguments for a further depreciation, and so on. Hence, an exchange rate target must be nominal and it really makes sense only if it is to be fixed more or less for ever thereafter; otherwise two problems emerge. The first stems from the impossibility of defining criteria for change – the IMF's problem with this under the Bretton Woods system. The other is that nearly all the benefits of a fixed rate disappear once there is a possibility that it may be altered, because the benefits depend upon domestic and overseas agents' expectations that the rate will not alter (for both points, see Gowland, 1983b, Chapter 9). Advocacy of exchange rate targets is therefore close to arguments for the revival of the gold standard. A fixed rate makes the price of traded goods determinate at a level dependent upon the price in other countries (exogenously equal to it for small countries). Walters (1990) presents a brilliant and surprisingly impartial review of this latter literature.

The case for an exchange rate target is best seen in the context of a small, open economy in which all goods are traded; in reality, perhaps Luxembourg is the largest economy to satisfy this. The smallness of an economy in international economics is not a measure of its physical size, but of ability to influence the world price; a small economy is defined as an economy which is unable to influence world prices. Nevertheless, physical size is crucial to the existence of non-traded goods; restaurant meals, for example, are probably tradeable in Luxembourg because diners could switch their patronage to a Belgian or a German restaurant, whereas no one in Iceland could. Hence, while

Iceland is a small economy for (internationally) traded goods, it has a non-traded goods sector.

In the simple model (that is, without non-traded goods) presented in Chapter 2 every domestic firm is a price taker at the world price expressed in its own currency. Let us say the world price of leets is $1. The price in the small country of *A*, whose currency is the α, of a leet will be $1 times the exchange rate expressed as αs per $ (or divided by it if expressed UK style as $s per α). If the exchange rate is $1 = 1\alpha$, the price in *A* will be 1α and all domestic producers will be price takers at a price of 1α; that is, they face a horizontal marginal revenue curve as in Figure 12.5. If the exchange rate fell to $1 = 2\alpha$ (or 1α = 50 cents) they would face a horizontal marginal revenue curve at 2α – the world price expressed in αs. Output for a firm could be determined where marginal cost equals marginal revenue; that is, Q_1 when the exchange rate is $1\alpha = \$1$ and Q_2 when it is $2\alpha = \$1$. Thus, the world price and the exchange rate determine the domestic price level and the exchange rate and marginal cost determine output. Thus, by adjustment of the exchange rate, the authorities

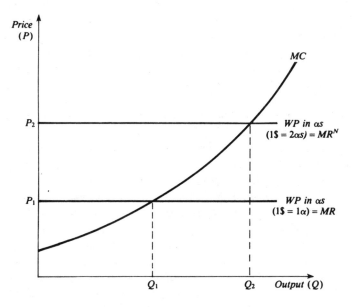

Figure 12.5 A small open economy

can influence price and output in either a discretionary fashion or by fixing a target exchange rate. Indeed, it seems a classic dilemma model: higher prices are the price of lower unemployment (higher output) and lower employment the price of less inflation. Alternatively if they peg the exchange rate the price level will be the world price level – hopefully that of a low-inflation country like Germany. The money supply, by contrast, except insofar as it determines the exchange rate, determines only net imports. It does this by determining (aggregate) demand and so, in Figure 12.6, a rise in the money supply would shift domestic demand from AD_1 to AD_2, but this would merely increase imports from $(Q_3 - Q_1)$, the exchange rate being fixed. Any reduction in domestic demand will leave output unaltered and merely cause a fall in imports or a rise in exports (and vice versa for an increase in domestic demand).

This model is incomplete in one respect: the exchange rate also influences domestic costs. Domestic costs can be divided into

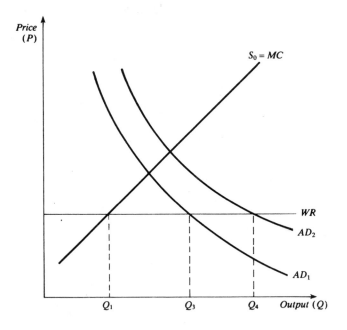

Figure 12.6 An increase in the money supply

imported raw materials and wages. Imported raw materials'
prices automatically rise by the amount of a depreciation. Wages,
it can be argued, will also rise by the amount of a depreciation
unless there is money illusion, either because of a trade union
bargaining theory or because supply-and-demand curves shift in
nominal terms by the amount of the depreciation. In this case the
situation is represented in Figure 12.7. A depreciation initially
increases output and prices, as the economy moves from 1 to 2
(Fig. 12.7). However, the marginal cost curve shifts from MC_1 to
MC_2 so that, in the long run, the economy settles down at 3 with
output back at its original level. This trade-off between short-
term unemployment and long-run inflation is reminiscent of
Friedman's model, although based upon different foundations.
Of course, if the marginal cost does not shift all the way to MC_2,
a long-run trade-off exists (between unemployment and inflation)
but at a worse price than in the short run (if unemployment is the
primary target; a lower cost if inflation is). In this model, the
exchange rate is the obvious target, whichever marginal cost (or

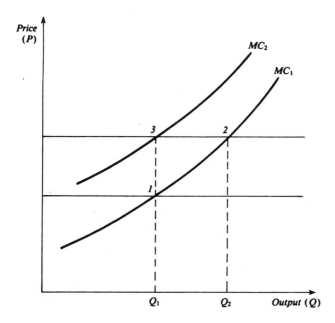

Figure 12.7 A small open economy in the long run

aggregate supply) curve is adopted. If a non-traded goods sector is added, the model can be changed radically, unless this sector is perfectly competitive, as in Scandinavian models (Gowland, 1984b, Chapter 10). If this sector is competitive, the basic framework remains unchanged, although more assumptions are needed to generate the long-run independence of output from the exchange rate.

It is clear that in a large economy an exchange rate target is foolish – but only the USA is large in this technical sense. In a small economy an exchange rate target is optimal. However, there is no clear theory about medium-sized economies such as Germany, France, Japan or the UK. One strong argument against exchange rate targets is that one is committed to the world's inflation rate and loses any ability to have either a higher or a lower rate. However, this is rather two-edged – perhaps one regards this as the best/least attainable. It seems worth reviewing the arguments for and against UK membership of the ERM in the light of the above analysis. In general the impact of a move to genuinely and fully fixed exchange rate means that one can analyse a country such as the UK in exactly the same way that one normally analyses a region within it. Hence, for example, balance of payments problems show up as regional unemployment. If the exchange rate mechanism allows for adjustment of parities, a whole host of traditional problems arise: one-way options, etc. These arguments are analysed in for example, Gowland (1991a). Here it is only necessary to analyse the impact of exchange rate fixing on macroeconomic policy.

Membership of an exchange-rate-fixing agreement involves a commitment to support one's currency. Say the parity is fixed at £1 equals 3DM, then every time anyone presents the Bank of England with £1, they must exchange it for 3DM (or 10 French francs etc. for all the currencies in the ERM). This means that the UK would need sufficient foreign exchange to meet all such demands; the ERM puts prime responsibility on a country to maintain the value of its currency, not to stop it rising too fast – if the pound rose in value against the DM it is Germany's problem not the UK's. Usually there is little problem in keeping a currency within its limits but sometimes most people believe that it is overvalued and seek to sell it. This is called a crisis of confidence.

This is a special problem for the UK given that the pound is held internationally on a far wider scale than continental European currencies. This is why the UK government argued that a necessary condition for UK membership was that our inflation rate be equal to Germany's. In this case it is reasonable to expect the pound to maintain its value against the DM so there is little incentive to convert pounds into DM. Otherwise, the UK argued, membership would involve excessive heavy expenditure (buying DM for pounds) that would not be successful.

If a country does not have enough reserves on such occasions it has three options – to leave the ERM, to impose direct exchange controls or to change its economic policy in such a way that it convinces people that the currency is worth holding. This leads to three arguments against membership of the ERM (see 1–3 below).

1. British membership of the ERM could prove an expensive fiasco

The UK joined the previous version of the ERM in 1972 and had to leave after a few weeks because it did not have enough revenue. The effect was not only to humiliate the UK but also to set back the cause of European economic integration.

2. Membership may involve actions that impede European economic integration

To ease the problem described above, most of the members of the European Community have used exchange control, that is regulations which forbid some or all transactions in a foreign currency. An Italian, for example, could not have a UK or German bank account, nor any other sterling or DM asset without government permission until 1990. Hence he or she could not convert lire into DM so it is much easier to support the lira's value against the DM. These restrictions impede the European Community's goal of a single market. Hence the UK's requirement that the remaining members of the EC abandon their exchange control before the UK joined the ERM. They promised to do this at Hanover in June 1988 (with a waiver for Italy until 1992 and Portugal, Spain and Greece until 1995). Following further British pressures at the Madrid summit in 1989, France and Italy abandoned their exchange control in the first half of 1990. It remains to be seen how the ERM functions without it.

3. A country may be forced to change its macroeconomic policy so as to remain a member of the ERM

For example, the French government in 1983 had to abandon a Keynesian policy of reflation adopted after the election of President Mitterand. Usually this is regarded as a consequence of a wider proposition.

4. If the UK is a member of the ERM, it loses autonomy of domestic policy

The exchange rate is linked to the money supply (and other domestic targets such as interest rates). Hence if one fixes the exchange rate, it is impossible to retain complete control over the other variables, just as a monetary target involves sacrifice of other objectives. Hence the UK government would not be able to manage the UK economy. However, some may think this a good thing – argument 5.

5. The Bundesbank will manage the UK economy better than UK politicians

Many economists and people in the City welcome the possible loss of autonomy. They argue that if membership of the ERM involves management of the UK economy by the Bundesbank (the German equivalent of the Bank of England), the better would be economic management of the economy. This is the same economic argument as 4 with a different interpretation. In effect this solves the credibility problem. However, Karl Pohl's resignation in 1991 showed that there were problems in maintaining the Bundesbank's credibility. These doubts had already arisen because of arguments about the economic consequences of German reunification. Hence, on the one hand, it was argued that if even the Bundesbank was not independent, then it was foolish to rely on an independent central bank. On the other hand, it was argued that these problems revealed the need for the

European Community to strengthen the independence of central banks.

6. *If the UK is a member of the ERM, it cannot use the exchange rate as a weapon of domestic policy*

UK governments have used a high exchange rate to reduce inflation and a low one to reduce unemployment. Obviously if the exchange rate is fixed, it cannot be varied in this way, nor to achieve any other objective, p.41.

7. *Joining the ERM will lead to a lower level of inflation*

It was argued above that under some circumstances the UK price level is determined by the exchange rate and world prices. If the exchange rate is fixed the UK's prices would be determined only by world prices – in practice within the EMS, Germany's prices – and Germany has a low inflation rate.

8. *Membership of the ERM would increase the credibility of UK anti-inflation policy*

Given the importance of expectations in determining inflation, it is desirable if people expect a low rate of inflation. This means that inflation policy will work only if people have confidence in it (credibility). Membership of the ERM has increased the credibility of anti-inflation policy in France. In effect, the hope is that instead of inflationary expectations being determined by domestic inflation, they will be determined by German inflation. This makes it possible to test the impact of the ERM on an economy by seeing whether this does happen.

9. *Membership of the ERM would facilitate trade with Europe and European integration generally*

On the whole many of the problems stem from lack of confidence that the UK will stay in (or cannot maintain the original parity) and many of the benefits from confidence that it will! For example, lack of confidence could lead to very high interest rates (argument 3) whilst a credible anti-inflation policy could lead to lower ones (argument 8). As often in economics a policy will work but only if people believe in it – a point first made by Keynes (1936, p.209) above (p.267). Keynes' own views, however, would have been against the ERM:

> We are determinded that, in future, the external value of sterling shall conform to its internal value, as set by our own domestic policies, and not the other way round. Secondly, we intend to keep control of our domestic rate of interest. Thirdly, whilst we intend to prevent inflation at home, we will not accept deflation at the dictates of influences from outside. In other words, we abjure the instruments of bank rate and credit contraction operating through an increase in unemployment as a means of forcing our domestic economy into line with external factors. I hope your Lordships will trust me not to have turned my back on all I have fought for. To establish these three principles which I have just stated has been my main task for the last twenty years. (Reprinted in Keynes, 1971, Vol.XXII, p.234.)

A Poole-type argument can be constructed that if shocks are mainly external a monetary target is preferable, but if mainly domestic an exchange rate target is better (for example Artis and Currie, 1982). This seems to tilt the balance for a monetary target. However, some authors have sought a compromise in the concept of contingent targets.

12.7 Which quantity?

It has been pointed out by various authors, of whom Artis and Currie were probably the first (1982), that arguments in favour of a monetary target were really arguments in favour of any quantity target. In a world of certainty a money target or a target for any other stock (such as bonds, credit or liquidity) or flow (*PSBR*, *DCE*, nominal income or current account balance of payments) would be equivalent. That is, if a flow-of-funds matrix and a series of sector balance sheets were calculated, the implications of a monetary target for the size of any other financial variable could be derived. The effect on the economy of a money supply target would be equivalent to that of any of the others since each would imply the money supply target just as it was itself implied by the monetary target. Moreover, even in a world of uncertainty any target expressed in current prices, whether stock or flow, suffices to make the price level determinate. The case for preferring a monetary target had to be based on an explicit comparison incorporating uncertainty.

This led to a discussion of the case for alternative quantity targets. The New Cambridge School, intellectual gurus of the Labour left, had long argued for a public sector financial deficit target.[5] In a curious and unconscious alliance, Beenstock (1980) argued for public sector debt as a suitable target variable (the stock whose change is the New Cambridge *PSFD*). A group of moderate Keynesians argued for a nominal *GDP* target (Meade, 1982; Tobin, 1981; Corden, 1981 – all in Griffiths and Wood, 1981). Other authors analysed or argued for credit and the Radcliffean 'liquidity' argument appeared more fashionable than it had done for years. Ben Friedman (1983) and others revived the arguments for credit.

The comparison of the case for alternative targets was a complex one and probably pointless. It was usually done in the context of a formal model since, otherwise, it was impossible to introduce any sort of uncertainty or imperfect information so as to distinguish the effects of different targets. However, in this case the results became totally model specific and not really of general applicability. Moreover, a point stressed by Laidler (1982) in a slightly different context is crucial; that is, the debate presupposes a degree of knowledge which renders pointless not only the monetarist argument but also any case for targeting as opposed to discretion. To construct a model implicitly assumes an enormous degree of knowledge since (implicitly) it is taken to be an accurate description of the structure of the economy. The monetarist proposition is that one has not this degree of knowledge; that is why there is a case for a monetary target. This is best seen in the debate about the case for a nominal income target. The monetarist case has always been that a monetary target is the best means of achieving a nominal income target. Every monetarist would agree that fixing nominal income growth at x per cent would be preferable to monetary growth of y per cent *if it were possible*. The argument is that there is no better way of controlling nominal income than by controlling money. The reasons are based on the workings of officials and ministers in an imperfect world with defective information. The argument for adjusting instruments to an indicator or proximate target (such as money) rather than a final one (such as nominal income) can never be illuminated by papers about the nature of aggregate supply in a world in which it is presupposed that one can control either (for example, Bean, 1982).

An earlier paper, by Waud (1973), had provided the strongest case for a nominal income target. His argument was simple. The government has a target (nominal income) and an instrument or instruments, such as its (re)discount rate, a reserve ratio or the level and structure of interest rates. It is known that the instruments determine the money supply and the money supply, in turn, income; in both cases the relationship is not precise – there is a random (stochastic) term in it. This model captures the essence of the monetarist view of the world.

Waud showed that the deviation of nominal income from its target would normally be minimised by operating a policy rule which adjusted the instrument according to the value of the final target rather than of the intermediate one. For example, Waud's model implies that the authorities should reduce the rediscount rate when nominal income is below target, and vice versa, irrespective of the level of the money supply. The exception is when there are counteracting errors in the two relationships – instrument (rediscount rate) to intermediate target (money) and intermediate to final target (income). This can be interpreted as an argument for no target, as by Mr Lawson. The crucial counter is that the target may tell you earlier. In early 1988 Mr Lawson argued that as inflation was about 3 per cent his policy was right. Monetarists had predicted disaster since late 1985 and various schools of Keynesians from different points in 1986. In late 1988 nemesis arrived – accelerating inflation, a huge balance of payments deficit and the need for very sharp corrective action.

This Waud argument has been accepted in small part by Friedman, by Minford and by the Swiss authorities. All have advocated, and in the Swiss case practised, a system in which the authorities fix some money base (high-powered money or cash or a legally defined reserve base) and allow market forces to determine the money supply and so income. The arguments for a monetary target can be used to justify base control as the best attainable degree of control of money so long as there is a relationship between the base and money. Most UK analysts, monetarist and non-monetarist alike, doubt that such a link either exists or could be created; see the analysis in Gowland

(1982, Chapter 3). If it were possible, the idea of a non-mandatory cash-base system is attractive in that problems of defining the money supply disappear since deposits are automatically weighted by the banks' reserve ratio, which is a measure of the assets' effective moneyness. (For example, if banks choose to hold a reserve against time deposits equal to half that held against demand deposits, the best definition of money would include demand deposits and 50 per cent of time deposits.)

It is a reflection of the dependence of monetarism upon Keynes' 'dark forces of ignorance and uncertainty' that rational expectations models give very little support for any rule in preference to any other or for any target variable. Output is invariant with respect to any anticipated path of any variable in rational expectations models. In consequence, a monetary rule is either equivalent to any other (quantity) rule or at least equivalent in its effect on output. The case for a monetary target rests on ignorance. Monetarists believe that fallible policy makers in a situation of such imperfect information and uncertainty are likely to make so many mistakes, if given discretion, that it is thought a simple rule will optimise economic welfare. If enough were known to test this belief, then *a fortiori* it would be better to do something else. Some monetarists, but not all, would take a similar perspective on the control of the money supply and so argue that the target should be the reserve base or some other alleged determinant of the money supply. Moreover, different monetarists could disagree about the definition of the money supply in a particular economy. Hence, the case for looking at a range of financial aggregates is powerful, but the question is what should the authorities do if they diverge? Possible answers may be found in multiple or contingent targets.

12.8   Contingent and multiple targets

An obvious solution to the problem of which variable to select as the target of economic policy is to compromise. A compromise may take the form of either a contingent or a multiple target, in which case more than one target is set. Buiter (1980b) and others have pioneered the notion of contingent or open-feedback targets. In this case the level of the primary target is dependent upon the behaviour of the secondary variable. A plausible contingent target for the UK might be 5 per cent growth in £M_3 plus 1 per cent for every 4 cents by which the exchange rate exceeds $1.30. As the exchange rate rises its contractionary but anti-inflationary effects are balanced by the higher rate of monetary growth, and vice versa. Buiter and his allies find it easy to demonstrate that some contingent rule would be preferable to a fixed monetary rule.

This stems from the fact that a conventional ('closed-feedback') target is necessarily a special case of Buiter's contingent target. One of the possible relationships between the monetary target and the exchange rate is that the target is independent. Buiter's variant can be selected from an almost infinite range of targets, including the conventional target, so necessarily it will do at least as well and is almost certain to do better, so long as one knows the model's structure or has the benefit of hindsight. Laidler's objection is valid: there is no fair test of the two as the monetarist argument is based on ignorance. Moreover, by a similar criterion, one can establish that discretion is preferable to any rule; the set from which the discretionary policy maker chooses includes all Buiter's rules and other choices besides, so the discretionary policy will show up as being never less successful than the target, contingent or fixed.

To illustrate this, a simple example may be useful. Imagine that an exercise is being conducted with perfect hindsight to determine the optimal economic policy for four years. It has been established that the best policy would have been monetary growth of 8, 14, 6 and 12 per cent in the four years respectively. The best monetary rule would have been 10 per cent growth per annum. A Buiterite cannot do worse than this; he or she seeks to find a formula relating the target to some other variable, such as 'x plus y exchange rate'. If y is set equal to 0 (and x to 1) the Buiterite must do as well as the monetarist and almost certainly must find a value of x and y which will produce results closer to the optimal values. This can be claimed as an argument for the superiority of contingent to fixed rules – indeed, it is Buiter's argument. However, a believer in official discretion can make similar claims for this policy, since in these circumstances the optimal values can be selected. Buiter's contingent rule is a subset of the fine-tuner's range of options and the monetarists of

Buiter's, so the ranking of policy rules in a world of perfect knowledge is clear. One cannot do worse by adding extra options. Imperfect knowledge on the part of the policy makers can be introduced to show that discretion will be impracticable, but Laidler's critique (1982) is still apposite – how can one appraise a policy by a test which gives the appraiser knowledge a policy maker could not have? To summarise, on their own terms, Buiter's contingent rules are clearly preferable. Nevertheless, there is no agreed methodology to compare them with alternatives.

In fact, Poole had already made a point similar to Buiter's in his article (1970). He suggested that a target which was a weighted average of both interest rates and the money supply was likely to be superior to either a monetary target or an interest rate one. Suppose that in a world of certainty the optimal monetary target was a growth rate of 5 per cent and the optimal interest rate 10 per cent. Poole argued that a rate such as keeping the sum of interest rates and monetary growth equal to 15 per cent was more likely to keep income closer to its optimal value than maintaining either monetary growth at 5 per cent or interest rates at 10 per cent. Leroy and Waud (1977) extended this analysis. They showed that such a combination would in general be superior to either single target.[6] Moreover, they argued that it was purely semantic which variable, if any, was designated the primary target. In the above example, all of the following are equivalent:

1. Money is the primary target – the target is that its growth rate (M) will equal 15 per cent less the rate of interest (r) ($M = 15 - r$).
2. The interest rate is the primary target – it will be pegged at 15 per cent less the growth rate of money ($r = 15 - M$).
3. Neither is the primary target – their sum will be maintained at 15 per cent ($r + M = 15$) – sometimes called an index.

However, it is clear that this argument has not been widely accepted. It is clear that policy makers do regard the choice of primary target as being of great significance. Given the psychological nature of many of the arguments for targets, this is not unreasonable. Moreover, contingent targets may not be practicable. For example, it is conceivable that the means necessary to control one variable may render the other variable unobservable or beyond the authorities' ability to control (Gowland, 1984b).

Contingent targets must be simple enough to be meaningful for those forming expectations, at least in financial markets. Unfortunately, it cannot be established *a priori* what target would or would not carry conviction and be comprehensible. Moreover, the case for contingent targets assumes a considerable degree of very short-term control of monetary aggregates. Most central bankers would argue that it is impossible to vary monetary policy in response to the foreign exchange markets. It is impossible, they argue, to change monetary policy from one day to the next and back again according to frequent exchange rate fluctuations. Any attempt at this degree of flexibility ignores the period it takes markets, and banks, to react and would consequently produce confusion.

Ironically, Buiter, Artis and others cite the greater responsiveness of exchange rates as a reason for contingent targets. Exchange rates are a 'jump' variable and so very likely to 'overshoot' in response to a shock (unlike sticky variables like the price level). The discovery of North Sea oil might have raised the equilibrium levels of exchange rate by 10 per cent and of output by 20 per cent. In the short term, output could not rise by more than 5 per cent, so extra upward pressure on the exchange rate would cause it to jump by 30 per cent (all numbers illustrative). This overshoot would have adverse effects. Indeed, it is cited as a cause of the UK depression of 1981–3. Artis and others use this as a crucial argument for exchange rate targets, to avoid such overshooting. Overshooting has been extensively analysed, by Dornbusch (1989), without changing the basic argument. Walters (1990, p.32–3) brilliantly reviews the argument. Not for the first time, greater depth of analysis has revealed that we know less than we thought we did – Laidler's bottom line?

One alternative to either single targets or contingent targets which has always appealed to the author is the setting of multiple targets (Gowland, 1978, p.151; 1982, p.153). These involve the authorities determining target values for a range of financial aggregates rather than for a single definition of money. These might take the form of a primary target with a range of supplementary ones such that the primary target was reassessed when the supplementary ones were breached. Alternatively, all could have equal status and either a below-target level of one could cancel out an above-target level of another, or attempts could be made to meet all (usually by varying the structure of interest rates). The Federal Republic of Germany has frequently had more than one target – for example, for M_2 and M_{1b} in 1983 – but one has always had such priority that the system has always been operated as if a single target were in force. The UK introduced multiple targets of a sort in the 1982 budget, but as identical target ranges were set for three variables (M_1, £M_3, PSL_2) it appeared to be at least as much a PR exercise as an economic change. (Identical ranges would be desirable only if wealth, income and interest rate elasticities were identical for all three demand functions.)

The case for multiple targets is pragmatic. If either M_1 or M_4 may be the best target variable, the case for having a target for both is self-evident. Similarly, if changes in the structure of the financial system may distort any monetary aggregate, the implication is that more than one definition is relevant.

12.9   Summary and conclusions

There are a large number of alternative methods of controlling the supply of money. These include:

1. Price effects on bank deposits.
2. Quantity controls on bank deposits.
3. Regulations.
4. Variation of the *PSBR*.
5. Price effects on non-bank private sector lending to the public sector.
6. Quantity effects on non-bank private sector lending to the public sector.
7. Price effects on the demand for bank lending.
8. Quantity controls on bank lending.
9. Reserve-base and reserve-ratio control of the supply of bank credit.
10. Price effects on the overseas influence on the money supply.
11. Quantity controls on the overseas influence on the money supply.

None of these is without costs. In particular, while all quantity controls permit more stable and lower interest rates, they lead to the growth of black markets. These are likely to render the control ineffective and to deprive the authorities of the information they need to forecast a coherent or rational policy.

In practice monetarism amounts to a belief that policy makers should set targets for monetary growth and, moreover, should adhere to them even, indeed especially, when this involves sacrifices. Adherence to a monetary target means that at least some of interest rates, exchange rates and public sector finance must be subordinate to this end. Although respectable arguments can be constructed for varying monetary targets over time in response to shifts in the demand for money function and in aggregate supply, most monetarists believe that monetary targets should be constant over time. Such a fixed target will act as an automatic stabiliser (of output), restrain government folly and both influence private sector expectations and facilitate economic efficiency by providing the private sector with information. However, there is a case that these objectives could be achieved by other devices as well as a monetary target. Monetarists disagree. They reject targets set in terms of prices, such as the exchange rate or an interest rate or Tobin's preferred variant, a variable related to share prices. On the one hand, they argue that a quantity target is necessary if the price level is to be determinate (and so hyperinflation avoided). On the other, monetarists believe that the financial sector is more stable than the goods sector and that shocks are more likely from overseas than domestic sources. They also believe that money is a direct substitute for all other assets, not just a narrow range of financial assets. These plausible propositions are sufficient to establish the case for monetary targets. The argument for a target expressed in terms of money rather than any other financial aggregate is much weaker, as is the case for a single against a contingent or multiple target. The monetarist case is in essence an argument for a simple, easily understood rule in an uncertain, complex world of imperfect, indeed defective, information; in the 1980s this case has been largely accepted, at least in Europe. In the UK, for example, the main opposition to monetarists now comes from those who support exchange-rate fixing, usually in the context of the European Monetary System. At the national level, the argument for such a system is also for a simple and easy to understand rule in a world of imperfect information. However, even in Europe, the main debate between monetarists and their opponents will continue. The European Community as a whole needs to decide whether it needs the flexibility of discretion, or the simple, simplistic, advantages of a monetary target.

Notes

1. There are problems in determining which countries adopted monetary targets and when. Foot cites the Netherlands as 'very much a borderline case' because they have a monetary target for M_2 but do not 'actively seek to control M_2'. Moreover, in most countries monetary targets were introduced in stages and it is arbitrary to select a specific date. Finally, DCE targets have been very widespread but are not generally regarded as monetary targets (see p.20).
2. See Ward and Neild (1978), Musgrave in Caves (1968), Hansen (1969), Heller *et al* (1968) and note 2 on page 148 above.
3. An important exception to this is Cagan's proposition. He argues that it is reasonable to assume that the money market is subject to a large number of short-term shocks, but is stable in the longer term. The reasons for the short-term shocks are such events as large, oversubscribed share issues which boost the money supply for a few days when a private issue is made, but reduce it when the issue is made by the public sector, for example the British Telecom issue reduced the UK money by about £x billion for a few days in early December 1984. The goods market, on the other hand, is subject to long-term shocks but is stable from day to day. By a simple application of Poole's model (p.288) the authorities should stabilise interest rates from day to day (and let the money supply fluctuate) but on a quarter-to-quarter basis they should stabilise the money supply and let interest rates fluctuate. This is both a good rationalisation of Central Bank practice and a neat attempt to get a handle on a complex problem but is clearly too simplistic to provide a complete answer.
4. On the problems of seasonal adjustment of monetary data, see *Bulletin*, Vol.24, No.2 (June 1983), p.311 and references mentioned there.
5. For the New Cambridge School, see Godley and Cripps (1983), Gowland (1979, p.57 and 1983b, pp.71–6), Cuthbertson (1979), Crystal (1979), Cripps and Godley (1976).
6. The optimal combination being calculated by Kalman filters.

Bibliography

Ackley, G. (1961) *Macroeconomic Theory*, Macmillan, New York

Adeney, M. (1989) *The Motor Makers*, Fontana, London

Akerlof, G. and Milbourne, R. (1978) 'New Calculations of Income and in Interest Elasticities in Tobin's Model of the Transactions Demand for Money', *Review Economics and Statistics*, Vol.60, No.4 (November), pp.541–6

Akhtar, M.A. (1983) *Financial Innovation*, BIS, Basle (Economic Paper No.9, December)

Allais, M. (1948) '*Economie et intérêt*', Imprimerie Nationale, Paris

Alt, J.E. (1979) *The Politics of Economic Decline*, Cambridge University Press, Cambridge

Anderson, P.S. (1989) *Inflation and Output*, BIS Economic Paper, No.24, Bank for International Settlements, Basle

Ando, A. and Modigliani, F. (1963) 'The "Life Cycle" Hypothesis of Saving', *AER*, Vol.53 (June), pp.55–84

Appelbaum, E. and Schettkat, E. (1988) 'Determinants of Employment Developments: Comparison of the US and Germany', *OECD Working Paper*, No.98, OECD, Paris

Arestis, P. (ed.) (1988) *Post-Keynesian Monetary Economics*, Edward Elgar, Aldershot

Arrow, K.J. (1974) *Essays in the Theory of Risk Bearing*, North Holland, Amsterdam

Arrow, K.J. and Debreu, G. (1954) 'Existence of an Equilibrium for a Competitive Economy', *Econometrica*, Vol.22 (July 1974), pp.265–90

Arrow, K.J. and Hahn, F.H. (1970) *General Competitive Analysis*, Holden Day, San Francisco

Artis, M.J. and Currie, D. (1982) 'Monetary Targets and Exchange Rates' in Eltis and Sinclair (1982)

Artis, M.J. and Lewis, M.K. (1981) *Monetary Control in the United Kingdom*, Philip Allan, Oxford

Bain, A.D. (1981) *The Economics of the Financial System*, Basil Blackwell, Oxford

Bandyopadyay, T. and Ghatak, S. (1990) *Current Issues in Monetary Economics*, Harvester Wheatsheaf, Hemel Hempstead

Barro, R.J. (1974) 'Are Government Bonds Net Worth?', *Journal of Political Economy*, Vol.82, pp.1095–117

Barro, R.J. (1989) *Modern Business Cycle Theory*, Basil Blackwell, Oxford

Barro, R.J. (ed.) (1990) *Modern Business Cycle Theory*, Basil Blackwell, Oxford

Barro, R.J. and Grossman, H.I. (1976) *Money, Employment and Inflation*, Cambridge University Press, Cambridge

Baumol, W.J. (1952) 'The Transactions Demand for Cash: An Inventory Theoretic Approach', *Quarterly Journal of Economics*, Vol.56 (November), pp.545–7

Bean, C. (1982) *Targeting Nominal Incomes: An Appraisal*, Discussion Paper 144, Centre for Labour Economics, LSE

Beckerman, M. (1972) *The Labour Government's Economic Record 1964–70*, Duckworth, London

Beenstock, M. (1980) *A Neoclassical Analysis of Macroeconomic Policy*, Cambridge University Press, Cambridge

Beenstock, M. (1982) *The World Economy in Transition*, 2nd edn, Allen and Unwin, London

Begg, D.K.H. (1982) *The Rational Expectations Revolution in Macroeconomics*, Philip Allan, Oxford

Benassy, J.-P. (1982) *The Economics of Market Disequilibrium*, Academic Press, New York

Blanchard, O.J. (1990) 'Suggestions for a new set of Fiscal Indicators', *OECD Working Paper, No.79*, OECD, Paris

Blanchard, O.J. and Fischer S. (1989) *Lectures on Macroeconomics*, MIT Press, Cambridge, Massachusetts

Bleaney, M. (1985) *The Rise and Fall of Keynesian Economics*, Macmillan, London

Blinder, A.S. (1989) *Macroeconomics under Debate*, Harvester Wheatsheaf, Hemel Hempstead

Blinder, A.S. and Solow, R.M. (1973) 'Does Fiscal Policy Matter', *Journal of Public Economics*, Vol.2, pp.319–38

Brittan, S. (1981) 'How to End the Monetarist Controversy', *Hobart Paper No.90*, Institute of Economic Affairs, London

Browning, P. (1986) *The Treasury and Economic Policy*, Longman, London

Brunner, K. (1981a) 'Monetary Policy', *Lloyds Bank Review*, No.139 (February), p.1

Brunner, K. (ed.) (1981b) *The Great Depression Revisited*, Martinus Nijhoff, The Hague

Brunner, K. and Meltzer, A. (1967) 'Economics of Scale in Cash Balances Reconsidered', *Quarterly Journal of Economics*, Vol.81 (August), pp.422–36

Brunner, K. and Meltzer, A. (eds.) (1980a) *On the State of Macroeconomics*, Carnegie Rochester Conference Series Vol.12, North Holland, Amsterdam

Brunner, K. and Meltzer, A. (eds.) (1980b) *Monetary Institutions and the Policy Process*, Carnegie Rochester Conference Series Vol.13, North Holland, Amsterdam

Brunner, K. and Meltzer, A.H. (1989) *Monetary Economics*, Basil Blackwell, Oxford

Buchanan, J.M. and Brennan, H.G. (1981) 'Monopoly in Money and Inflation', *Hobart Paper No.88*, Institute of Economic Affairs, London

Buchanan, J.M. *et al* (ed.) (1986) *Deficits*, Basil Blackwell, Oxford

Buiter, W.H. (1980a) 'The Macroeconomics of Dr Pangloss', *Economic Journal*, Vol.90 (March), pp.34–50

Buiter, W. (1980b) *The Superiority of Contingent Rules over Fixed Rules in Models with Rational Expectations*, Bristol Discussion Paper 80/80

Buiter, W.H. (1981) 'The Superiority of Contingent Rules over Fixed Rules in Models with Rational Expectations', *Economic Journal*, Vol.91 (September), p.1

Buiter, W. (1990) *Principles of Budgetary and Financial Policy*, Harvester Wheatsheaf, Hemel Hempstead

Buiter, W.H. and Miller, M. (1982) 'Monetary Policy and International Competitiveness' in Eltis and Sinclair (1982)

Cagan, P. (1965) *Determinants and Effect of Changes in the Stock of Money 1875–1960*, NBER Studies in Business Cycles, No.13, Columbia, New York

Cagan, P. (1986) 'The conflict between short-run and long-run objectives' in Campbell, C.C. and Dugan W.R. (eds.), Alternative Monetary Regimes, Johns Hopkins University Press, Baltimore

Carleton, J.F. and Cooper, T.J. (1976) 'The Term Structure and Rationality', *Journal of Finance*, Vol.63 (January), p.837

Carlin, W. and Soskice, D. (1990) *Macroeconomics and the Wage Bargain*, Oxford University Press, Oxford

Carson, D. (ed.) (1963) *Banking and Monetary Studies*, Irwin, Homewood, Illinois

Caves, R.E. (1968) *Britain's Economic Prospects*, Allen and Unwin, London

Chick, V. (1973) *The Theory of Monetary Policy*, 2nd edn, Basil Blackwell, Oxford

Chick, V. (1983) *Macroeconomics after Keynes*, Philip Allan, Oxford

Chouraqui, J.C. *et al* (1988) 'The Effects of Monetary Policy on the Real Sector', *OECD Working Paper No.51*, OECD, Paris

Chouraqui, J.C. *et al* (1990) 'Indicators of Fiscal Policy: A Re-examination', *OECD Working Paper No.78*, OECD, Paris

Ciarrapico, A.M. (1991) *Sovereign Debt*, Dartmouth, Aldershot

Clayton, G., Gilbert, J.C. and Sedgwick, R. (eds.) (1971) *Monetary Theory and Monetary Policy in the 1970s*, Oxford University Press, Oxford

Clower, R.W. (1965) 'The Keynesian Counter-Revolution: A Theoretical Reappraisal' in Hahn and Brechling (1965); reprinted in Clower (1969)

Clower, R.W. (ed.) (1969) *Monetary Theory*, Penguin, Harmondsworth

Clower, R.W. (1971), 'Theoretical Foundations of Monetary Policy' in Clayton *et al* (1971)

Clower, R.W. (1986) *Money and Markets*, (essays ed. Walker, D.A.), Cambridge University Press, Cambridge

Coddington, A. (1983) *Keynesian Economics*, Allen and Unwin, London

Coghlan, R.T. (1980) *Theory of Money and Finance*, Macmillan, London

Coghlan, R.T. (1983) *Money, Credit and the Economy*, Allen and Unwin, London

Cohen, D. and McMenamin, J.S. (1978) 'Fiscal Policy in a Financially Disaggregated Model', *Journal of Money, Credit and Banking*, Vol.10, No.3, pp.322–36

Creedy, J. (1990) *Foundations of Economic Thought*, Basil Blackwell, Oxford

Cripps, T.F. and Godley, W.A.H. (1976) 'A Formal Analysis of the CEPG Model', *Economica*, Vol.43 (November), pp.335–48

Crystal, K.A. (1979) *Controversies in British Macroeconomics*, 2nd edn, Philip Allan, Oxford

Cuddington, J.T. *et al* (1984) *Disequilibrium Macroeconomics in Open Economies*, Basil Blackwell, Oxford

Culbertson, J.M. (1957) 'The Term Structure of Interest Rates', *Quarterly Journal of Economics*, Vol.71 (November), pp.485–517

Culbertson, J.M. (1972) *Money and Banking*, McGraw-Hill, New York

Currie, D.A. and Peters, W. (eds.) (1980) *Contemporary Economic Analysis Vol.2*, Croom Helm, London

Cuthbertson, K. (1979) *Macroeconomic Policy*, Macmillan, London

Cuthbertson, K. (1985) *The Supply and Demand for Money*, Basil Blackwell, Oxford

Darby, M.R. (1972) 'On economic policy with rational expectations', *Journal of Monetary Economics*, Vol.3, No.2, pp.118–26

Davidson, P. (1978) *Money and the New World*, 2nd edn, Macmillan, London

Desai, M. (1981) *Testing Monetarism*, Frances Pinter, London

Di Cagno D. (1990) *The Regulation of Banks*, Dartmouth, Aldershot

Dixit, A.K. (1976) 'Public Finance in a Keynesian Temporary Equilibrium', *Journal of Economic Theory*, Vol.12, pp.242–58

Dixit, A.K. (1977) 'The Balance of Trade in a Model of Temporary Equilibrium with Rationing', *Review of Economic Studies*, Vol.XLV, p.393

Dornbusch, R. (1989) *Exchange Rate Economics*, MIT Press, London

Dornbusch R. and Fischer S. (1990) *Macroeconomics*, 5th edn, McGraw-Hill, New York

Dow, J.C.R. (1964) *The Management of the British Economy 1945–60* (NIESR, Social and Economic Studies 22). Cambridge University Press, Cambridge

Dow, J.C.R. and Saville, I.D. (1988) *A Critique of Monetary Policy*, Oxford University Press, Oxford

Dow, S.C. and Earl, P.E. (1982) *Money Matters*, Martin Robertson, Oxford

Eatwell, J., Milgate, M. and Newman, P. (1989) *Money*, Macmillan, London

Eichner, A.S. (1979) *A Guide to Post-Keynesian Economics*, Macmillan, London

Eltis, W.A. and Sinclair, P.J.N. (eds.) (1982) *The Money Supply and the Exchange Rate*, Basil Blackwell, Oxford

Evans, G. (1980) *The Stability of Rational Expectations*, Discussion Paper No.80, University of Stirling

Favier, J. (1963) *Enguerran de Marigny*, Presses Universitaires de France, Paris

Fforde, J.K. (1983) 'The UK – Setting Monetary Objectives' in Meek (1983)

Finley, M.I. (ed.) (1974) *Studies in Ancient Society*, Routledge and Kegan Paul, London

Fisher, D. (1978) *Monetary Theory and the Demand for Money*, Martin Robertson, Oxford

Fisher, D. (1989) *Money Demand and Monetary Policy*, Harvester Wheatsheaf, Hemel Hempstead

Fisher, I. (1911) *The Purchasing Power of Money*, Augustus M. Kelly, London

Fitoussi, J.-P. (1983) (ed.) *Modern Macroeconomic Theory*, Basil Blackwell, Oxford

Fleming, J. (1976a) 'The Cost of Capital, Finance and Investment', *Bank of England Quarterly Bulletin*, Vol.16, No.2 (June)

Fleming, J. (1976b) 'The Cost of Capital and Corporate Profitability: A Note', *Bank of England Quarterly Bulletin*, Vol.15, No.2 (June)

Foot, M.D.K.W. (1981) 'Monetary Targets: Their Nature and Record in the Major Economies' in Griffiths and Wood (1981)

Ford, J.L. and Driscoll, M.J. (1982) 'Real Parameter Instability and the Optimal Choice of Monetary Policy', *Journal of Macroeconomics* (Summer), Vol.4, No.2, pp.339–48

Frank, J. (1987) *The New Keynesian Economics*, Wheatsheaf, Brighton

Friedman, B.M. (1983) 'The Role of Money and Credit in Macroeconomic Analysis' in Tobin (1983)

Friedman, B.M. (1988) *Day of Reckoning*, Random House, New York (UK edition, Pan Books, 1989, London)

Friedman, M. (1953) 'The Methodology of Positive Economics', in *Essays in Positive Economics*, University of Chicago Press, Chicago

Friedman, M. (1956a) 'The Quantity Theory of Money – A Restate-ment' in Friedman (1956b) and Friedman (1969), pp.51–68

Friedman, M. (ed.) (1956b) *Studies in the Quantity Theory of Money*, University of Chicago Press, Chicago

Friedman, M. (1957) *Theory of the Consumption Function*, Princeton University Press, Princeton, New Jersey

Friedman, M. (1962) 'Should there be an Independent Monetary Authority?' in Yeager (1962); reprinted in Friedman (1968b)

Friedman, M. (1968a) 'The Role of Monetary Policy', *American Economic Review*, Vol.LVIII (March), p.1

Friedman, M. (1968b) *Dollars and Deficits*, Prentice Hall, New York

Friedman, M. (1969) *The Optimum Quantity of Money and Other Essays*, Aldine, Chicago

Friedman, M. (1970a) 'The New Monetarism: A Comment', *Lloyds Bank Review* (October), pp.52–3

Friedman, M. (1970b) *The Counter Revolution in Monetary Theory* (First Wincott Memorial Lecture, London, 16 September 1970), Occasional Paper 33, Institute of Economic Affairs, London

Friedman, M. (1974) 'A Theoretical Framework for Monetary Analysis' in Gordon (1974)

Friedman, M. (1975) *Unemployment vs. Inflation: An Evaluation of the Phillips Curve with a British Commentary by David Laidler*, Occasional Paper 44, Institute of Economic Affairs, London

Friedman, M. and Meiselman, D. (1963) 'The Relative Stability of Monetary Velocity and the Investment Multiplier in the United States, 1897–1958', *Commission on Money and Credit, Stabilisation Policies*, Englewood Cliffs, New Jersey

Friedman, M. and Schwartz, A.J. (1963) *A Monetary History of the US 1867–1960*, NBER Studies in Business Cycles No.12, Princeton University Press, Princeton, New Jersey

Frydman, R. and Phelps, E.S. (eds.) (1983) *Individual Forecasting and Aggregate Outcomes*, Cambridge University Press, Cambridge

Gilbert, J.C. (1982) *Keynes's Impact on Monetary Economics*, Butter-worths, London

Godley, W. and Cripps, F. (1983) *Macroeconomics*, Fontana, London

Godley, W.A.H. and Coutts, K. (1984) *Some Proposals for the Simplification and Reorganisation of Macroeconomic Theory*, mimeo, Cambridge

Goodhart, C.A.E. (1970) 'The Importance of Money' (June 1970); reprinted in Goodhart (1984), p.21

Goodhart, C.A.E. (1975) *Money, Information and Uncertainty*, Macmil-lan, London, 1975. This is retained despite Goodhart (1989) because much valuable material is omitted in its successor

Goodhart, C.A.E. (1982) 'Monetary Trends in the US and the UK: A British Review', *Journal of Economic Literature*, Vol.20 (December), pp.1540–51

Goodhart, C.A.E. (1984) *Monetary Theory and Practice: the UK Experience*, Macmillan, London

Goodhart, C.A.E. (1989a) *Money, Information and Uncertainty*, 2nd edn, Macmillan, London

Goodhart, C.A.E. (1989b) 'Keynes and Monetarism', pp.106-21 in Hill (1989) plus replies by Dow, Fletcher and Brothwell

Goodhart, C.A.E. and Gowland, D.H. (1977) 'The Relationship between Yields on Short and Long-Dated Gilt-Edged', *Bulletin of Economic Research*, Vol.29 (November), pp.96–112

Goodhart, C.A.E. and Gowland, D.H. (1978) 'The Relationship between Long-Dated Gilt Yields and other Variables', *Bulletin of Economic Research*, Vol.30 (November), pp.59–70

Gordon, R.J. (ed.) (1974) *Milton Friedman's Monetary Framework*, University of Chicago Press, Chicago

Gowland, D.H. (1975) 'Money Supply and Share Prices' in Parkin and Nobay (1975)

Gowland, D.H. (1978) *Monetary Policy and Credit Control*, Croom Helm, London

Gowland, D.H. (ed.) (1979) *Modern Economic Analysis*, Butterworths, London

Gowland, D.H. (1982) *Controlling the Money Supply*, 2nd edn, Croom Helm, London

Gowland, D.H. (ed.) (1983a) *Modern Economic Analysis 2*, Butterworths, London

Gowland, D.H. (1983b) *The Political Economy of Monetarism*, Paper delivered to Political Science Association Annual Conference, Newcastle (13 April 1983)

Gowland, D.H. (1984) *International Economics*, Croom Helm, London

Gowland, D.H. (1989) *Whatever Happened to Demand Management?*, RJA (Books), Bedford

Gowland, D.H. (1990) *Understanding Macroeconomics*, Edward Elgar, Aldershot

Gowland, D.H. (1991a) *Monetary Control in Theory and Practice*, Routledge, London

Gowland, D.H. (1991b) *The Microeconomics of Monetary Policy*, Edward Elgar, Aldershot

Graham, A.D.W.M. (1980) 'Demand Management in Changing Historical Circumstances' in Currie and Peters (1980)

Gramlich, E. (1990) 'Fiscal Indicators', *OECD Working Paper No.80*, OECD, Paris

Grandmont, J.-M. (1977) 'Temporary General Equilibrium Theory', *Econometrica*, Vol.45, pp.535–72

Grandmont, J.-M. (1983) *Money and Value*, Cambridge University Press, Cambridge

Griffiths, B. (1970) 'Competition in Banking', *Hobart Paper No.70*, Institute of Economic Affairs, London

Griffiths, B. and Wood, G.E. (eds.) (1981) *Monetary Targets*, Macmillan, London

Griffiths, B. and Wood, G.E. (1984) *Monetarism in the UK*, Macmillan, Basingstoke

Guisso, L. and Teruzzese D. (1990) 'Time Consistency and Subgame Perfection', *Banca D'Italia Discussion Paper No.141* (July), Banca D'Italia, Rome

Gurley, J. and Shaw, E. (1960) *Money in a Theory of Finance*, Brookings Institute, Washington, DC

Hahn, F.H. (1982) *Money and Inflation*, Basil Blackwell, Oxford

Hahn, F.H. and Brechling, F.P.R. (eds.) (1965) *The Theory of Interest Rates*, Macmillan, London

Hamburger, M.J. (1973) 'The Demand for Money in 1971: Was there a Shift?', *Journal of Money, Credit and Banking*, Vol.5 (May), pp.720–5

Hamouda, O.F. and Smithin, J.N. (1988) *Keynes and Public Policy After Fifty Years* (2 Vols.), Edward Elgar, Aldershot

Hansen, A.H. (1953) *A Guide to Keynes*, McGraw-Hill, New York

Hansen, B. (1969) *Fiscal Policy in Seven Countries*, OECD, Paris

Harcourt, G.C. (ed.) (1977) *The Microeconomic Foundations of Macroeconomics*, Macmillan (for the International Economic Association), London

Hare, P. and Kirby, M. (eds.) (1984) *An Introduction to British Economic Policy*, Harvester, London

Hayek, F.A. (1976) *Choice in Currency*, Institute of Economic Affairs, London

Heller, W.W. *et al.* (1968) *Fiscal Policy in Balanced Economy*, OECD, Paris

Hendry, D.F. (1980) 'Econometrics: Alchemy or Science?', *Econometrica*, Vol.47 (August), pp.387–406 (a modified version appeared in the *New Statesman*, 23 November 1979)

Hewitt, G.E. (1977) 'Financial Forecasts in the UK', *Bank of England Quarterly Bulletin*, Vol.12, No.2 (June)

Hey, J.D. (1979) *Uncertainty in Microeconomics*, Martin Robertson, Oxford

Hicks, J.R. (1935) 'A Suggestion for Simplifying the theory of Money', *Economica*, Vol.2 (February), pp.1–19; reprinted in Lutz and Mints (1951)

Hicks, J.R. (1937) 'Mr Keynes and the Classics', *Econometrica*, Vol.5 (April), pp.147–59

Hicks, J.R. (1946) *Value and Capital*, 2nd edn, Oxford University Press, Oxford

Hicks, J.R. (1967) *Monetary Theory and Policy: A Historical Perspective*, The Seventh Edward Shawn Memorial Lecture in Economics, University of Western Australia Press, Perth, 1967; partially reprinted in Clower (1969)

Hicks, J.R. (1983) 'IS–LM: An Explanation' in Fitoussi (1983), pp.

49–63; this originally appeared in the *Journal of Post-Keynesian Economics*, Vol.III, Winter 1980–1

Hill, R. (ed.) (1989) *Keynes, Money and Monetarism*, Macmillan, London

Hillier, B. (1977) 'Does Fiscal Policy Matter?', *Public Finance*, Vol.32, pp.374–89

Hillier, B. (1986) *Macroeconomics*, Basil Blackwell, Oxford

Hillier, B. (1991) *The Macroeconomic Debate*, Basil Blackwell, Oxford

Hodgson, G. (1989) *Institutionalist Economics*, Basil Blackwell, Oxford

Jaffee, D.W. (1975) *Credit Rationing and the Commercial Loan Market*, Wiley, New York

Jenkinson, N.H. (1981) *Investment Profitability and the Valuation Ratio*, Bank of England Discussion Paper No.17

Johnson, C. (ed.) (1956) *The De Moneta of Nicholas Oresme and English Mint Documents*, Nelson, London

Johnson, C. (1989) *Measuring the Economy*, Macmillan, London

Johnson, E.S. and Johnson, H.G. (1978) *The Shadow of Keynes*, Basil Blackwell, Oxford

Johnson, H.G. (1972) *Further Essays in Monetary Economics*, Allen and Unwin, London

Johnston, R.B. (1984) *The Demand for Non-Interest Bearing Money*, Government Economic Service Working Paper No.66

Judd, J.P. and Scadding, J.L. (1982) 'The Search for a Stable Money Demand Function: A Survey of the post-1973 Literature', *Journal of Economic Literature*, Vol.20, No.3 (September), pp.993–1023

Kaldor, N. (1970) 'The New Monetarism', *Lloyds Bank Review* (July 1970), pp.1–17; reprinted in Walters (1973). See also Kaldor's reply to Friedman (1970a) in *Lloyds Bank Review* (October 1970), pp.54–6

Kaldor, N. (1982) *The Scourge of Monetarism*, Oxford University Press, Oxford

Kalecki, M. (1944) 'Professor Pigou on the Classical Stationary State – a Comment', *Economic Journal*, Vol.54 (April), pp.131–2

Karni, E. (1974) 'The Value of Time and the Demand for Money', *Journal of Money Credit and Banking* (February), Vol.6, pp.45–64

Kaufman, H. (1986) 'Debt: The Threat to Economic and Financial Stability', *Economic Review*, Federal Reserve Bank of Kansas City, Vol.71, No.10, pp.3–11

Kennet, W. (ed.) (1982) *The Rebirth of Britain*, Weidenfeld and Nicolson, London

Keynes, J.M. (1930) *A Treatise on Money* (2 vols), Macmillan, London, reprinted as Keynes (1971), Vols V and VI

Keynes, J.M. (1936) *The General Theory of Employment, Interest and Money*, Macmillan, London; also in Vol.VII of his *Collected Writings* (see below)

Keynes, J.M. (1937) 'Alternative Theories of the Rate of Interest', *Economic Journal*, Vol.XLVII, June, pp.241–52

Keynes, J.M. (1971) *The Collected Writings of John Maynard Keynes*, Macmillan (for the Royal Economic Society), London

Keynes, M. (1975) *Essays on John Maynard Keynes*, Cambridge University Press, Cambridge

Klamer, A. (1984) *The New Classical Macroeconomics*, Wheatsheaf, London

Kydland, F.E. and Prescott, E.C. (1977) 'Rules rather than Discretion: the Inconsistency of Optimal Plans', *Journal of Political Economy*, Vol.85, No.3 (June), pp.473–91

Laidler, D.E.W. (1975a) 'The End of Demand Management: How to Reduce Unemployment in the 1970s' in Friedman (1975)

Laidler, D.E.W. (1975b) *Essays on Money and Inflation*, Manchester University Press, Manchester

Laidler, D.E.W. (1980a) *Memorandum to House of Commons Select Committee on the Treasury and Civil Service Monetary Policy*, HC 720, HMSO, London

Laidler, D.E.W. (1980b) 'The Demand for Money in the United States – Yet Again' in Brunner and Meltzer (1980a)

Laidler, D.E.W. (1982) *Monetarist Perspectives*, Philip Allan, Oxford

Laidler, D.E.W. (1984) 'The Buffer Stock Notion in Monetary Economics', *Economic Journal*, (Royal Economic Society – Aute Conference Supplement to Vol.94, p.16

Laidler, D.E.W. (1985) *The Demand for Money*, 3nd edn, International Textbook Company, Scranton, Pasadena, California

Laidler, D.W. and Parkin, M. (1975) 'Inflation: A Survey', *Economic Journal*, Vol.85, pp.741–59

Leibenstein, H. (1976) *Beyond Economic Man*, Harvard University Press, Cambridge, Massachusetts

Leijonhufvud, A. (1968) *On Keynesian Economics and the Economics of Keynes*, Oxford University Press, New York

Leijonhufvud, A. (1969) *Keynes and the Classics*, Institute of Economic Affairs, London

Leijonhufvud, A. (1981) *Information and Coordination*, Oxford University Press, Oxford

Leroy, S.F. and Waud, R.N. (1977) 'Applications of the Kalman Filter in Short-Run Monetary Control', *International Economic Review*, Vol.17, pp. 195–207

Levacic, R. and Rebmann, A. (1982) *Macroeconomics*, 2nd edn, Macmillan, London

Lutz, F.A. (1940) 'The Structure of Interest Rates', *Quarterly Journal of Economics*, Vol.55 (November), pp.36–63

Lutz, F.A. and Mints, L.W. (1951) *Readings in Monetary Theory* (Vol.5 of American Economics Association Articles on Economics), Irwin, Homewood, Illinois

McKinnon, R.I. (1979) *Money in the International Exchange*, Oxford University Press, Oxford

Malinvaud, E. (1977) *The Theory of Unemployment Reconsidered*, Basil Blackwell, Oxford

324 *Bibliography*

Marris, R. (1964) *Economic Theory of Managerial Capitalism*, Macmillan, London

Masera, R.S. (1972) *The Term Structure of Interest Rates*, Clarendon Press, Oxford

Mattesini, F. (1990) 'Financial Markets, Asymmetric Information and Macroeconomic Equilibrium', *Quaderni ISE*, LUISS, Rome

Mattesini, F. (1992) *Financial Markets, Asymmetric Information and Macroeconomic Equilibrium*, Dartmouth, Aldershot

Matthews, R. (1968) 'Why has Britain had Full Employment since the War?', *Economic Journal*, Vol.78, No.3, pp.555–69.

Mayer, T. (ed.)(1978) *The Structure of Monetarism*, Norton, London

Mayer, T. (1990) *Monetary Theory*, Edward Elgar, Aldershot

Meade, J.E. (1982) 'The Restoration of Full Employment' in Kennet (1982)

Meek, P. (ed.) (1983) *Central Bank Views on Monetary Targeting*, Federal Reserve Bank of New York

Metzler, A.H. (1969) 'Money, Intermediation and Growth', *Journal of Economic Literature*, Vol.7 (March), pp.27–56

Miller, M. and Orr, D. (1966) 'A Model of the Demand for Money by Firms', *Quarterly Journal of Economics*, Vol.80 (August), pp.413–36

Minford, P. (1981) 'Equilibrium Model Defended', *The Times*, 3 March

Minsky, H.P. (1975) *Keynes*, Columbia University Press, Columbia, New York

Minsky, H.P. (1982) *Can 'It' Happen Again*, M.E. Sharpe Inc. Armonk, New York

Modigliani, F. (1963) 'The Monetary Mechanism and its Interaction with Real Phenomena', *Review of Economics and Statistics*, Vol.45 (Supplement), pp.79–107

Modigliani, F. and Sutch, R.C. (1966) 'Innovations in Interest Rate Policy', *American Economic Review*, Vol.56, No.2 (May), pp.178–97

Moggridge, D.E. (1976, 1980) *Keynes*, 2nd edn, Macmillan, London

Moore, B.J. (1988) *Horizon Talism*, Free Press, New York

Morgan, J. (1991) 'Inventory Methods and Recessions' in *Economic Review*, Federal Reserve of Kansas City, Vol.21, No.3, pp.3–18.

Musgrave, R.A. (1968) 'Fiscal Policy' in Caves (1968)

Nicoletti, G. (1988) 'Private Consumption, Inflation and the Debt Neutrality Hypothesis', *OECD Working Paper No.50*, OECD, Paris

OECD (1979) *Monetary Targets and Inflation Control*, OECD, Paris

OECD (1982) *Budget Financing and Monetary Control*, OECD, Paris

Orr, D. (1970) *Cash Management and the Demand for Money*, Praeger, New York

Parkin, M. and Nobay, A.R. (eds.) (1975) *Current Economic Problems*, Cambridge University Press, Cambridge

Patinkin, D. (1956) *Money, Interest and Prices*, Harper and Row, Evanston, Illinois

Patinkin, D. (1959) 'Keynesian Economics Rehabilitated: A Rejoinder to Professor Hicks', *Economic Journal*, Vol.69, pp.582–7

Patinkin, D. (1969) 'Money and Wealth', *Journal of Economic Literature* Vol.7 (December), pp.1140–60

Patinkin, D. and Leith, J.C. (1977) *Keynes, Cambridge and the General Theory*, Macmillan, London, 1977

Pegues, F.J. (1962) *Lawyers of the Last Capetians*, Princeton University Press, Princeton, New Jersey

Percival, N.J. (1982) *Types of Asset*, University of York, mimeo

Pesek, B.P. and Saving, T.R. (1967) *Money, Wealth and Economic Theory*, Macmillan, New York

Phillips, R. (1979) *The Corporate Transactions Demand for Money*, University of York, mimeo

Pigou, A.C. (1943) 'The Classical Stationary State', *Economic Journal*, Vol.53 (December), pp.343–51

Pippenger, J.E. and Phillips, D. (1977) 'Rationality and the Term Structure of Interest Rates' (unpublished mimeo), University of Wisconsin

Polak, J.J. (1957) 'Monetary Analysis of Income Formation and Payments Problems', *IMF Staff Papers*, Vol.6, pp.1–50

Policano, H.I and Grossman, A.J. (1977) 'Money Balances, Commodity Inventories and Inflationary Expectations', *Journal of Political Economy*, Vol.83, No.6 (December), pp.1093–111

Podolski, T.M. (1986) *Financial Innovation and the money supply*, Basil Blackwell, Oxford

Poole, W. (1970) 'Optimal Choice of Monetary Instruments', *Quarterly Journal of Economics*, Vol.84, pp.197–216

Price, L.D.D. (1972) 'Demand for Money in the UK: A Further Investigation', *Bank of England Quarterly Bulletin*, Vol.12, No.1 (March), p.43

Radcliffe (1959) *Committee on the Workings of the Monetary System*, Cmnd.827, HMSO, London

Roll, E. (1961) *A History of Economic Thought*, Faber and Faber, London

Ross, D. (1954) *The Nicomachean Ethics of Aristotle*, Oxford University Press, London

Rotwein, E. (1972) *David Hume: Writings on Economics*, Books for Libraries Press, Freeport, New York

Sargent, T. J. (1979) *Macroeconomic Theory*, Academic Press, London

Sargent, T.J. (1986) *Rational Expectations and. Inflation*, Harper and Row, New York

Sastry, R.A.S. (1970) 'The Effect of Credit on the Transactions Demand for Cash', *Journal of Finance*, Vol.XXV (September), pp.777–82

Sawyer, M. (1982) *Macroeconomics in Question*, Wheatsheaf, London

Shackle, G.L.S. (1968) *Keynesian Kaleidics*, Edinburgh University Press, Edinburgh

Shackle, G.L.S. (1974) *Expectations, Investment and Income*, 2nd edn, Oxford University Press, Oxford

Sheffrin, S.M. (1983) *Rational Expectations*, Cambridge University Press (Surveys), Cambridge

Sinclair, P. (1987) *Unemployment*, Basil Blackwell, Oxford

Skidelsky, R. (1983) *John Maynard Keynes*, Vol.1: 1883–1920, Macmillan, London

Smith, A. (1776) *An Inquiry into the Nature and Causes of the Wealth of Nations*, best modern edition, Oxford University Press, Oxford

Spencer, P.D. (1990) 'House Prices' in *ROOF* (May–June) pp.3–9

Spencer, P.D. and Muellbauer (1990) 'House Prices and the UK Economy', *CEPR Discussion Paper No.13*, London

Sprenkle, C. (1969) 'The Uselessness of Transactions Demand Models', *Journal of Finance*, Vol.24 (December), pp.835–47

Sprenkle, C. (1972) 'On the Observed Transactions Demand for Money', *Manchester School*, (September), pp.261–8

Sprenkle, C. and Miller, M.H. (1980) 'The Precautionary Demand for Narrow and Broad Money', *Economica*, Vol.47 (November), pp.407–21

Stein, J.L. (1982) *Monetarist, Keynesian and New Classical Economics*, Basil Blackwell, Oxford

Strayer, J.R. (1980) *The Reign of Philip The Fair*, Princeton University Press, Princeton, New Jersey

Surrey, J.J.C. (1976) *Macroeconomic Themes*, Oxford University Press, Oxford

Sweeney, R.J. (1988) *Wealth Effects and Monetary Theory*, Basil Blackwell, Oxford

Temin, P. (1976) *Did Monetary Forces Cause the Great Depression?*, Norton, New York

Tew, B. (1969) *Monetary Theory*, Students Library of Economics, Routledge and Kegan Paul, London

Thorn, R.S. (1974) 'A Transactions Theory of the Demand for Money', *Weltwirtschaftliches Archiv*, Band 110, pp.430–44

Tobin, J. (1956) 'The Interest Elasticity of the Transactions Demand for Cash', *Review of Economics and Statistics*, Vol.38 (August), pp.241–7

Tobin, J. (1958) 'Liquidity Preference as Behaviour Towards Risk', *Review of Economic Studies*, Vol.XXV, No.66 (February), pp.65–87

Tobin, J. (1963) 'Commercial Banks as Creators of Money' in Carson (1963); reprinted in Tobin (1972)

Tobin, J.M. (1964) 'An Essay on the Principles of Debt Management', reprinted in Mayer (1990), pp.99–112

Tobin, J. (1969) 'A General Equilibrium Approach to Monetary Theory' *Journal of Money, Credit and Banking* Vol.1, No.1 (March)

Tobin, J. (1972) *Essays in Economics, Vol.1: Macroeconomics*, North Holland, Amsterdam

Tobin, J. (1980) 'Government Deficits and Capital Accumulation' in Currie and Peters (1980)

Tobin, J. (ed.) (1983) *Macroeconomics, Prices and Quantities*, Basil Blackwell, Oxford

Tobin, J.M. and Baumol, W.J. (1989) 'The Optimal Cash Balance Proposition' (Maurice Allais contribution) *Journal of Economic Literature*, Vol.XXVII, No.3 (September), pp.1160–3

Turnovsky, S.J. (1977) *Macroeconomic Analysis*, Cambridge University Press, Cambridge

Vicarelli, F. (1983) (ed.) *Keynes' Relevance Today*, Macmillan, London

Volcker, P.A. (1977) 'A Broader Role for Monetary Targets', *FRBNY Quarterly Review* (Spring), pp.23–8

Walters, A.A. (ed.) (1973) *Money and Banking*, Penguin, Harmondsworth

Walters, A.A. (1986) *Britain's Economic Renaissance*, Oxford University Press, New York

Walters, A.A. (1990) *Sterling in Danger*, Fontana/Collins, London

Ward, T.S. and Neild, R.R. (1978) *The Measurement and Reform of Budgetary Policy*, Heinemann (for the Institute of Fiscal Studies), London

Wattel, H.L. (ed.) (1985) *The Policy Consequences of John Maynard Keynes*, Macmillan, Basingstoke

Waud, R.N. (1973) 'Proximate Targets and Monetary Policy', *Economic Journal*, Vol.83 (March), p.1

Weintraub, E.R. (1979) *Microfoundations*, Cambridge University Press, Cambridge

Weintraub, S. *et al* (1973) *Keynes and the Monetarists and Other Essays*, Rutgers University Press, New Brunswick, New Jersey

Weston, J.F. and Brigham, E.F. (1987) *Managerial Finance*, Holt, Rhinehart and Winston, New York

Williamson, J. (1986) *The Open Economy and the World Economy*, Basic Books, New York

Wood, J.C. (ed.) (1983) *John Maynard Keynes: Critical Assessments* (4 Vols.), Croom Helm, Beckenham

Wrightsman, D. (1983) *Monetary Theory and Policy*, 3rd edn, Free Press, New York

Yeager, L.B. (ed.) (1962) *In Search of a Monetary Constitution*, Harvard University Press, Cambridge, Massachusetts

Further reading

General

Goodhart (1975) and (1989a) are significantly different, the newer volume concentrating more on finance and micro topics. Together they are by far the best advanced text available, providing an excellent advanced coverage of all the material included in this book. Palgrave (Eatwell *et al* 1989) provides magisterial surveys of many areas. Fisher has produced a series of texts of which (1989) and (1978) are the most useful. On any advanced macroeconomic topic Blanchard and Fischer (1989) is unrivalled. Coghlan (1980) and Chick (1973) are also excellent texts, although not covering the full range of monetary economics. Surrey (1976) includes many of the journal articles referred to in this text. Mayer (1990) includes even more articles: Baumol (1952), Miller and Orr (1966), Sprenkle (1969), Akerlof and Milbourne (1978), Hicks (1935), Tobin (1969), Tobin (1964), Friedman (1956a), Patinkin (1969).

1. Necessity of monetary theory

Money creation is analysed in Gowland (1982). The causality debate is well reviewed in Coghlan (1980).

2. Quantity theory and portfolio balance

Friedman's restatement can be found in (1956b) and (1969) as well as the readings cited above. Gowland (1984) summarises international monetarism and its critics. Chick (1973) – especially Chapter 6 – is superb in its analysis of portfolio balance models.

3. Demand for money

Laidler (1985) is still the best introduction to this topic, although he has since modified his views (1980a). Fisher (1978) is still the best advanced specialist work. Empirical work is summarised in Judd and Scadding (1982). See also Ben Friedman's retrospective in Mayer (1990).

4. IS–LM model

The ubiquitous IS–LM can be found in Laidler (1985), Surrey (1976) and virtually all macroeconomic texts; for example, Levacic and Rebmann (1982) and subsequent editions or Dornbusch and Fischer (1990).

5. Tobin's model

The best analysis of Tobin's approach is still in Chick (1973), especially Chapter 6. Goodhart (1970) demonstrates the crucial significance of what is a direct substitute for holding money.

6. Flow of funds

On the narrow issue of financial forecasting, Hewitt (1977) is very useful. On flow-of-funds analysis, Tew (1969) and Coghlan (1980, Chapter 6) are the best simple analyses. The relative impact of alternative methods of financing expenditure and creating money is considered in virtually every macroeconomic textbook. No treatment stands out.

7. Inflation and unemployment (I)

Patinkin (1969), Metzler (1969) and Sweeney (1988) stand out as unrivalled surveys of the theoretical material covered in this chapter. The application to the UK is presented in more detail in Gowland (1990, Chapters 5 and 10).

8. Inflation and unemployment (II)

The best survey of the bulk of the material covered in this chapter is Weintraub (1979). Post-Keynesian thought is presented in Dow and Earl's contributions to Hare and Kirkby (1984) and in Arestis (1988). For some interesting extensions, see Leijonhufvud (1981) and Harcourt (1977), especially the contributions by Goodhart and Leijonhufvud. Goodhart's paper is a superb review of the literature on why money exists. It is admirably complemented by Hahn (1982). For a critical review of this school from a sympathetic viewpoint see Sawyer (1982).

9. Debt management and government finance

Hillier (1977) presents an interesting exposition and extension of the Blinder–Solow model. Turnovsky (1977) is hard going but thorough in his development of more advanced models.

10. Term structure of interest rates

Masera's introduction (1972) is an excellent summary of the theory in this area and still unrivalled.

11. Bank sector and money supply

Coghlan (1980, 1983) provides an interesting and sophisticated analysis of the money supply process. Goodhart's three chapters are essential reading (1984, Chapters 4, 5 and 6): see also the special issue of the *Journal of Money Credit and Banking* (1978) and Di Cagno (1990).

12.   Monetary policy

On all the material covered in this chapter Goodhart (1984) is superb and strongly recommended. On techniques of monetary control, Gowland (1982) covers the material presented in Section 12.2 in greater depth and detail. Shorter presentations can be found in Artis and Lewis (1981) and in Gowland (1979, Chapter 1; 1983a, Chapter 1). On monetary targets the collection edited by Griffiths and Wood (1981) is invaluable, especially the introduction and the papers by Foot, Minford and Corden. Sumner in Brunner and Meltzer (1980a) is equally valuable as a comprehensive survey. Volcker (1977) is fascinating for obvious reasons, for its insight into US monetary policy 1979–87. Fforde (1983) is equally illuminating.

Index

332